Matt 5:17-18
The law is 4
Renovate to
to restrict ... repair
or activity

praise for *unlikely*

"*Miracle Grow* for your soul! The perspective and guidance are wonderful! It is a great conduit to remind all of us how to live as a Christian."–Michael McGee

"*Unlikely* is simply one of the most inspirational books I have ever read. Its directness and thought-provoking style backed with biblical truths are a refreshing approach to God's truth for your life. It would seem impossible for anyone to read this book and not be changed by the message!"–Dr. Ken Roddy

"*Just think, if God's spoken words can cause all of creation to leap into existence, imagine what reading His written Word can do to your life!* This thought increased my desire to read and study God's word and to really know Him even more. Thank you for writing this book!"–Rhonda Thurman

"Dr. Goodman's journey of self-examination and conviction to affirm his relationship with God should serve as inspiration to every person of faith who has ever asked the question '*Why me?*'"–Joshua Kotula

"Discover in these pages a moving encounter with an authentic life transformation as *religion* is lost and *faith* is found. With a clear vision for the plain teachings of scripture, Dr. Goodman invites all those who don't look, smell, dress, think, or act 'right' into the journey of God's amazing plan for salvation in Jesus Christ. A great read for all who long for a living faith and a more excellent way."–Pastor Mark B. Hunt

"My walk with God will forever look dramatically different having read this work. It brought conviction, humility, and most importantly a call to action to pour into the lives of others. If you ever wondered why God chooses the most unlikely people to fulfill His purpose, you will wonder no more!"–John Bizal

"Dr. Goodman's book explores the nature of simple human experience, the challenge of faith, the church as [the] Christian community, and the surrender to Christ. We yearn for this sustenance on our Christian journey. Spiritual wisdom found in real life experiences. What a gift for us all!"–Melanie Nichols

"This book is an ideal read for those who are struggling with the concepts of Christianity and desperately seeking clarity."–Lori McPherson

"I am a first-hand witness to the change that has happened in George's life: a change that can only come from God himself. *Unlikely* is obviously the culmination of God's work in George, and will certainly be a blessing to others who are on that journey of discovering who they are and how they relate to God!"–Doug Mason

"There are so many people that desire something more in their lives, and what they are missing is God. I think we all know this deep within and desire to have a close relationship with God. It may be a new relationship or rebuilding a relationship with God. Your book has opened my heart and answered questions so many of us have."–Delinda Burger

"I have had the opportunity to read your first draft and now this one. The constant in both cases is my belief that God is speaking through your heart, which in my estimation is why this book will minister to those who are truly seeking what God has in store for them. I've got a feeling that when it is your time, God will say, 'Hi. George, my good and faithful servant.'"–Dave Osborn

unlikely

Marlene

unlikely

The Simple Truth about

Finding God's Will and

Plan for Your Life

Dr. George Goodman

TATE PUBLISHING & *Enterprises*

Published by Tate Publishing & Enterprises, LLC
127 E. Trade Center Terrace | Mustang, Oklahoma 73064 USA
1.888.361.9473 | www.tatepublishing.com

Tate Publishing is committed to excellence in the publishing industry. The company reflects the philosophy established by the founders, based on Psalm 68:11,
"The LORD *gave the word and great was the company of those who published it."*

Book design copyright © 2008 by Tate Publishing, LLC. All rights reserved.
Cover design by Leah LeFlore
Interior design by Jonathan Lindsey
Published in the United States of America

ISBN: 978-1-60604-843-6
1. Christian Living   2. Spiritual Growth
3. Inspiration   4. Motivational
12.02.10

dedication

To all the *"unlikely"* people of the world.

May you begin to see yourselves as God sees you.

This book is dedicated to the many Christians that sit
in church and wonder how they can serve our LORD
in a more meaningful way. Whether you are a new
believer or whether you have known our LORD for a lifetime, get ready—God has a plan for you and an incredible journey that He wants you to embark upon.

Jesus answered, "I am the way and the truth and the life.
No one comes to the Father except through me."

John 14:6—NIV

And now I will show you the most excellent way.

1 Corinthians 12:31—NIV

acknowledgements

I want to thank my LORD and Savior for the vision that He has given me to write this book. The process of watching a work such as this come full circle, from concept to reality, has been truly amazing. Being a part of God's plan and purpose has been more of a blessing to me than I can possibly begin to communicate. I thank God for the opportunity to be a part of something so wonderful.

In the early drafting stages, John, my accountability partner, was instrumental in helping to shape the outline. Over the last few years, he has been there for me, especially when times were tough and I needed a Christian brother to encourage me. He never gave up on me and was always there to speak the truth, sometimes the painful truth, seasoned with grace, when I needed it most. Our friendship has meant a lot to me over the last few years. God allowed John and me to cross paths so that He could ultimately be glorified. This work (ministry) and the credit for it all belongs completely to Him.

I would also like to thank my wife, Judy, for the wonderful example that she is of a patient, kind, loving Christian wife. She desires, in all things, to bring glory to God by how she chooses to live her life. Her relationship with God is very real to her.

More than any woman I know, she displays the fruits of the spirit by daily living out her faith with conviction. She helped me through the countless hours that I spent in my office, in front of my computer, seeking God for inspiration (reading, researching, pondering, and writing). She prayed for me, encouraged me, challenged me, and most importantly, she always believed in me. God has blessed me with someone who understands me, accepts me, loves me, and laughs at all my quirks.

My sister, Melanie, was the first person to read my manuscript for this book. I must say that she has been one of my biggest fans. She has read, reread, proofread, and contributed so much along the way as this book developed. I will always be grateful to her for the constant encouragement that she consistently gave me throughout this process. She is a great example of what a big sister ought to be. I love her and thank God that He put her in my life.

A big "thank you" goes out to my good friend Dr. Paul Karpecki for agreeing to take time out of his incredibly busy schedule to read and critique this book prior to submission for publication. In my profession, Paul lectures, publishes, and practices on the cutting edge. He must be the hardest working man I know. Paul is a great man of God whom I deeply respect for his wisdom and gentle nature. He is one of many godly men that has been placed in my life to help me through my Christian journey. Considering all his accomplishments, he is very modest. I am honored to know him and call him my friend.

In their own unique ways, my children (Aaron, Hannah, Ethan, and Ryan) inspired me to keep working. All I have to do is look at them to find inspiration. I thank God that He blessed me with such awesome children. I don't just say they are great because they are mine, I say it because they are truly sweet spirited and God centered. They are the clearest and purest examples of God's love for me in my life. Their childlike faith inspires me and reminds me how, as adults, we need to put everything aside and seek God and pray without fear, shame, reservation, or motive. Listening to my kids pray as I tuck them in at night is a truly humbling experience.

After putting the kids to bed and praying with each of them, I would often begin writing. While most of my writing took place while they were sleeping, occasionally, during the day, inspiration would come, and when I needed to get away and put on paper what was burning inside of me, they were so sweet and patient with me. They will never know what they mean to me and how much I love and appreciate them for who they are.

 He created everything there is—nothing exists that He didn't make.

John 1:3—TLB

God will provide for His children; this book and the story behind why I wrote it are no exception. God provided for me: the vision, the material, the time, the means, the accountability relationship, and the publisher. It is my goal in this book to present simple truths about what having a meaningful relationship with our LORD Jesus Christ is all about.

I also want to thank all my favorite Christian authors who have never ceased to inspire me to personally put into words the vision that God placed in my heart. When I struggled through dark times in my life, books by these great men and women of God lifted my spirits and gave me renewed focus and purpose. It is a rare and glorious thing to be able to both grasp what it means to be a Christian and have the gift to articulate that to the reader in a meaningful way. Someday I hope to meet some of these writers, shake their hands, and personally thank them for the inspiration and motivation that they unknowingly gave me to attempt and complete this book. Most of all, I want to thank them for giving me the courage to take the leap of faith. I now know what goes into the making of a book, and I deeply respect these writers for their contributions to the Christian world of literature, as well as their contribution to my Christian journey.

I also want to thank all the wonderful people at Tate Publishing for believing in me. From the beginning, they were able to see and share in my vision. They made this book possible. As an author, especially a new author, I cannot express how wonderful it is to be able to write a book, say what you want to say, and have a publishing company see the vision and believe in the project and then have the means to make the dream of publishing this book a reality. The process of writing an entire book can be a daunting yet wonderfully fulfilling and exhilarating experience. Prior to this experience, if I had been an established author desiring to write a second or third book, then this process would probably have been less intimidating for me, because the door to the world of writing and publishing would have previously been opened for me. However, walking through this door for the first time, as I am doing, has truly been a blessing for me and a rare opportunity, which I humbly realize. I really appreciate the faith that Tate Publishing has placed in me and in my work. I also appreciate the freedom they have given me to express what I believe that God has placed on my heart, without compromise.

When I received my publishing contract, I read through it carefully, like I would any contract. As I approached the end of the document, right before the signing page, I noticed there was included, as part of the contract, a page that read, "Tate Publishing's Statement of Belief."[1] While I read through this part of the document, I found myself getting more and more excited. Their explanation of what they believe about God and the Bible was thorough and completely biblically sound. As I read it, I realized that these people really knew and believed everything about the Gospel message that I hold dear. I found nothing contained therein that I had any disagreement with. I like knowing that Tate Publishing's thoughts about God, Jesus, salvation, redemption, etc., are in total agreement with what I believe the Bible to communicate. Their "statement of belief" is included in every contract so that every author who signs with them clearly understands their doctrinal position.

In this day and age, it is refreshing to know that there are still believers who have a reverence for God and elevate Him to His rightful place in their lives, in their jobs, and throughout the marketplace. I am proud to be associated with a wonderful Christian company who raises high the banner of Christianity in all aspects of what they do. Without a doubt, I know that I have been led, by God, to the right publisher for this book. I pray that God would continue to guide the staff of Tate Publishing, because they are giving Christian authors a means of getting their work into the marketplace. May God continue to bless these fine people of faith for their ministry, their commitment to pursuing excellence, and for putting God first in all things.

> The LORD gave the word: great was the company of those
> that published it.

Psalms 68:11—KJV

table of contents

foreword

After reading *"Unlikely"* by my good friend and colleague Dr. George Goodman, I felt a strong sense of emotion, because I could relate to so much of what was written and the great lessons that were captured in this must-read book.

Recently, in the span of one year, I watched my father (who was my closest friend) pass away from terminal cancer, went through the difficult task of leaving a very abusive relationship (that I felt bound to for some reason), left my current job at a very well-respected medical center, and had three friends pass away at an early age. I truly couldn't imagine what all of this could mean and how anyone could see the benefit of a year such as this, what my purpose could be, or how God could take a life like mine and make it extraordinary ... yet it was a year that changed my life for the better. Although I deeply miss my father and dear friends who went on to be with God, I am grateful for all that happened to me and how it opened my eyes and my heart to the intimate relationship with God that I could previously only imagine—to experience real joy, passion for life, and gratitude to the fullest. It was only at that point that my life finally started changing for the better. My way would never have led to the abundance of God's way. George's writing about God's plan and His will for our lives and the importance of surrendering ourselves and our plans to Him was so insightful.

George's insights into the concepts of ask and you will receive, the importance of prayer, and the purpose of trials and tribulations will be immensely valuable to many readers. Accountability and the importance of friendship is so well elucidated in his writings and the positives of accountability and their contribution to a life of abundance of love, faith, joy, and peace are explained in a way that will allow the reader to feel that accountability and other such traits are positive terminology. I found so many of the chapters valuable in my life and some areas such as *"God's opinion is all that really matters,"* helped me and will likely help many readers who sometimes try to please others or seek their approval, when we really need to only be pleasing God—in return, we will find true happiness for ourselves.

Finally, as George states, God selects the *"unlikely"*—those that feel unlovable or imperfect at times. What a blessing to be the *"unlikely"* ones that God can guide to create extraordinary lives by living His *"good, pleasing, and perfect will."* Everyone who has ever experienced questions in understanding their life, as well as difficulties and tribulations, and has wondered how God can make a divine purpose of our life should read this fantastic and insightful book.

Dr. Paul M. Karpecki

March 13, 2008

a must-read
introduction

The purpose of this book is to cause us to question the manner in which we live out our Christian faith. Have we developed a deep, abiding, and unshakable faith, or do we just have a religious veneer that we can hide behind that keeps everyone from seeing the person that we really are behind our mask? Asking Christ to come into our lives and change us is just the beginning of our journey. For some of us, our spiritual growth stops there.

For many of us, we have walked the path of religion, but we haven't fully grasped the relationship aspect of our faith and found the liberation of our hearts to fully trust God for our every need. Is it our heart's cry to intimately know our LORD and Savior Jesus Christ and seek out His *good, pleasing, and perfect will*" (Romans 12:2—NIV) for our lives? If it is your earnest desire to grow into a closer relationship with our LORD, then this book is definitely for you.

There are many spiritual truths contained in this book. Some of them are easier to learn about than others. As disciples of Christ, our ultimate goal should be for us to be conformed into the image of Christ, no matter what difficulties present themselves along the way. Change is never easy. When we are being shaped by God's truth, it can be painful, especially if our pride is injured. Being receptive to hearing from God and having a willingness to change areas of our life that are not submitted to Him is a huge step in our spiritual development.

Occasionally, as we learn about the deeper truths and mysteries of God's Word, we discover things about ourselves that are tough for us to face.

It is my prayer that you would stop and pray, *before* you read this book.

I want you to ask God that He would prepare your heart to receive His truths as He reveals them to you. My tendency as a writer is to "shoot it to you straight" while trying to speak the truth in a loving way, without watering down the message. For the faint of heart, this can seem brutal at times. Believe me; I mean no disrespect whatsoever. I just believe that my calling and purpose in writing this book were to communicate (sometimes with boldness) what God has revealed to me, through His Word, as I have struggled through learning to live out my Christian faith.

> If you cling to your life, you will lose it; but if you give it up for me, you will save it.
>
> Matthew 10:39—TLB

Personally, it is my heart's desire that when God shows me an area of my life that is not in line with His Word, I want to be receptive to admitting my faults and to making the necessary changes to align my life with His plan, as it is revealed in His

Word. I pray that you will read through this book and maintain the same receptive attitude. Your toes will be occasionally stepped on and your foundation will be shaken at times, but I am asking you to endure the tough questions and truly seek God in all things contained herein. Substantial spiritual growth always awaits you if you will incline your heart to receive it.

I will often refer to God's *"good, pleasing, and perfect will"* for your life because I believe we all have a "will" that God specifically created for each of us. It is our job and responsibility as disciples to get to know God in a personal way so that He will reveal His will to each of us. I hope that in some small way God will use me to help show you His *"good, pleasing, and perfect will"* for your life.

I mentioned previously that I have strived to speak the truth, in love, seasoned with grace, without diluting it in any way. While some of it is easy to hear, some of it is not. I promise you, everything in this book is intentionally presented in such a way as to urge you to live to a higher standard (the standard to which, as disciples of Christ, we have been called) and, in the process, help you develop a deeper, more meaningful, more intimate relationship with the LORD. I know that the only way that you will fully discover God's *"good, pleasing, and perfect will"* is to encourage each of you to grow in your faith and commitment to Him by revealing to you what the Bible says about His will for you. Learning more about Him helps you to better understand and embrace His plan and His purpose for your life.

In almost every instance in this book, I have chosen to acknowledge and present God's Word first, and then follow it with discussion, rather than reversing the order and manipulating God's Word by bending it and trying to make it say what I want it to say. It is my intent to give glory to God by allowing Him to speak first and then present my thoughts afterward as they align with His thoughts. This may seem like a simple distinction to you, but to me, it was extremely important and it allowed, in a symbolic way, the opportunity to show God the respect and reverence that He deserves. I also did this because I feel that too many people try to twist the Bible to say things that were not intended; therefore, I want to honor God in this way—by giving Him first priority. I did my very best to communicate the message He intended and not take scripture out of context to justify my position, as so many people do these days.

The answers to all of life's most important questions can be found in God's Word. In order to discover these answers, we must learn to prioritize our time so that we will read and study God's Word. When we realize and decide to make God's Word the *"final authority"* in all our decision making and live according to its instruction, we will realize that God's *"good, pleasing, and perfect will"* is more easily discovered than we may have previously thought. My challenge to you, as you read this book, is to make it a point to get in the Bible and start reading. Miraculous things will happen in your life if you will start setting out to discover God in the pages of His Word.

Key Thought:

Just think, if God's spoken words can cause all of creation to leap into existence, imagine what reading His written Word can do to your life!

We must always keep in mind that, this side of heaven, our journey is a process and not just a destination. We must seek out

His will for our lives in order to discover the abundant life we all wish for. Ultimately, I want you to come to know our Creator and Savior in a personal way, because I want your walk with Him to be all that it was meant to be.

Chapter 1

unlikely

But small is the gate and narrow the road that leads to life, and only a few find it.

Matthew 7:14—NIV

Are you on the path?

I think that every one of us wants to believe that we are on the right path in life. Think about it: do we really *know* what path we are on? Maybe we think that we know, but perhaps, instead, we are actually lost, but we don't even know it because our surroundings seem strangely familiar to us, somehow strangely comfortable. If the "road" is so narrow, how do we even know that we are on it? Maybe we are in the wrong lane; going in the wrong direction. Maybe we are off on the shoulder, or maybe, we have spun off the road and found ourselves in the ditch, feeling stranded. Who knows? Maybe we are off the road completely and out in "left field" and seem content to be off the road, in our state of *"lostness."*

Consider Moses. Here is a man that ran away from Egypt and his problems and became lost in the desert (his "left field").

It was in this place that God met up with Moses and revealed to him His divine purpose for Moses' life. Upon hearing the news, Moses questioned God and even told Him that he was not the man for the job. In his own mind, Moses was the most *"unlikely"* person to carry out God's purpose.

That's exactly the point!

This is so important! The way that you see yourself is not the way God sees you. God sees so much more than we are capable of seeing. We tend to see only the physical world around us (our surroundings), but God sees everything. His eyes see both the spiritual and physical world, as well as our hearts and our minds. He knows us better than we know ourselves. Never forget that!

God generally calls people who are completely *"unlikely."* The Bible is loaded with examples that show us that God doesn't usually call people that seem suited for the task. However, once God calls you for His purpose, He will equip you for the task and begin to work His wonders through you! Ultimately, God is not dependent upon you, but He loves you and He wants you. God wants your heart ... not part of it, but all of it!

Fact:
Every single one of us has a divine calling on our lives, a purpose for existing.

Ask Yourself This Question:
Do you really care to find out what this divine calling is?

We *all* play a small, but significant part in God's big plan. As an author, it is my expressed, specific intent to encourage you to personally examine this issue. Believe me when I say, it is much better to live a life in the shadow and protection of God's enormous purpose than to wander aimlessly in the open desert. Not only is the aimlessly wandering life barren, it is devoid of real life itself. Who wants to live a life without knowing your divine plan or purpose? Don't we all, deep down, want to know that our lives had real meaning and significance? Isn't there an innate desire in all of us to know that our lives had some lasting impact on our world? Don't we all want to leave this earth knowing that our legacy will live on through the lives of our children, and those we touched along the way, for generations to come? What is the legacy that we are leaving behind? Is it a legacy that testifies to the kingdom of God?

> I tell you, now is the time of God's favor, now is the day of salvation.
>
> 2 Corinthians 6:2—NIV

Many times the Bible says, *"He who has ears, let him hear."* I want to share truth with you and I want to know that you are hearing me with spiritual ears. How can I say what I want to say to reach out and effectively grip your heart? If you are ready to make a lasting change, find God in the desert that you are in, and get on that narrow road that leads to life and an eternal civilization, then let's cry out to Him and seek Him together. Today is the day!

> Ask and it will be given to you; seek and you will find; knock and the door will be opened to you. For everyone who asks receives; he who seeks finds; and to him who knocks, the door will be opened.
>
> Matthew 7:7–8—NIV

Question:

Are you knocking?

Are you curious about what lies on the other side of that amazing door? There are three things about this verse that we need to focus on:

- Knocking is an action.
- Asking is an action.
- Seeking is an action.

Key Thought:

God is right where you are, right now ... and He always has been. He is waiting for you to *knock* on His door, *ask* Him for His gift of grace, and *seek* His purpose for your life.

As any loving father, God earnestly desires to have a deeper relationship with you. When we are self-absorbed, God has many ways that He will use to get our attention. God will use situations and circumstances that get us out of our comfort zones in order to draw us closer to Him. He is patient and He is waiting for us to come to the point where we will reach out to Him and lean on Him for our every need. We must remember that His "door" literally separates the realms of spiritual life and death.

Question:

Are you ready to do the "unlikely" thing?

For some of you, the unlikely thing may be to finally seek God for Him to reveal to you what your purpose is in His big plan. For the rest of you, the unlikely thing may be that you need to reach out to a loving Father Who has been patiently waiting the whole time. He has allowed you to have the time that you needed to discover that you desperately need Him and you can no longer make it through your life on your own, by your own sufficiency. Regardless of what your *"unlikely"* thing is, we all desperately need our Heavenly Father. The problem is that many of us haven't figured that out yet.

Are you ready for your relationship with your Heavenly Father to become intimate? Are you tired of drifting aimlessly through your life on the open sea without a compass or even a port of safe harbor? Are you ready to live each day knowing that you are actually living out God's *"good, pleasing, and perfect will"* (Romans 12:2) for your life? If you are, then I suggest that you read on.

If you will open your heart and mind to the possibility that you can have an intimate relationship with the Creator of the universe and draw strength from Him for your every need, you will find Him when you "knock, ask, and seek," and He will be there waiting for you to walk alongside you. When you are ready to depart from the old way of living, God is ready to take you on a journey of discovery and reveal to you what your divine purpose has been all along. It is about time that you knew your part in God's big plan.

●●●

When you look at some of the main characters mentioned in the Bible, there are some excellent examples of the *"unlikely"* type of people that God chooses. As you look at their individual sto-ries (background, experiences, strengths, weaknesses, etc.), you will see how God called them and what He did through them in mighty ways. After learning their stories and looking at the seeming contra-indications for their effective service, it is clear to see that God obviously sees things differently than we do. We need to thank God for that! I have often thought to myself, "If God could speak to Balaam through the mouth of a donkey (Numbers 22), then He is perfectly capable of speaking through me or you." Just as we are to walk by faith and not by sight (2 Corinthians 5:7), we must understand that God sees the begin-ning, the middle, and the end. He knows how many hairs we have on our heads (Matthew 10:30) and the number of our days on this earth (Hebrews 9:27).

MOSES
JACob
David
Jonah
Paul/Saul

Again, let's look at the life of Moses:

Moses was born into slavery in Egypt. Pharaoh had ordered that all Hebrew males who were born be thrown into the Nile River. To avoid his capture and execution, Moses' mother placed Moses in a basket and set him in the reeds of the Nile River. Moses was found by Pharaoh's daughter when she went to the river to bathe. Pharaoh's daughter sent for Moses' mother to nurse him. Moses was adopted by Pharaoh's daughter and raised as an Egyptian, a prince of Egypt. As an adult, after killing an Egyptian for beat-ing a Hebrew, Moses fled to the desert for fear of his life. While

Moses was living as an outcast, God met up with him in the desert in the form of a burning bush. God called Moses to go back to Egypt and free His people from slavery. Moses resisted ... God insisted. God worked mightily in the life of Moses.

Basic Facts:
- Moses was a Hebrew—Raised as an Egyptian.
- Moses was a criminal—A fugitive who fled from justice.
- Moses was "slow of speech and tongue"—Not an eloquent or convincing spokesperson.
- Moses was sent back to confront Pharaoh—Who would dare give Pharaoh (the king of Egypt) an ultimatum?— God protected Moses.

There are many other examples of biblical characters that God called to do amazing things. The truth is, the list of *"unlikely"* people in the Bible is seemingly endless. (If you want to know about other specific examples, then look into the lives of some of the following biblical figures: Abraham, Isaac, Jacob, Joshua, Joseph, David, Noah, Isaiah, Jonah, Jeremiah, Nehemiah, Paul, Peter, Ruth, Esther ... and the list goes on.)

Just as God called some pretty interesting (and seemingly unqualified) people to carry out His purpose, He has also called me to become an author, so as to take this burden that He placed on my heart and deliver it to yours.

As a fellow believer, I feel that I should start this book by sharing some of my testimony with you. It is my belief that you should know a little bit more about whom it is that is writing to you. Although my experiences in life differ from your experiences, there are universal components of every person's story that need to be expressed. It is in these fundamental similarities that, as believers, we may begin to form a bond with one another, through Christ.

My Testimony:

I want to acknowledge the impact that my children have had on my spiritual life. It is amazing how our children observe our lives as parents. I have heard it said that, as parents, we may be the best (or worst) example of Jesus that our children ever get to see. As I prepared to write this book, I didn't even know that I was preparing to write a book. All I knew was that, more than anything, I wanted to find God's will for my life. Every night when I prayed with my children, I would ask them to pray for me to know God's will for my life. All they knew was that I wanted, more than anything, to know, beyond the shadow of a doubt, without hesitation, God's will for my life and where I could best serve Him in ministry. They were aware that I had applied for positions of ministry and that I had been seeking counsel with pastors from my church. They were also aware that I had been reading everything that I could get my hands on. It blessed me so much to get calls from my children during the day and hear them ask, *"Do you have your answer? Did God tell you what you are supposed to do yet?"*

After I began the process of writing, my children colored pictures and left me little notes of encouragement. Early in the writing process, my oldest son, Aaron (who was nine years old at the time), left me a note that still blesses me and makes me smile every time I read it.

Dad,   3/19/06

I hope your book becomes
a best-seller. You are doing
really good on it. ✝ ⊕

                    Love You
                    Aaron

I placed these notes and pictures by my computer as inspiration to keep striving toward the goal of finishing this project. It means so much to me that my kids believe in me so much. More than that, it really blesses me that they, at such a young age, have such a clear concept of who God is and a faith in God that guides their thoughts and actions. God has blessed me and entrusted me with four of the most precious souls on the planet. Every one of my children is completely unique, and it never ceases to amaze me what pearls of wisdom and insight, and pure innocence, comes from "the mouth of babes." They remind me what "child-like faith" is all about. I am blessed by being able to see God's hand at work through the lives of my children.

Sadly, I haven't always been the Christian that I should have been. My "Christian" life began as a child. I grew up in a "Christian" home. We always attended church but never had any joy about doing so. I was raised in an atmosphere that was legalistic, Bible-thumping, and quasi-militaristic. Although my father is now a patient and loving man, he wasn't that person while I was a child. As the fifth of six children, I was mostly well behaved. The truth is, I was well behaved, but it was more out of fear than out of respect. My father wouldn't hesitate to discipline us. The problem was that his discipline wasn't delivered in a loving manner; instead, it tended to be cruel and harsh. I know what he was trying to accomplish, but something was lost in translation and in delivery.

Today, my father is a completely different person, and I mean *completely* different. After my mother got sick (a disease that ultimately took her life), I guess my father got a wake-up call on the value of life and the importance of relationships. I often ask my sister, "Who kidnapped our father and replaced him with this person?" Time has mellowed my father and been very good to him. He is now an openly loving, patient person. I love my father very much, and I have definitely grown to respect him over the last few years. When I was a kid, he wasn't the person that I thought I needed him to be, and now, as an adult, the loving father that was missing during my childhood has left a giant hole in my heart that nothing or no one else but God can fill.

I have made it my mission to love my kids and make them feel secure and loved unconditionally. Like my father, I have also mellowed with time, but thankfully, I have the relationship with my kids that I always dreamed of my father having with me. That is really important to me. I want them each to know, beyond the shadow of a doubt, that I think the world of them and that I thank God for each of them. They know that they are a gift in my life from God.

> You intended to harm me, but God intended it for good to accomplish what is now being done, the saving of many lives.
>
> Genesis 50:20—NIV

The difficulty I had with my father while I was a child, as I know now, was all part of God's plan for my life. The pain, heartache, and resentment that I had toward my father was totally consuming. As an adult, when I finally mustered the courage to tell him how I felt about how he had hurt me in the past, he just looked at me as if he had no clue whatsoever about what I was saying. The ridiculous part of all of it is that for all those years, I harbored unforgiveness toward him that was not hurting him at all but, instead, was killing me and my spiritual life. Something drastic changed in my heart that day. God used that moment in my life to slap me across the face and shake me. It was all so clear to me. Looking back at that moment, I can remember having the overwhelming thought come over me that I needed to accept, forgive, love, trust, and move past. It was a God-moment. My prayer is that God will always do whatever he has to do to get my attention, no matter what it takes.

Key Thought:

It is amazing how we tend to see our Heavenly Father in the same light that we see our earthly fathers.

Growing up, I was taught to have a reverential fear of God. As I sit here and look back on my childhood, I think that my views on who God is were shaped in large part by my father. I perceived God as being more stern and less loving. For this reason, I feel that I struggled for a long time with having a healthy understanding of who God really is and what His nature is really like. Over the years, I have come to realize that God loves me and wants to have a meaningful relationship with me. He wants me to serve Him, but He wants me to love and respect Him. Yes, He expects me to live up to His standards, but even when I fail, I now know that He loves me just the same.

> Instead, we will speak the truth in love, growing in every way more and more like Christ, who is the head of his body, the church.
>
> Ephesians 4:15—NLT

I have always been around church, and I thank God for that. God has given me a gift of remembering scriptures and applying them to everyday life. This is only a gift when it is used out of love and not out of legalism. When used out of legalism, the Word of God can be more of a sledgehammer than an instrument of sharing His loving grace and mercy. I am ashamed to admit it now, but I spent many miserable years poisoned by legalism. I now realize that when we learn to speak the truth in love, we will begin to bless people with God's Word instead of bashing them with it. As believers, we must remember that it is the Holy Spirit's responsibility to convict people of their sin, not ours! Legalism helps no one. It stunts our spiritual growth and robs us of our joy. I am speaking from personal experience. Don't fall into this trap!

Recently, I watched an interview in which two Christian leaders were discussing the concept of speaking the truth in love. During this interview, two statements were made that really made me stop and think:

- Speaking the truth without love leads to cold-hearted legalism.
- Speaking love without the truth leaves people bereft of direction.

When the truth is spoken without love, people get hurt. In contrast, when love is spoken without the truth, people are left with no guidance. However, when the truth of God is spoken in a loving manner, people are exposed to the life-changing power of the Word of God. Lives will be changed. People will be drawn to the cross.

Until October 2005, I had head knowledge about God, but that knowledge had never completely found its way to my stubborn, hardened heart. Through a series of life-changing, painful events, God literally turned my life upside down and shook it. In a short period of time, God allowed me to experience the pain of many things. I lost my business, experienced bankruptcy, endured an unwanted divorce, lost custody of my children and had them move four hours away, and was hit with almost $40K in taxes from the misadvised sale of a business. I was devastated on all levels. I experienced deep depression. I really felt like I had lost everything. But I hadn't! I realized that I had lost everything *except* that which was most important of all: *my faith* in my LORD and Savior. I cried out to Him and rededicated my life to Him, and I believe that for the first time in my life, I really came into a relationship with Him. For the first time, I had lost my "religion" and found my "faith" in a right relationship with my Creator. The truth of the following verses finally registered with me.

> And you have forgotten that word of encouragement that addresses you as sons: "My son, do not make light of the LORD's discipline, and do not lose heart when he rebukes you, because the LORD disciplines those he loves, and he punishes everyone he accepts as a son." Endure hardship as discipline; God is treating you as sons. For what son is not disciplined by his father? If you are not disciplined (and everyone undergoes discipline), then you are illegitimate children and not true sons.
>
> Hebrews 12:5–8—NIV

The truth of this passage is a hard one for many to accept. The fact is that I had made God second place in my life by living out an appearance of godliness, when in reality, in my hardened heart, I had been harboring unforgiveness, living for my own selfish desires, and God wasn't even on my radar. God lovingly allowed my foundation to be shaken to get my attention back on Him.

Question:

Did God cause these terrible things to happen to me?

Absolutely not! He *allowed* them to happen. Remember this: It was my own selfishness and stupidity that got me into that mess in the first place. Those events were brought on by me. I could have been a better husband, a better father, a better businessman, etc. I could have avoided much of that pain if I had put God in His proper place in my life and lived according to His plan.

We need to know that God will forgive us, and He does forgive us when we sin against Him, *but* He still allows us to experience the *consequences* of our sins. I stand here today, thankful that He disciplined me. I am thankful because it just proves to me once again that He really does love me as a son (Hebrews 12:6). I endured His discipline and have grown tremendously because of it, and I now know that I need Him more than ever (Hebrews 12:7). To try and live life without Him is nothing short of crazy. Imagine if I had lived out the rest of my days not knowing this truth. What a waste that would have been. In contrast, if I had not received His loving discipline, then I would not be considered to be His son (Hebrews 12:8). If I were not His son, that would mean that I was lost and did not know Him. I would be on the road to destruction. We all have a choice: eternal death *or* temporal chastisement for your own good? For me, that choice was easy. I'll take a second helping of discipline. *"Thank you, may I have another ... ?"*

Key Thought:

The things of this world will pass away,
but our relationship with God will last forever.

It has always bothered me that I couldn't look back on my life and call out a specific time or instance where I knew that I had given my life over to God. It is not as if the day, time, or place has to be recited as proof of salvation. What matters is that God gets a hold of us and we completely surrender to Him. On a Thursday night in October 2005, I got on my knees and cried out to God to change me. I was tired of being angry. I was tired of being miserable. I was tired of hurting everyone in my life that was important to me. I had been selfish and immature and downright bitter. I had been an arrogant jerk for way too long. It was time for a change.

The months that have followed have been enlightening and amazing. God continues to challenge me and show me His character, as He is developing mine. I am certain that I know Him and that He has my life and my complete attention. I know that my best effort is completely insufficient. I confess that I absolutely could not make it through this life without Him. I praise God for being the lover of my soul! I thank Him for never giving up on me. No matter how stubborn, selfish, controlling, etc. that I had been, He was always doing a work in me in preparation for things to come.

> Being confident of this very thing, that He who has begun a good work in you will complete it until the day of Jesus Christ.
>
> Philippians 1:6—NKJV

I am confident that the good work that He has begun in me He is still perfecting. How wonderful to have such a gracious and loving Heavenly Father. It is my prayer that as I submit my will to God and write out the words in this book (that I am convinced are flowing from Him), you will come to see clearly how to draw closer to our LORD and seek Him for His will for your life.

Recently, my friend Mike (one of my best friends, who happens to be a non-believer) asked me a question that made me step back and evaluate some profound, but basic, truths about my life and my faith. It was such a ridiculously simple thought that it almost made me feel stupid for never having wrestled this idea before. It was much like the feeling that I got when I read *Mere Christianity* by C.S. Lewis for the first time. I like to think that I am a pretty intelligent guy, but when I read works from guys like C.S. Lewis, I feel like I am intellectually challenged. I have to read a little bit and put the book down and process what I have just read and then pick it up again; otherwise, I tend to lose the deeper meaning of the passage. (Anyone who has read *Mere Christianity* knows what I mean. C.S. Lewis thought on a different plane than most of us. He was a true intellectual and spiritual giant in my eyes.)

The question my friend Mike asked me is this:
"What is the difference between *truth* and *reality*?"

Wow! I really struggled with this seemingly simple, yet profound, question. I tend to be a deep thinker, and I like to work things out in my mind, so after a few days of meditating on this question, I came to a few conclusions.

- *Truth is absolute.* No matter what, real *truth* is always true. Real *truth* is not situational. Real *truth* is not relative. Real *truth* is constant; it is irrefutable. The best example of all is God's Word. God's Word is the real *truth*. It is absolute. It is non-negotiable. It is fact! It is God's recorded Word. We can trust it with our very lives.
- *Reality is relative. Reality* (in the sense to which I am referring to it here) is what we *believe* to be true. It is our own private perception. I believe that each of us live in a world that consists of our own private *reality*. In our respective worlds, we believe what we believe and we stay in our comfort zone until, out of the blue, real *truth* comes along and knocks us around. It is during these times that we are faced with a real dilemma.

If we would be truly honest with ourselves, we would quickly realize that we have been wrong about a few beliefs that we held as our own individual "truths." The problem is that our *reality* (perception) can be jaded when compared to the real *truth* that we find in God's Word. The real *truth* reveals to us that we are often misguided and/or uninformed; that is our real *reality*. The Bible wasn't written to accommodate our lifestyles and our choices for how our life should be, according to our plan. Instead, the Bible has been given to us to show us the path to holiness and how our lives are to be lived, according to God's plan.

"That was then; this is now ..."
It seems to me that we live in a culture that thinks of morality (right *vs.* wrong) as something that is relative only to what society, as a whole, thinks at that given moment in time. It seems we all want to find a way (even subconsciously) to justify our actions as appropriate (sometimes we even look for scripture to back up our misguided attempts to say that we are serving God, when in reality, we are just looking for excuses to justify our chosen path). This is like a house built upon a foundation of sand; it will crumble when the next wave of cultural beliefs washes in. While most people look at the world with a perspective that comes from this widely held belief of "moral relativism," we, as disciples, have God's Word to look to for true guidance. There is nothing morally relative about God. God's Word (in regard to how we should live our lives) is morally absolute.

Key Thoughts:

Moral relativism is a house built
upon a foundation of sand.

Moral absolutism is a house built
upon a foundation of solid rock.

The beauty of knowing God and learning about Him in His Word is that *God is the same yesterday, today, and forever* (Hebrews

13:8). What was wrong 100 years ago, 500 years ago, 1000 years ago, and even before that, is still wrong today. Likewise, what was right 100 years ago, 500 years ago, 1000 years ago, and even before that, is still right today! When we learn to accept that God is infinite and infinitely wise, we will have a much easier time accepting and adhering to His Word and His plan for our lives. He truly does know best!

When we search God's Word for its meaning (what is truly meant by the Bible), we will discover many things that we didn't know about God, and as we read His Word, we will also discover that many of the things we thought we knew, we had learned incorrectly. I find that so many Christians really think that they know a lot about God, when "in reality," they know very little. This reminds me of what my grandmother used to say. She'd say, "You know what happens when you *'assume.'*" (I "ass-u-me" you know what I mean.)

"Absolute Truth" *vs.* "Absolute Fact":

Whether or not we believe what the Bible says, it is God's Word; it is His Truth ... period. That does not change; no matter what we think about it and no matter how we try to rationalize it. As "rational" human beings, in our minds, because we feel so "enlightened," we have the tendency to elevate ourselves to a level that is most likely offensive to God. We live our lives without Him, learn for ourselves along the way, we size things up, and in the end we tend to accept everything that we have collectively assimilated and come to believe it as "absolute truth." Where we go wrong is that we accept these beliefs as "absolute fact." When these *self*-discovered "truths" and "facts" (beliefs) don't line up with God's truths, we have a real dilemma on our hands. The fact is that when we come to believe things that are not in line with God's Word (His Truth), we are absolutely wrong, no matter how strong our convictions may be about our position. This is further proof that we need to be reading God's Word and praying for a renewing of our minds. If we are going to be spiritually convicted about something, it better line up with God's Word. Otherwise, our sincerity is misplaced and we are sincerely wrong!

Question:

What level are you operating on?

Are you willing to admit that your reality (perception) *might* be wrong? Are you ready to admit that God knows best and that any other point of view is ultimately futile? Think about it this way:

Question:

What is it that we are concerned about?

Are we focused on *eternity*? Are we focused on the fact that we are going to spend *eternity* with our Creator? That we are going to live forever? Our real future, as believers, is with God, in heaven. Or ...

Are we focused on *temporary*? Life is a vapor. It is like a flash ... and then it's gone.

We have to ask ourselves these questions:
- Are we looking for God? If so,
- Where are we looking for Him?

> In his heart a man plans his course, but the LORD determines his steps.
>
> Proverbs 16:9—NIV

One of two scenarios is true for each of us. We are either walking on our own path and waiting for God to join us (FYI, this is *not* going to happen), or we are conforming our will by submitting to His will and we are walking on the narrow road that He has laid out for us. When we are walking with God, we have the assurance that we are on the narrow road. The only way that the narrow road is visible to us is while we are walking the road, with Him, living by faith.

A few months ago, I was being counseled by my associate pastor. He used an analogy to describe an idea to me. He described playing video games with his son. He talked about a combat game where, in order to complete your mission, you have to walk around in the dark searching for your objective. He said that you might take a step forward and suddenly you realize that there is a building in front of you that you couldn't see before. He paralleled this with walking by faith. He said that sometimes you just have to take that next step so that you can discover where God is leading you. You might take that step and realize that there is a roadblock and that you need to change your course slightly, or you may take that next step and realize that God has led you safely through spiritual land mines.

Key Thought:

God wants us to trust him.

Take Peter for example; he took that first step off the boat to walk out to Jesus on the water (Matthew 14:28–31). His faith allowed him to take that first step, but then he questioned the situation instead of continuing to trust God, and thus, he began to sink. If we could take that step of faith and continue to trust God to illuminate our next step along the path, we would grow tremendously in our faith. Through our obedience, with each passing step along the journey, our faith grows because we are developing a dependence upon God for His guidance and direction. Without His guidance and His direction, we have absolutely no hope of staying on the path. This is how we discover and develop a deeper, trusting relationship with God.

Question:

Do we even believe that God is real?

For since the creation of the world God's invisible qualities—His eternal power and divine nature—have been clearly seen, being understood from what has been made, so that men are without excuse.

Romans 1:20—NIV

Here is *truth* staring us right in the face again. We *must* acknowledge that God exists. His existence is undeniable. He has revealed Himself to us in so many ways. As Romans 1:20 points out, He has revealed Himself to us through the beauty and intricacy of nature. Just look around you; God is visible in all of creation. Forget all about "evolution" or "intelligent design." I believe in an Intelligent Designer!

I remember a time when I was a teenager when my church's youth group took a trip to Denver, Colorado, to attend a CIY conference (Christ in Youth). My youth group leader and I had a close bond, and he insisted that I go on this trip. I can vividly remember this trip because of an encounter that I had with God while I was at the conference. I also remember this trip because I got to meet Rich Mullins, the Christian singer. He was a fairly new artist at that time, and I remember him singing a song during one of our praise and worship times that said, "Live like you'll die tomorrow; die knowing you'll live forever." Though his time on earth was short, he made it count. He was an awesome example of Christianity in action. To everyone that knew him, he seemed to have an amazing faith. His relationship with our LORD was so real it was palpable and infectious.

At the time I took this trip, I was really struggling with the whole concept of God being real or not. At the time, I remember that He didn't seem very real to me. One day, toward the end of the conference, I remember sitting outside, alone, during a time that was set aside for individual prayer. I sat there and I prayed, but I was so frustrated. I really wanted to believe in God, but I had serious doubts. I prayed and asked God if He would make Himself real to me. I prayed this prayer and just sat there quietly for what seemed like forever. Nothing happened, that is, until I opened my eyes. When I opened my eyes, I looked to the west. What I saw will stay with me until I die. I saw the Rocky

Mountains. In that instant, I had the immediate sense that God had spoken to me. In my spirit I knew that He was showing me a glimpse of Himself in the beauty and grandeur of the Rockies. It was as if He called out to me and said, *"Here I am. Look at my handiwork."* He gave me exactly what I needed. He showed me and confirmed in my heart that He is real. I am so thankful that He shared that moment with me. It changed my life and gave me a different perspective.

The fool says in his heart, "There is no God."

Psalm 14:1 & Psalm 53:1—NIV

(Brace yourself for this next comment.)
Anybody who would give anything or anyone else, other than God Himself, credit for the wonder of creation might as well walk up to God and personally spit in His face. As bold as this statement is, it is so true. It is an affront to God to even consider that creation was an accident, or the result of evolution, yet much of society, and even some professing Christians that I have met, give credence to the "theory" of evolution. Evolution is not factual. It is a theory, accepted as a fact only by its proponents.

Key Thought:

It takes just as much faith, if not more, to believe in evolution as it does to believe in God.

How "logically" ridiculous can we be? We know that God made it all (read Genesis again in case you forgot) and He made it all in six days—then He rested. As far as the "Big Bang" theory, the only truth to it I am sure, is when God spoke the universe into existence—it happened with a "*bang*"!

Creation occurred with God's spoken words. *Poof!* We are not descendants of monkeys, nor are we descendants of fish or a puddle of "primordial ooze." Our real ancestors are Adam and Eve. They were also created by God Himself. Make no mistake about it. You may think that I am being harsh, but we either believe in God and acknowledge who He is and what He has created, or we are robbing Him of His glory and majesty. If we will just look around, His fingerprints are everywhere we look. It's time that Christians start acknowledging the glory and majesty of God and defend Him when His nature or character is challenged or questioned, or we must ask ourselves the following question about our beliefs:

Question:

Do we really believe all this Bible stuff to be true?

Now faith is the substance of things hoped for, the evidence of things not seen.

Hebrews 11:1—KJV

We have our faith as the substance of the evidence of things we can't see. Think about what I just said. We have more evidence of God because we have this substance, which is our faith. Reduce that down. We have evidence of God because of our faith. Just because we cannot physically see God at work in our lives, doesn't mean He isn't there. However, we can see the evidence of His presence and we can testify to His provision for us, because of our faith. If you are confused, just remember this: God is faithful. Period.

Key Thought:

You can't see the wind, but you can see the effect of the wind.

Our faith helps us to fill in the voids and bridge the gaps in our understanding. We are to believe specifically because we can't see with our own eyes. This makes us rely on other things to measure or quantify God's presence. Anyone can believe in someone they can see with their own eyes, but it takes real faith to believe in someone you can't see. We should be more faithful, because God is faithful. He believes in us even when we don't believe in Him.

Question:

Do we believe that we need Him?

Believing that He exists is just the first piece of the puzzle, but coming to the realization that we *need* Him is the next step in our spiritual evolution.

Trust me, He exists. Because He exists, we need Him! Many

of us haven't come to grips with this *truth* yet. I have personally learned this one the hard way. Please take heed to my warning! It took me a very long time to realize that I was not in charge and that my best efforts left my life in shambles.

> There is a way that seems right to a man, but in the end it leads to death.
>
> Proverbs 14:12—NIV

 When are we going to accept that our way is a dead end? God's way is the best way. He has a specific plan for us, as we are about to find out in the next chapter.

Chapter 2

God's plan

[Read the following chapter (Romans 12) *carefully* and *meditate* on what it is saying to you personally.]

> Therefore, I urge you, brothers, in view of God's mercy, to offer your bodies as living sacrifices, holy and pleasing to God—this is your spiritual act of worship. Do not conform any longer to the pattern of this world, but be transformed by the renewing of your mind. Then you will be able to test and approve what God's will is—his good, pleasing and perfect will. For by the grace given me I say to every one of you: Do not think of yourself more highly than you ought, but rather think of yourself with sober judgment, in accordance with the measure of faith God has given you. Just as each of us has one body with many members, and these members do not all have the same function, so in Christ we who are many form one body, and each member belongs to all the others. We have different gifts, according to the grace given us. If a man's gift is prophesying, let him use it in proportion to his faith. If it is serving, let him serve; if it is teaching, let him teach; if it is encouraging, let him encourage; if it is contributing to the needs of others, let him give generously; if it is leadership, let him govern diligently; if it is showing mercy, let him do it cheerfully. Love must be sincere. Hate what is evil; cling to what is

good. Be devoted to one another in brotherly love. Honor one another above yourselves. Never be lacking in zeal, but keep your spiritual fervor, serving the LORD. Be joyful in hope, patient in affliction, faithful in prayer. Share with God's people who are in need. Practice hospitality. Bless those who persecute you; bless and do not curse. Rejoice with those who rejoice; mourn with those who mourn. Live in harmony with one another. Do not be proud, but be willing to associate with people of low position. Do not be conceited. Do not repay anyone evil for evil. Be careful to do what is right in the eyes of everybody. If it is possible, as far as it depends on you, live at peace with everyone. Do not take revenge, my friends, but leave room for God's wrath, for it is written: "It is mine to avenge; I will repay," says the LORD. On the contrary: "If your enemy is hungry, feed him; if he is thirsty, give him something to drink. In doing this, you will heap burning coals on his head." Do not be overcome by evil, but overcome evil with good.

Romans 12:1–21—NIV

In this passage, the apostle Paul is explaining to the Roman Christians how to live their lives so that their behavior would be honoring and pleasing to God. If you examine this passage carefully, you will notice that it is *loaded* with practical applications for living your life as a disciple of Christ. The instructions contained within this passage apply to us as much today as they did when they were written.

Key Thought:

God desires you to surrender every part of your life to Him.

I would like to take some time to break down Romans 12 and look at some key thoughts on a verse by verse basis. There is so much in Romans 12 that it is hard to process it all. By taking the verses and focusing on them one by one, I want to reinforce some key aspects of living like a true Christ-follower.

> Therefore, I urge you, brothers, in view of God's mercy, to offer your bodies as living sacrifices, holy and pleasing to God—this is your spiritual act of worship.
>
> Romans 12:1—NIV

Sacrifice—An act of giving up something valued for the sake of something else regarded as more important or worthy.[2]

Key Thought:

If you want to be filled with God, you must be empty of everything else.

To be a *living* sacrifice, we must come to the realization that God is worthy of our best; He is worthy of all our being. Offering ourselves as living sacrifices has deep meaning and some serious implications. It's about dying to self and sacrificially giving Him our needs and desires. It's about worshiping God by living out our faith daily. If we value our LORD more than we value ourselves, we will communicate this belief to Him through our thoughts, prayers, and actions. It is in this way that we become living sacrifices that are *holy and pleasing to God*. If He is really our LORD, then we belong to Him—not in part, but in whole. Therefore, we are to serve Him and give Him our all as our spiritual act of worship.

> Do not conform any longer to the pattern of this world, but be transformed by the renewing of your mind. Then you will be able to test and approve what God's will is—his good, pleasing and perfect will.
>
> Romans 12:2—NIV

This verse contains one of the key themes of this book, which is, the pursuit of God's *"good, pleasing, and perfect will"* for our lives. (We will spend a lot of time in this book referencing this specific verse and the concept that this verse communicates to us as believers and disciples of Christ.) As you re-read this verse, you will see that there is a wealth of knowledge in this verse alone. (a) Don't conform to this world or its systems; (b) Be transformed (changed into something better) by the renewing of your mind, and then (after this transformation); (c) You will be able to test and approve what God's *"good, pleasing, and perfect will"* is for your life. Meditate on this truth for a moment. Let it sink in deep. To me, it is clear that when we stop going with the flow of society and start living for God, He will renew our minds so that we can discover what His perfect plan is for our lives. What an awesome blessing it is to discover God's will for our lives!

> For by the grace given me I say to every one of you: Do not think of yourself more highly than you ought, but rather think of yourself with sober judgment, in accordance with the measure of faith God has given you.
>
> Romans 12:3—NIV

This is a verse that is all about perspective. When we elevate God to His proper status in our hearts and humble ourselves in His sight and in the sight of others, we are then considering ourselves to be no better than anyone else. To rephrase, if we recognize who God really is and recognize who we are in relation to Him and to those around us, we then have the mindset that God requires. God gives grace to the humble.

> Just as each of us has one body with many members, and these members do not all have the same function, so in Christ we who are many form one body, and each member belongs to all the others.

> Romans 12:4–5—NIV

To put it simply, everyone who professes faith in God and has accepted Jesus Christ as their LORD and Savior is a member of the "body" of Christ (the "Church"). We are all members of the same spiritual family. We each have our own unique position within the family. As I sit here and meditate on this verse, I am reminded of a story that I heard once during a sermon. The pastor was preaching on being a "member" of the body of Christ. He said that once upon a time there was a "big toe" who complained all the time because he desperately wanted to be an "eye." Rather than assuming the role that he was given, he constantly complained that he wanted to be something else; something "better" in his opinion. So after months of constant complaining, God decided to grant his wish. He made the "big toe" into an "eye." From that day on, the "big toe" complained even more, because now, as an eye, all he could see was the inside of a dirty sock! The moral of the story is this: we all have our God-given purpose and place to serve as a member of the body as a whole. We can fight God's purpose and plan, but in doing so, we will never discover where we fit in God's perfect plan for our lives. When we humble ourselves and seek God above all else, He will show us what we are supposed to be and then He will empower us to live our lives in the role that He created us for. This is what I mean when I speak of finding God's *"good, pleasing, and perfect will"* for our lives. This is the only way that we will ever know true wholeness and maturity in our faith and walk with God.

> We have different gifts, according to the grace given us. If a man's gift is prophesying, let him use it in proportion to his faith. If it is serving, let him serve; if it is teaching, let him teach; if it is encouraging, let him encourage; if it is contributing to the needs of others, let him give generously; if it is leadership, let him govern diligently; if it is showing mercy, let him do it cheerfully.

> Romans 12:6–8—NIV

Just as we are all members of the body of Christ, we all have our own specific gifts that God has given to each of us by His grace. As we come to discover God's will for our lives, we also discover the gifts that He has given each of us. Knowing our place within the body is only the beginning. Once we know where we belong, we need to use the gifts that God has given to us for the betterment of the whole body. Some of us are teachers, yet we don't share our knowledge. Some of us are encouragers, yet we withhold the words of life from those that desperately need to hear from us. Some of us are blessed with abundance, yet we hoard what we have and don't share it with those in dire need. When we have a gift and fail to use it, we are robbing others of the blessings that God intends for us to share. In sharing what we have been given, not only is the person who receives blessed, but so are we as the givers. We are a family. We are all blessed in some area that we could use in a meaningful way to show others the abundant love that God has for His children.

> Love must be sincere. Hate what is evil; cling to what is good.
>
> Romans 12:9—NIV

This verse seems so simple, yet, in daily life, we all seem to struggle to overcome our humanity, that is to say, our depravity. We are to be sincere, loving people if we are to be effective witnesses for Jesus Christ. We are to despise evil because it is a destructive force in our lives. I love the quote *"Hate the sin, but love the sinner."* So many Christians have a hard time distinguishing between the two. If we would reach out to the sinner and show them God's love and grace (rather than condemning the sinner because of their sin), we would be more effective at letting our light shine for the world to see. When we find the good in life, we need to grab a hold of it and cling to it as if our life depended on it. When we find the good, we need to share it with everyone around us.

> Be devoted to one another in brotherly love. Honor one another above yourselves.
>
> Romans 12:10—NIV

We have already mentioned the concept of our membership and position in the body of Christ. As members in this spiritual family, we need to be committed to one another and honor each other by showing the decency and courtesy that, as children of God, we should be demonstrating toward one another. We are to be the "hands" and "feet" of Christ in this world. As such, we need to use His hands to reach out and grab a hold of those who need us, and we need to use His feet to run to those who are far off and show them the way home.

> Never be lacking in zeal, but keep your spiritual fervor, serving the LORD.

> Romans 12:11—NIV

We need to draw our strength from God, but we also need to be a source of encouragement to others. When I think of zeal, I think of raw enthusiasm. Are we enthusiastic about serving the LORD? Do we exhibit a spiritual "fervor" that is clearly visible to those around us? When we see someone who is down, we need to make it a point to lift their spirits by helping and encouraging them. When we feel down, we need to be reminded that God is in control and that we are in the palm of His hands. Our zeal (enthusiasm and passion) is so important. It is often our zeal and zest for life that draws those around us to begin to question us about the joy that consistently radiates from us. It is one of the best ways to share our faith with those who have yet to enter into a relationship with our LORD. From time to time, our zeal may seem mysteriously absent. It is during these times that we need to be reminded that we serve a loving, gracious, and relational God. If that doesn't restore our zeal, then we need to check ourselves for a pulse.

> Be joyful in hope, patient in affliction, faithful in prayer.

> Romans 12:12—NIV

We have hope because we have faith in God. Patience, however, doesn't come so naturally. For years, I have prayed for patience.

Some of my Christian friends have challenged me and asked me why I would pray for such a thing. To them, praying for patience means that God will allow you to weather some terrible storms so that your patience can develop. To me, I see asking God for patience as a way of asking God for maturity. My heart's desire is to grow in my faith by whatever means necessary. If God wants me to grow, then I want Him to stretch me, mold me, and shape me into the image of Christ. If that means I have to weather some storms, then all I can say is that He will do whatever He thinks needs to be done in order to develop my character. I am His child and He is my Heavenly Father. I trust my LORD to raise His child in the way that He sees fit. This verse just serves as a reminder that God is in control and we need to remain faithful to hope, persevere, and remain faithful, never ceasing to pray.

> Share with God's people who are in need. Practice hospitality.
>
> Romans 12:13—NIV

Sharing with those who are in need is a sign of a disciple putting their faith in action. Sharing may be a number of things. We may need to share our experience or knowledge. We may need to share our faith. We may need to share our food, shelter, or clothing. We may need to share our financial excess. Just like we spoke of using our gifts, this is an example of using our resources as well to the glory of God. God knows the need, and you will know too, if you are asking Him for guidance and discernment. So many Christians need to be reminded that we are to be hospitable. I have met way too many professing Christians who were some of the most frustrated, bitter, inhospitable people I have ever met. If you are one of these people, let me say that it is time that you returned to the joy of your salvation. There is every reason to have a smile on your face when you think of what Christ did on the cross for you so that you may have eternal life.

> Bless those who persecute you; bless and do not curse.

> Romans 12:14—NIV

When someone is persecuting you, it is exceedingly difficult to have the desire for God to use you to bless your persecutor. In our state of depravity, we would probably rather see a lightning bolt come down from heaven and, in a flash, vaporize our tormenter. This is possibly your first reaction, but it is obviously the wrong reaction, because it is decidedly unbiblical. It is during times like this, when you are being persecuted, that you need to call upon the power of the Holy Spirit in you to give you the strength to maintain a Christ-like perspective so that you could, in turn, love that person and bless them. Our depravity wants to curse this person, but God changes our hearts and gives us the capacity to love this person through the life-changing power that only He can give us.

> Rejoice with those who rejoice; mourn with those who mourn.

> Romans 12:15—NIV

If we are in tune with our fellow believers, then we are sharing life with them. As in any close family, when one of us hurts, we all hurt. If we truly have love for one another, we feel and share in the joys and pains of those closest to us. This is another benefit of being a part of a loving family. Imagine what an orphan feels or what a widow feels. To feel alone or abandoned, not to have someone to talk to or lean on when you are hurting, must

be amazingly isolating. We need each other. We need to be fel-
lowshipping with other believers and sharing the ups and downs
that are all a part of our journey through this life. Just because
we are on the narrow road that leads to life, doesn't mean that
we can't walk the road in the company of our closest friends and
fellow believers.

> Live in harmony with one another. Do not be proud, but
> be willing to associate with people of low position. Do not
> be conceited.
>
> Romans 12:16—NIV

Think of what harmony means. In a musical sense, harmony
can only exist when all notes of a chord combine to produce a
pleasing effect. Think about different instruments (and we are
God's instruments in this world) playing from the same sheet
music (the Bible) making music that blends to produce a beautiful harmony. Now think about different instruments playing
from different sheet music, but all playing simultaneously. This
would be unpleasant to say the least. When chords contain notes
that are in the wrong key and produce a non-pleasing effect, you
have disharmony ("dis-chord"). Spiritually, when we have harmony, we have peace, contentment, and joy. When we become
arrogant and prideful, we have discord because we are trying
to make our own music, instead of reading from God's sheet
music. The problem is that our music doesn't blend with the
music of those believers that are around us. Therefore, it is not
pleasing to the ears of God or to anyone else who happens to be
nearby. We need to strive to live at peace with fellow believers
by being humble and loving. God opposes the proud but gives
grace to the humble (James 4:6). Now imagine that we are all in
one accord, synchronized, in tune, giving our best, and focused

on our Conductor. I imagine Him saying that the music being played was music to His ears.

> Do not repay anyone evil for evil. Be careful to do what is right in the eyes of everybody.
>
> Romans 12:17—NIV

We are to strive to live a holy, righteous, and blameless existence. While this is a humanly impossible task, it is nevertheless our responsibility to try. When we repay evil for evil, we are not demonstrating God's love; instead, we are retaliating as if we had not become a new creation, as if the renewing of our mind had never occurred. We need to live out our faith by forgiving those that persecute us. When we live a life that is controlled by the supernatural power that lives in us (the power of the Holy Spirit), we bless others by not reacting as a non-believer would, but instead, we show God's grace to those who persecute us.

> If it is possible, as far as it depends on you, live at peace with everyone.
>
> Romans 12:18—NIV

If we could learn to live in a constant state of forgiveness, it would be much easier to live at peace with those around us. I think it is interesting to note that verse 18 says, *"as far as it depends on you."* I take this to mean that in an interaction with another person, we are called to be the peacemaker. Sometimes, I think that we forget that it takes two to have an argument. Interestingly, it takes more than one to be in "one accord." We can't control the other half of an exchange, but we can definitely control our half. It is our responsibility to take the "high road."

> Do not take revenge, my friends, but leave room for God's
> wrath, for it is written: "It is mine to avenge; I will repay,"
> says the LORD. On the contrary: "If your enemy is hungry,
> feed him; if he is thirsty, give him something to drink. In
> doing this, you will heap burning coals on his head."

> Romans 12:19–20—NIV

If we are truly peacemakers, then we shouldn't be seeking revenge. To me, this verse implies that when we take revenge on someone, we are trying to do God's job for Him. If this is the case, we are interfering where we don't belong. It is made clear to us that God will judge and avenge as He sees fit. No matter what the situation, God's wrath will bring about the right remedy in the situation (*"I will repay," says the* LORD.). As followers (not leaders), we need to remember this. We also need to remember that God is in control, and we need to allow Him to move in any and every situation, without our interference. When you show grace and mercy to your enemy, you are opening the door for God to work mightily. Never underestimate God.

> Do not be overcome by evil, but overcome evil with good.

> Romans 12:21—NIV

We are in this world, but we are not of this world. We have been born again and have experienced the renewing of our minds. We are called to be a light to this dark world. When evil seems overpowering, we are called to be overcomers and let our light so shine. No matter how much darkness there is around us, we need to know that even the smallest amount of light is visible from great distances. Light will always make darkness flee (conversely, when light is extinguished, darkness returns).

Any goodness that we have is from God. Without Him, we are hopeless. With Him, we can accomplish anything that He calls us to do.

●●●

Key Thought:

You need to conform your life to God's Word.

If we want to find God's will for our lives, we must be aware that we need to know how He expects us to conduct ourselves in our daily lives. Romans 12 is an excellent example of what it means to live the life of a disciple. Imagine how our lives would change if we could align our thoughts and actions with the truths spelled out in this passage. Far too many people get this completely backward. Many Christians want to conform God's Word to their life ... not conform their lives to God's Word. If we would get this simple point and burn it into our minds, we would be well on our way to understanding so much more regarding our Christian behavior and existence and what it means to live a life that is pleasing to God.

Conforming our lives to God's Word is a self-*less* act, whereas conforming God's Word to our lifestyle is self-*ish*. If we truly die to self, then it is much easier to live life God's way instead of twisting His Word to satisfy our own selfish, egocentric position on life. In other words, if your life was a universe, what is the sun? What is at the center of your universe? What revolves around it? In your universe, is your sun actually *you*? Does everything revolve around you and your wishes? Think about it and be honest with yourself.

Ask yourself these questions:
- Is God the center of my universe?
- Do I revolve around *Him*?

Question:

Who sits on the throne of your life?

This is a tough question and the answer to this question will shed light on where you are in your spiritual development and where you need to be in order to mature in your faith. If you are sitting in and warming up that chair, then you are completely missing God. Instead, if God is occupying that chair, then you are in the right position. It is like the old bumper sticker that says "God is my co-pilot." The person who wrote that probably meant well, but God had better be your pilot, and not your co-pilot, if you expect to fly straight (or fly around potential, avoidable storms) and land at the proper destination. The "throne" or "driver's seat" or "pilot's seat" or whatever you choose to call it had better be occupied by God if you are ever going to serve Him in the manner to which He intended.

Key Thought:

To discover God's will for your life, you need to discover God's plan for everyday living.

If today is the first day of the rest of your life, shouldn't we start today by trying to get it all together? Don't you want to live life the right way (God's way)? It is not hopeless; far from it.

●●●

Behavior Modification:

Try this: Change something about your behavior today. Pick something that you know isn't right, and make it right. Confess it. Lay it down. Turn away from it. If you can't think of something, ask God to reveal something to you. Get ready. It may not be easy, but give it a chance. What a *huge* opportunity for growth lays in front of you if you will do this.

Remember: Every journey begins with a single step; even if that step is a baby step. Forward progress begins with the first step. I pray that you take this opportunity very seriously!

works

Romans 12

Key Thought:

Holiness is not a single act; holiness is a lifestyle.

Holiness is a conscious choice to do life God's way. So many people just want to be happy and are not concerned with being holy. I believe that when we make holiness our focus, God will create a joy in us that comes from the sheer fact that we are living a life with purpose and meaning. Joy that comes from God will far exceed any happiness that you could ever find on your own. Why? Because it is a lasting joy, not like the fleeting happiness that we only momentarily discover through life. I'll take heavenly joy over earthly happiness any day of the week!

We have all heard it said that our actions speak louder than our words. Why can't our actions confirm to others the words that we speak (or ought to speak) regarding our life and our faith? Our actions should match up if we intend to be real about our faith and not be lukewarm or hypocritical. What we need to grasp is that God's Word should radiate from us like a beacon in the dark. We should know it because we read it and study it. We should live our lives according to His Word because it is an act of obedience and it is the road that leads us to finding what Romans 12:2 tells us—his *"good, pleasing, and perfect will."*

Let's look at Psalms 119:

> How can a young man keep his way pure? By living according to your word. I seek you with all my heart; do not let me stray from your commands. I have hidden your word in my heart that I might not sin against you. Praise be to you, O LORD; teach me your decrees. With my lips I recount all the laws that come from your mouth. I rejoice in following your statutes as one rejoices in great riches. I meditate on your precepts and consider your ways. I delight in your decrees; I will not neglect your word.
>
> Psalms 119:9–16—NIV

Don't you see it? We need to have this hunger for Him and this desire to seek Him and serve Him. We need to recognize Him as our everything. We need to really examine what this passage says. Look back over it and think about what it would be like to have a heart that is that hungry for the things of God.

> Knowing this first, that no prophecy of Scripture is of any private interpretation, for prophecy never came by the will of man, but holy men of God spoke as they were moved by the Holy Spirit.

2 Peter 1:20–21—NKJV

When we examine the Bible, verse by verse, we are looking at it *expositionally*. We are "exposing" it, verse by verse, learning what it has to say as a whole. I believe that it is important that we examine the Bible in this way. Where we must be careful is this: so many people look for a single verse that says what they want it to say to fit their specific situation. I believe many people use individual verses to justify their position or justify their inappropriate actions. Many times, what is being said in the passage is taken out of context by the reader (sometimes innocently, but sometimes intentionally).

Key Thought:

When you take a text out of context and form a pretext, you have misinterpreted the text.

Let that one soak in. Read it again and think about how it applies to biblical interpretation.

When we take a verse from the Bible and try to apply it to our situation without ...

- Understanding who the verse was written to (*audience*)
- What the circumstances were as to why it was written (*situation*)
- Considering what the intended message was (*meaning*)

... we miss the point. The Bible is not open to *private* interpretation. We need to learn the rules of biblical interpretation if we are to really understand it as God intended. Believe me; I am not talking about ridiculous approaches, esoteric meanings, or hidden codes that reveal nothing more than contrived phrases. I am sure that if I picked up any book on any shelf and dissected long enough, I would find that if I took every 521st letter, I could, at some point within that book, find a simple word or phrase that is formed to say something that could be considered meaningful. Does this mean that this new *"revelation"* is suddenly *"divine"* in nature, or has simple chance, through a concocted formula, created something that I am now going to base my faith on? Come on, people!

Question:

Is the substance of our faith that fragile?

What are we doing? We need *faith* ... not formulas! There is more than enough information in the Bible that is *clearly* spelled out for us to study it for the rest of our natural human existence. I think that so-called "Bible codes" are nothing more than a distraction from our enemy that cause us to get derailed and cause us to question our faith based on things that are nothing more than superficial or esoteric. This is just another example of how our humanity gets in the way of our spirituality! We have a tendency to look for "signs" that may or may not have meaning while we ignore what is clearly written in the Word of God!

Key Thought:

Jesus instructed us to share the Gospel message, not the Gospel formula.

When I refer to biblical interpretation, I am referring to a logical, systematic approach that takes into consideration what the Bible says, word for word, as a whole. I believe that when we read the Bible, we should look at it as a complete work. We should read it at face value—word for word as it was written. It is not something to be taken out of context and twisted to mean what we want it to mean. I personally believe that the Bible is God's inspired Word. Let me be more specific. I believe the Bible is a perfect and complete work, created by God, through man, by the leading of the Holy Spirit. It is His gift to us. It is the best "instruction manual" for living a holy and purposeful life, and it is the best "owner's manual" for knowing how our body, soul (mind, will, and emotion), and spirit operate.

Let's take a minute to discuss how we really should be interpreting the Bible. When we read God's Word, we do need to be very careful that we interpret it correctly. This brings up the subjects of *hermeneutics* and *exegesis*.

Hermeneutics is defined as the theory and methodology of interpretation of a text (especially of scriptural text).

Exegesis is defined as a critical explanation or interpretation of a text (especially of scriptural text).

In the biblical sense, true *hermeneutics* is the interpretation of scripture according to its own context, according to the inspiration of the men who originally wrote it. Basically, this means that scripture must be interpreted by itself, and by examination of the facts. We need to look at what comes *before* and *after* a passage, as well as critically examine what the Bible says about the given subject matter in other passages before we arrive at what we believe the actual interpretation of the passage to be. In its original written language (primarily Hebrew and Greek), I whole-heartedly believe that the Bible is completely inerrant. When read in its original language, I believe that it will not contradict itself, ever. It is a perfect work.

There have always been debates over which translation is the best. I have no desire to open this can of worms because it seems that everybody has their own opinion on the subject. Let's remember that *no* translation will ever communicate the original Hebrew and Greek to the fullest extent of its intended meaning. When any document is translated into another language, some of the meaning is invariably lost. Words communicate concepts, and some languages just don't fully allow the deeper truths to be revealed to the same extent as the original language. If we can't seem to reconcile something that is contained in the Bible in the form in which we read it today, then we need to accept that, this side of heaven, we will never completely understand it in its entirety. We must also accept that it is God's inspired Word and that it is the complete and final authority on all things pertaining to life and godliness.

Remembering that our Bible has been translated from its

original language into English is *exceedingly* important. If we could read the Bible in its original language, we would better grasp its rich meaning because we wouldn't have to deal with the issue of meaning that gets *"lost in translation."*

Key Thought:

The Old Testament is the New Testament *concealed*

The New Testament is the Old Testament *revealed*

Lately, I have been feeling the urging to attempt to learn Hebrew. This urging seems to come from the fact that I am growing in my faith and in my desire to know more about my Christian roots. When I look at the Old Testament, I realize that my familiarity with it pales in comparison to my familiarity with the New Testament. As Christians, we have the tendency to spend all our time in the New Testament and seem to neglect the Old Testament. Except for our knowledge of the most common Bible stories, the Old Testament is a mystery to most of us. To be able to read the Word of God in its original language would be an amazing thing. I hope to be able to do this someday.

I have always been intrigued by the Jewish faith. I believe that this, in part, is due to my upbringing. When I was a child, my family observed many of the Old Testament holy days (the Feast of Unleavened Bread, the Feast of Weeks, and the Feast of Tabernacles, etc.). When I tell this to most Christians, they look at me and ask, *"What are the holy days?"* This just goes to show you how unfamiliar most of us are about Old Testament writings.

When I was in high school, I dated a Jewish girl for about a year and a half. She was raised as an Orthodox Jew.³ She worked with me and showed me how to read and pronounce some basic Hebrew words. I have to admit, it was pretty cool. Sometimes, I attended the synagogue with her and celebrated Passover, as well as some of the other Old Testament holy days, with her family. It was very interesting to learn about the Jewish culture and traditions (not to mention, the food was great). It was all very educational.

One of my favorite memories from that time is of reading a book at her house entitled *The Tabernacle of God in the Wilderness of Sinai.* When you learn about the design of the Tabernacle of God in the Sinai desert as described in Exodus, it helps you to better understand what occurred in the New Testament at the moment that Christ died on the cross:

> And when Jesus had cried out again in a loud voice, he gave up his spirit. At that moment the curtain of the temple was torn in two from top to bottom. The earth shook and the rocks split.
>
> Matthew 27:50–51—NIV

In the Tabernacle design there were two specific places that I want to draw your attention to. Both of these places are found in what was called the *"Tent of Meeting"*:
- Holy Place
- Most Holy Place (also known as the "Holy of Holies")

The Holy Place and the Holy of Holies were divided by a thick curtain. In the Holy Place was a golden table for the bread of the Presence, a golden lampstand, and an altar of incense. The Holy Place was an area for the high priest. The Holy of Holies was where the Ark of the Covenant was kept. God's spirit would dwell in the Holy of Holies. This place was sacred and off-limits to everyone except the high priest. The high priest could only enter the Holy of Holies once a year.

The thick curtain that separated the Holy Place and the Holy of Holies was also present in the Temple in Jerusalem as well. The symbolism of the curtain is important when you look at the difference between our relationship with God prior to and after the death of Jesus. Prior to Jesus' death, sins were forgiven by a sacrifice in the Temple (or previously in the Tabernacle). After Jesus' death, the curtain was torn from top to bottom. This symbolizes something that only God can do. It was as if God reached down, grabbed the curtain, and personally ripped it from the top to the bottom (if man had done this, it would have been ripped from bottom to top). This curtain previously separated us from God's presence until Christ's sacrificial death satisfied God's requirement that a sacrifice be made for the remission (forgiveness) of our sins. From that moment on, we have had direct access to God's presence. This is a great example of the fact that we serve a relational God.

I want to learn to read Hebrew because I have a hunger to learn God's Word in its original form so that I may better understand its truth and richness. On that note, I want to tell you about my younger brother. He is amazing. He speaks fluently in English, Spanish, Portuguese, and some French, Italian, and most recently, Tagalog. He also taught himself to read Hebrew and Greek. He is not like anyone I have ever met. It is so amazing to open my Bible software program that has multiple translations and have him sit there and read the Hebrew and Greek texts to me. He is unbelievable. He has inspired me to want to learn Hebrew for myself.

Now let's talk about sanctification. What does sanctification really mean? Sanctification means *to set apart, to make holy*. The Bible teaches us that, as believers, we have already been sanctified. I once heard it said that sanctification is when your practice (behavior) matches your spiritual position (saved). I have always liked that definition because it implies that the change that took place at the moment of our salvation causes us to live out our faith and our convictions in accordance to our new spiritual position. If we are taken out of darkness and placed in the light, we should reflect that change in our behavior. God has set us apart because He is in the business of making us holy. Understand this: *We are sanctified*. We are set apart. By, and through, the blood of Jesus, we are made holy. We have been redeemed. We were bought for a price—the shed blood of Jesus. He has given us a special place and a special purpose, and we must understand this truth if we are to fully grasp what He did for us on the cross.

> "For I know the plans I have for you," declares the LORD, "plans to prosper you and not to harm you, plans to give you hope and a future."
>
> Jeremiah 29.11—NIV

The church that I attend has four sayings that we, as a congregation, repeat on a regular basis. I cherish these sayings, and I want to share them with you because they are so meaningful to me.

I. Our mission statement:
To lead people to become fully devoted followers of Christ.

Note that as Christians, we are not just trying to convert people

to Christianity. The responsibility doesn't stop there. We are trying to lead people into a deeper, more meaningful relationship
with our LORD and Savior. Notice that I said *relationship*, not
religion! Our love of God does not stem from our religion. Our
love of God is born out of having a real relationship with Him—
knowing that we know Him, not just knowing about Him.

The message of salvation is not about knowing *about* Him.
The message of salvation is about *personally* knowing Him.

There is a *monstrous* difference in those statements.

Key Thought:

God has no grandchildren.

I believe that real faith can only be found when you have a real
relationship with Jesus. Just because my parents were Christians,
doesn't make me a Christian by default. It's not a birthright!
There are no second generation Christians; therefore, God has
no grandchildren. You either personally know Him (first generation, direct connection) and have a relationship with Him, or
you really don't know Him at all. Being in church doesn't mean
that you have a relationship with Him. It's a great place to start,
but it is just a building. Going to church doesn't make you are a
Christian any more than standing in your garage means you have
become a car. Remember, it is not about *where* you are, it is about
what you are.

Some people say in life that *what* you know matters most,

while others say *who* you know matters most. Well, I say that in matters of faith, *who* you know (Christ) and *what* you know (His plan of salvation), in that order, is what really matters. It is all about relationship!

II. Our purpose:
   Bring in ... Build up ... Train ... Send out.

In order to effectively spread the message of the Gospel, we need to concentrate on more than just conversion. We are called to teach, train, and send out. Think about the last thing that Christ said while on this earth, prior to His ascension into heaven.

   Therefore go and make disciples of all nations.

   Matthew 28:19—NIV

We are called to *"go and make disciples."* We can't all sit in church for the rest of our lives and not attempt to reach the world with the Gospel of Christ. I am not suggesting that we all pack up and leave for foreign missions, but someone has to do it. For the rest of us, we need to look at our own sphere of influence. Your community—that is your mission field and you are called to it. Why do we think that we must be a pastor to share the Gospel? What people are attracted to is the fact that when God's presence is around you because of how you act and speak, people want to know what is so different about you. Are you living a life that reflects God's presence, or are you living a life that appears devoid of God to those around you? When we really know God, we should stand out in a crowd.

III. Our service starts:

God is good, all the time, and all the time, God is good.

We all need to be reminded of God's goodness from time to time. We may not always understand God's methods, but we need to know that He is always good. Being good is His very nature—it is His essence. He is not good some of the time; He is good *all* of the time. When we are faced with trials in our lives, it helps to be reminded of what Romans 8:28 says to us:

> And we know that in all things God works for the good of those who love him who have been called according to his purpose.
>
> Romans 8:28—NIV

No matter what is going on in your life, remember, in *all* things *God* works for the *good.* That is definitely a reality check. God is in charge ... lest we forget.

IV. Our service ends:
   Whoever finds God, finds life.

One of our greatest responsibilities as a believer is to introduce people to the new life that is found only in salvation. To find God is to find life itself. A new life—a life everlasting.

> Where there is no vision, the people perish.
>
> Proverbs 29:18—KJV

This verse is one of my personal all-time favorites. Even though I know the word *"vision"* in this verse doesn't pertain to eyesight, as an eye doctor, I have always gravitated to this verse because

Character

of the word picture. The thought of people perishing for lack of vision always stuck out to me. Where there is no vision, there is blindness. For those of us blessed with functional vision, imagine what it would be like to be completely blind. Imagine living in a world that is completely dark. I believe that if I were blind, all alone, in the middle of nowhere, I would likely perish.

In Proverbs 29:18, if you substitute the word "knowledge" for "vision" and re-read it, you get a stronger sense of what the verse is saying. Look at it again:

> Where there is no [knowledge], the people perish.
>
> Proverbs 29:18—KJV

If the people perish for lack of "knowledge," then what is this "knowledge" that the verse is speaking of? Before we answer that question, let's dig a little deeper. In this verse, the actual Hebrew word for "vision" is "Chazown" (pronounced khaw–ZONE). "Chazown" means "a dream, revelation, or vision." Whether we realize it or not, we all have our own personal "Chazown." In other words, we all have a God-given purpose and plan for our lives. Once we find our God-given purpose and discover His plan, we find energy we didn't know we had because we see God's vision for our lives and we can't wait to embrace God's best for us. This is essentially what finding God's best is all about, or at least, this is where the journey begins. The problem for many of us is that we don't have any idea what this purpose for our lives actually is. We have not had the Romans 12:2 experience; we have not discovered His *good, pleasing, and perfect will.*

The question that each one of us should be asking is *"What is God's 'good, pleasing, and perfect will' for my life?"* (In Chapter 5, we will specifically ask this question. Be thinking about this question and ask God to reveal to you the answer. As you continue to read, I believe that you will discover the answer.) To answer my original question, I believe that the people perish for lack of "knowledge" because they lack the "knowledge" of God's plan for their lives; therefore, they wander through life aimlessly and miss the mark. They miss out on God's best. What a tragedy!

Key Thought:

Where God guides, God provides.

I attend an amazing church in Oklahoma City. My pastor's name is Craig Groeschel. He is a nationally recognized and respected pastor to whom God gave an absolutely amazing vision. Craig's "*Chazown*" began to come into focus over a decade ago. He had "*a dream, revelation, or vision*" for reaching out to people in a fresh, new way, and in 1996, after much prayer, he started a new church and named it LifeChurch. To quote Craig, "*It wasn't just about doing things to create a different church. It was about creating a church that did things differently.*"

Over the last decade, as Craig has lived out his "*Chazown,*" he has faced many obstacles, endured a lot of criticism, and seen God perform miraculous things that he could never have imagined possible. Today, with God's blessing, LifeChurch is one of the fastest growing churches in America. LifeChurch is a multi-campus church with locations all over the country connected via satellite with numerous weekly worship experiences in which several thousand people attend. What a tragedy it would have been if Craig had never discovered his *"Chazown"*! Imagine all the lives that would not have been impacted for Christ!

A few months ago, our church launched its "internet campus." At first, I must admit, I had my reservations about it, but then all the wonderful benefits about it hit me. What a blessing to be able to access our service and chat in the on-line "lobby" from almost anywhere in the world via the internet! If I traveled for a living or went on vacation or was physically unable to attend service, I don't have to miss a single message or miss out on being able to fellowship with other believers. What a wonderful age we live in!

I firmly believe in the assembling of Christians for fellowship (Hebrews 10:25) and I encourage it, but I believe in an old adage that I learned, while getting my doctorate, regarding therapy: *start where a person is and then take them where they are not.* Meaning? Let me put it this way: you don't feed a newborn baby solid food, nor do you yank crutches away from someone who depends on them to stand. Start on the appropriate level that someone is operating and then, over time, guide them to a point beyond their original starting point. This process of therapy equates to progressive growth and maturity. What I am trying to say is that we (the body of Christ) need to reach out to a lost world by whatever means necessary to connect to people and show them God's love. Church over the internet seems a bit unconventional, and maybe controversial, but if it brings people into a relationship with Christ, then so be it. Personally, I think the internet could use a little more godly material.

On the church's website,[4] they have made available, free of charge, all of our past video message series and all of our creative content (digital media, images, etc.) for other pastors and churches to use to help facilitate delivering the message of Christ to a lost world. It is not about selling books or DVD message series for profit. It is about getting the message of salvation out to a world that desperately needs it. I deeply respect the fact that our church leadership thinks that it is more important to make all of this material freely available, free of charge, instead of copyrighting all of it and trying to market it for profit. Just sitting back and watching my church leadership live out their convictions about spreading the Gospel message and reaching as many people as possible, really, really blesses me. I believe it is because of acts like this that God blesses our church so abundantly!

Let me get back to the biblical truth of *"Chazown."* I now understand this truth because I have read the Bible passage and studied my pastor's teaching on the subject. A few years ago, Craig developed a sermon series called "Life Development Plan." This series revealed some important spiritual truths that we all need to know:

- Everyone ends up somewhere, but few people end up somewhere on purpose.
- If you don't stand for something, you'll fall for anything.
- If you don't know where you are going, you won't know when you get there.
- When you fail to plan, you plan to fail.
- Accountability closes the gap between intentions and actions.

The most recent development in the "Life Development Plan" concept is an awesome book that my pastor wrote entitled *Chazown: A different way to see your life.* One of my favorite things in his book can be found on page 19. On this page, my pastor wrote the following:

Made for This

I'll bet your life is busy. Mine is, too. For me, raising six small children is challenging enough. Add to it the task of leading a large church with multiple campuses, and I often don't know if I'm coming or going.

My friends ask, "Craig, how do you do it all? Aren't you afraid you'll burn out?" What they really mean is, "Are you sure you're not heading for the psych ward?"

I can say with all honesty that my job and my family are never burdens. Sometimes I get tired. But I'm nowhere near burnout.

Why? Because this is what God created me to do. I have no doubt about it. I'm wired for this. This is the vision God put in me. And when God gives you His vision, He also gives you the ability to get it done. When you are living God's vision for your life, you will spring out of bed with excitement. When someone asks if you like what you do, you shout, "I love it!"

I have enjoyed watching this concept grow and touch the lives of so many people. It must be amazing to be a part of leading thousands of people to the knowledge of God's plan and purpose for their lives. In Craig's book, the symbolism of a wheel with five spokes is used to pictorially show five extremely important and fundamental areas of our lives. Each of the "spokes" are listed as follows:
• Relationship with God
• Relationships with People
• Financial Health
• Physical Health
• Work Life

If we imagine that each of these areas in our lives are actually spokes on a wheel, the next question is whether or not our wheel is in balance. When the wheel of our life spins, does it roll smoothly because we have achieved balance in our lives, or does it shake and vibrate violently because it is out of shape and off balance? If you have ever ridden in a car with a tire that was out of balance, you know first-hand what a rough ride is like. It will nearly rattle the teeth out of your head. Is your life like that? Are you rolling along the narrow path on new treads, or are you bouncing and swerving on and off the narrow road uncontrollably? When are you going to get tired of being off in the ditch? It's time to get things in balance.

Key Thought:

When God reveals His "good, pleasing, and perfect will" for your life, get ready. Things are going to change.

It is at this point that I want to explain how my book (*Unlikely*) really came about. As I mentioned in my testimony in Chapter 1, I got my first glimpse of what a *relationship* with God really looked like in October 2005. After years of having a *religious*, legalistic mindset and being devoid of the joy of my salvation (head knowledge *vs.* heart knowledge), I finally experienced not only a renewing of my mind, but a real change in my heart. (We will discuss the heart in Chapter 3). I began to really want to seek God, die to self, and depend on Him to get me through every day. This journey began with a true repentance and a hunger for truth. I knew that all my years of being controlling and manipulative had led me nowhere except down paths of pain and failure. After reading countless books, I got to the point where I was still searching to find God's will and purpose for my life but could not seem to find the answer. The good news is that all the reading that I had done had built me up and prepared me for the journey that lay ahead of me.

For most of my adult life, I have had the desire to preach or teach. During the months that followed that wonderful day in October 2005, I often thought of being a pastor and how much I thought that I would enjoy standing and delivering God's Word. Even though I knew that my finances at the time were holding me back, I knew that God was bigger than my situation and that if He opened a door for me to go into full-time ministry, I would walk through that door by faith. So I surrendered to this calling and applied for two different ministry positions; one as a pastor and another as an associate pastor. I just knew, deep down, that I would get one of the positions, because after all, I was called to preach and my resume, as a doctor, was loaded with all sorts of stuff (lectures, publications, adjunct faculty, etc.) that would impress ... or so I thought. I waited and waited, but the door for my "calling" never opened. After pondering on the events and lack of response to my applications, I began to doubt what God's plan for me really was. Surprisingly, all along, I knew that there was something specific that I was supposed to do, but I kept putting it off because it didn't seem to go along with *my* vision for my future. I kept feeling the prompting of the Holy Spirit to sit down and write out every experience or topic that I believed that I could speak or teach on with some degree of knowledge or experience. When I finally surrendered and obeyed His leading, I couldn't believe what came out of me as I finally sat down and began to put it all on paper. I was totally and absolutely blown away! It blessed me so much to see, on paper, in black and white, all of the life experiences that God had brought me through. It was at that moment that I realized that I should consider writing.

After praying about it, I sensed that I needed to write a book about finding God's will for our lives as believers and learning what it means to live a life dependent upon Him for our every need. After all, this was the quest that I was on; it was where He was leading me. I knew that this topic is what I was supposed to be writing about. So I began to form an outline of this topic. The first night, I had four pages of single-spaced typed outline. I was so excited! The next night, I had four more pages, and I was amazed at what was beginning to take shape. I then called my friend John (my accountability partner) and began to explain to him what was going on. I said, "John, you're not going to believe what is happening. I believe that I am supposed to be writing a book." Prior to this conversation, John had been aware of my desire to find God's calling on my life and my desire to be in ministry. He responded to me by saying, "That's awesome, man. God is so good. I want to see it." He shared with me his thoughts, and I told him that we should get together and go over the outline. The following Thursday night, he came over to my house, and we sat down and began to go over the outline. By the end of the evening, we had added four more pages of single-spaced outline. At that point, we sat back and looked over all twelve pages. It hit us both like a ton of bricks. We were looking at the perfect outline for a complete book. God *is* good!

I was so excited at what God was doing. I knew that I was on to something great. The next night, I sat down and began to look over the twelve-page outline and within thirty minutes, I had divided the outline into sections and named each one of them. What I hadn't even realized was that when I was finished, I had twelve chapters with names that just screamed out at me. I could clearly see the framework for a book, complete with chapters and titles. I called John and told him what had happened. I knew at that moment, beyond the shadow of a doubt, that this was something divine and wonderful that God had placed in my hands. God had given me a vision.

During the months that I spent writing this book, I learned so much about God and about myself. This work has turned out to be as much about ministering to me as it is about ministering to others. When I was about halfway through writing, my associate pastor told me that I should take my manuscript and sit down with a publisher and share my vision with them, even though I wasn't finished with the book yet. I took his advice and I sat down with the staff of Tate Publishing, and did that very thing. I explained to them that I had been writing this book out of obedience and that I had personally grown tremendously through the process. I told them that I believed that this work was to be published, but that if it were to happen, it was all up to God. I told them that if the book never grew beyond that point, if it were never published, I was still better off for having written it. They could sense my passion as I presented the vision to them. I left there that day believing that they got a real glimpse of the vision for the book.

I had been told that the manuscript review process could take six to nine weeks, so I decided to just relax and give it to God. I had a serene peace that God had the situation in control and that everything was going to work out fine. Everyone began asking me how I thought the meeting with the publisher went, and all I could say was that I sensed that it went very well. I knew that they only accepted a small fraction of the manuscripts that are submitted to them, but I just had this calm reassurance that this book would make the cut. A few *days* later, not six or nine weeks later, I got the phone call that I had been waiting for. The news brought tears to my eyes. As I processed the news, I sat there and trembled. Tate Publishing called and said that they loved the book, that they wanted to publish it, and that they would be honored to have it under contract. I cannot put into words the emotions that I experienced at that moment. I felt sheer joy for knowing that God was still confirming to me that He was behind this whole venture. I also felt humbled by the fact that I had truly found what God would have me to do at this point in my life. I knew that God had finally revealed His *"good, pleasing and perfect will"* to me. He hadn't prepared me for preaching from a pulpit. That was *my* vision ... not His. Instead, He had given me a much bigger audience—one that isn't limited to four walls, one language, or regional geography. I had never dreamt of the possibility of reaching so many people with the burden that He placed on my heart. I am so amazed by God! He has given me the opportunity to reach so many more people than I had ever thought possible by providing a way for me to use the talents that He has given me, but in a way that I never expected.

Key Thought:

God's vision for your life is so much better than anything that you can possibly imagine for yourself. Seek Him and ask Him to reveal to you what His "good, pleasing, and perfect will" is for your life.

Many of our philosophies and beliefs come from our personal experiences. I believe that these experiences help us (or possibly hinder us) in the process of living out our faith. If everything is handed to us in life without us having to earn it or experience it for ourselves, will we really have an appreciation for it when we get it? I seriously doubt it.

Think of a spoiled child. Why is this child so horrible to be around? Why does this child get on our nerves so quickly? The answer is simple. Human nature is carnal and generally, inherently selfish. A selfish person unconsciously says to themselves, *"Gimme, gimme, gimme, and then gimme some more. I want it all for myself. It's all about me!"* In the course of our development, both emotionally and spiritually, it is necessary and even helpful to *not* always get what we want. My belief is that when we get everything that we want, we generally don't appreciate it and always seem to want more to satisfy our endless appetite for self-gratification. We all have "*me*" programmed into our core. This is called depravity. This is what entered into the world when Adam and Eve inherited a *"sin nature"* in the Garden of Eden. The moment that they ate the forbidden fruit that God had instructed them not to eat, depravity entered the picture. Because of this, we are all inclined to sin. We are bent toward it. This is why we so desperately need a savior. Not only to save us from ourselves, but to save us from eternal separation from God.

To stop from having something

(?)

Question:

What is it that leads us to want to give complete control of our lives over to God?

Blessings   Peace   joy   eternity

We may say that we want God to be in control, but do we really mean it? Are we willing to say every day that we need Him to control our lives? Do we really believe that He is capable of doing a better job than we are? Most people are simply not willing to let God take control. Most think that they can do the job without any help or supervision. The truth is, it simply takes a step of faith to relinquish our control and completely lean on God for understanding when we simply don't have the answers. For each of us, it takes different circumstances to let go of our control. For some it is absolute tragedy and a sense of hopelessness that causes us to cry out and give our control over to God. For others, it is simply the realization of who God is and who we are as sinners, lost in a world that desperately needs a savior. Regardless of the circumstance, if you are living a life that God is in control of, then praise Him for opening your eyes to the truth. If you are currently living a self-centered existence and you are fighting to steer your own ship, please know that there are rocks ahead and you are headed for your own tragedy. We need to remember that the Bible says in Philippians 2:10–11 that *every* knee shall bow and *every* tongue confess that Jesus is LORD.

Do yourself a favor. Search your heart. Seek God. Confess to Him that you need Him to take control of your life. The sooner you get this figured out, the better off you will be. Please listen to me! Don't waste valuable time being distracted from what is real and what is true. Life is too short and this truth is too important to miss.

Question:

Do we want Him to completely guide our lives?

Let me rephrase the question.

Are we willing to give complete control over to Him?

For me, it took brokenness to let go and trust Him to take care of me. After complete failure, I realized that my way led to nowhere. Instead, His way leads to peace, joy, and fulfillment. Oh, if I could only share the burden I have in my heart and the pain I experienced to show you the answer. (By the way, the best answer to the previous question is emphatically "*yes!*") Just do it. Give control over to Him. You will *never* regret it. You will grow by leaps and bounds. You will find the rest of the answers. God will shape your life into something wonderfully amazing and breathtaking.

Key Thought:

The LORD doesn't use people to complete tasks. Instead, He uses tasks to complete people.

Let's face it. If God can speak the universe into existence, He doesn't really need us to accomplish His tasks. The simple truth is that He is creating character in each of us by allowing the experiences of this life to mold us and shape us. Recently, someone said something to me that made me completely rethink my relationship with God. They said, *"What if God allows you to go through storms in your life because He wants you to need Him more?"* When I think about God as a Father, I think about what it is like for me as the father of four children. I love it when my children need me. I love it when they run to me for reassurance and unconditional love. If I imagine what it is like for me as a father, I can begin to get a glimpse of what it must be like for God as our Father. What loving Father wouldn't want to be needed and loved by His children? When we turn to Him, He is there to wrap His loving arms around us and shower us with a peace and reassurance that only He can give. That is what a real relationship is all about. This is where intimacy begins.

Question:

Are you really willing to be used by God?

If you are willing to allow God to work through you, what will it cost you? What are you willing to give up to be used by God? There is no one single answer, but I assure you that one of the most important answers is that it will cost you your will. Allowing God to reshape your will, plan, and view of the future is essential to your spiritual development.

Question:

What in my life is keeping God from making His appeal through me?

I believe it boils down to a simple point ... choices. Every day we make choices. Are we living our lives by His calling or by our own choices? Are we leading, or are we following? Are we controlling, or are we trusting? Does your attitude reflect your desire to be closer to God and do your actions communicate this truth? If your attitude and actions don't reflect this, you need to seriously consider why they don't. If you plan to find God's will for your life, you need to get your heart and mind in the right place.

Question:

How do we find God's will and plan for our lives?

As you have read so far, there is no single answer to this question, but the good news is the overall process is rather simple. It's a process made up of choices that create a lifestyle. We must recognize who God is and recognize our need for Him. We must seek Him through prayer, reading His Word, fasting, etc. The process requires faith and patience.

Question:

Do we want His will and plan for our lives?

We can say that we want His will and plan, but do we really mean it? Are we willing to let go of our own agenda and grab a hold of God's agenda? Finding His plan requires self-*less*-ness on our part; whereas, finding our own plan requires self-*ish*-ness on our part. What is holding us back? Why can't we just trust Him?

To quote a familiar cliché, *"Let go, let God."* For most of us, what is holding us back is that we actually fear not being in control. Our carnal, fleshly nature drives us to want to "take charge" of our lives, when in reality, all we are doing is pushing God out of the way and saying, "Hey! I can do this better than you." To surrender our will, we must believe deep down that our way is not the best way, but instead, we must whole-heartedly believe that God's way is absolutely the best way. *This takes faith.* It also takes trust. How better to build our faith in our Creator than to surrender to Him all that we hold dear? This is easier for some than others. For me, until recently, it was a very difficult thing to do. You could say that I was the "strong-willed" child. What did it for me was that God allowed areas of my life that were not surrendered to Him, to literally disintegrate. Once I recognized that everything that I had planned for and expected out of life was one broken dream after another, He showed me that when I put my plans ahead of His, there are consequences for such actions. He knows best what will ultimately make me complete and content with this life. As soon as I confessed my sin of selfishness, He began to reveal to me so many truths about His character and about my need for a loving, patient Father.

> But the fruit of the Spirit is love, joy, peace, patience, kindness, goodness, faithfulness, gentleness and self-control. Against such things there is no law.
>
> Galatians 5:22–23—NIV

For most of my Christian life, I can remember hearing about the "fruits of the Spirit." Over the years, I have heard countless sermons on the subject and overheard many conversations about it. When you stop and take a long look at each of the fruits of the Spirit, it really makes you think about your own life. It makes you seriously evaluate your attitudes and your relationship with God. If we would stop and be honest with ourselves, we would likely want these nine characteristics to be accurate descriptions of our own life. I mean, who wouldn't want to be described in this way? Who wouldn't want their lives to be seen by others as the embodiment of these spiritual fruits?

I believe that if we will humble ourselves and surrender our lives and our wills to God, we will see God's plan for our lives beginning to unfold. For most of us, being humble and surrendering to God is not an easy task. We like being in control and we have a hard time letting it go and putting ourselves in a position of being completely dependent upon God. Maybe it is fear or possibly pride that keeps us from realizing the freedom that comes from trusting God and learning to walk by faith. For others of us, we need divine intervention and a change of heart in order to begin to bear spiritual fruit. What does a life look like that is actively bearing spiritual fruit? Well, a life that is lived with God leading, guiding, and teaching us, is a life that shows evidence of spiritual fruit. In contrast, a life without God does lead to a type of fruit, but not the spiritual kind. This type of life leads to "fruits of the flesh." This type of fruit consists of strife, greed, selfishness, bitterness, etc. There is way too much of this type of fruit in the world.

As we all learn more about God's plan, we become increasingly aware that we really need to have a change of heart.

Chapter 3

change of heart

These people honor me with their lips, but their hearts are
far from me.

Matthew 15:8—NIV

After receiving the news and marveling over the fact that my
first book was going to be published, God quickly taught me
another lesson. This time He reminded me of who He is and
who I am by allowing me to have an enlightening conversation
with my associate pastor. As I was walking up to the front door
of the church, my associate pastor gave me a high-five and began
congratulating me on the recent news that my book was going
to be published. The first thing that came out of my mouth was
"Wow! I can't believe it is going to be published!" These words
had no more left my lips and I felt convicted for my choice of
words. I should have said, "I am so blessed that God has given
me this vision and a means of expressing it," or something to
that effect.

Key Thought:

We should never act astonished by the miracles that God performs in our lives.

What a blessing it is to know that God is using me to reach others with the message contained within these pages. I felt that my original comment to my associate pastor had robbed God of the credit that He, and He alone, deserves. To some this discussion would seem like a frivolous distinction, but to me, it is an opportunity to expound on what it means to revere God and how we can bless Him by being careful about what we say to others and how we say it.

As disciples of Christ, we really need to be cautious of how we communicate God's blessings to others and not deny Him the glory that is His. After uttering those words, I kept thinking about how the Bible says that God is a jealous God. When I show faithlessness or take credit that belongs to Him, I am pushing Him out of the spotlight so that I can get the credit and the glory. I am sure that, at that moment, God cannot be pleased with me. All the glory goes to Him. Think of it as a means of showing Him the respect He deserves. We need to honor Him and worship Him through our thoughts, actions, and spoken words.

Key Thought:

Some of us can talk the talk and sound like a devout Christian, but are we really just giving lip service to God?

Let that sink in. Are we hiding behind our religious façade hoping that no one will recognize the real person that we are inside, behind the mask? Are we sinners saved by God's grace, or are we playing the part of the Pharisee by just acting religious? People around us may think that we are sold out to God, but don't be deceived, God knows exactly where our heart is. Has the knowledge of God in our heads found its way to our hardened hearts? We all need a renewing of our minds, but we also need a heart transplant. We need a pride-ectomy! We need the Great Physician to do radical surgery on our hardened, selfish, and prideful hearts.

> I will give you a new heart and put a new spirit in you; I will remove from you your heart of stone and give you a heart of flesh.
>
> Ezekiel 36:26—NIV

Don't get me wrong on this point; I really want us to evaluate who we really are in our hearts and minds. Are we the new creation that we read about in the Bible and hear about in church, or are we just the rotten candy hidden in a pretty wrapper? Looks great until you open it, but once you see what's inside, you realize that it is awful and nauseating. Has any *real* change taken place in our hearts? We spoke the words, and we prayed the prayer. What happened?! Why are we not different?

Where does the rubber really meet the road? Think of it like the old Wendy's commercial with the old woman looking down at a tiny hamburger on a big bun and asking, "Where's the beef?" Let me say it another way: Where is the meat of our existence? Where is the substance of our lives? Personally, I think it boils down to the idea of realizing one very key point.

Question:

Do we, as professing Christians, know our true identity in Christ?

Identity in Christ?! Most would ask, *"What are you talking about?"* Believe me; this concept is much bigger than you even realize at this point. This truth is *huge*! Understanding how God sees each of us is absolutely essential to deepening our relationship with our LORD and Savior. Once we begin to see ourselves as God sees us, we will begin to realize how liberating it is to know who we are in Christ. Once and for all, we will see our true identity—the identity that He gives us!

This was never more true to me than after I read *Lifetime Guarantee: Making Your Christian Life Work and What to Do When It Doesn't* by Bill Gillham. In this book, Bill gives a list of verses that reveal to us our true identity. I want to list some of these for you and I want you to get your Bible out and read each one of them. When I read those verses and internalized them, it changed me forever. You really need to see this truth. I am urging you to take the time to read these verses. Get out your Bible, put this book down, and don't read on until you have done the following assignment:

Look up the following verses and discover how God sees you! *free from guilt*
Romans 3:24—You are *justified* and *redeemed.* *+ so free from consequences of sin*
(You have been made righteous. You were purchased and rescued.)
Romans 6:6—Your old self was *crucified.* *No longer slaves of sin*
Romans 8:1—You are not *condemned.* *Blamed of sin*
(God doesn't condemn the performer, just the performance.)
Romans 8:2—You are *free* from the law of *sin* and *death.*
Romans 15:7—You are *accepted.*
1 Corinthians 1:2—You are *sanctified.*
(You are holy and set apart.)
1 Corinthians 1:30—You have *wisdom, righteousness, holiness,* and *redemption.*
2 Corinthians 5:17—You are a new *creation.*
2 Corinthians 5:21—You are the *righteousness of God.*
Galatians 4:7—You are not a slave; You are an *heir.*
Ephesians 1:3—You are *blessed* with every spiritual blessing.
Ephesians 1:4—You are *chosen, holy,* and *blameless* before God.
Ephesians 1:7—You are *redeemed* and *forgiven.*
Ephesians 1:13—You are *sealed* with the Spirit.
Ephesians 2:5—You are *alive* and *saved* by Grace.
Ephesians 2:10—You are *created* for good works.
Ephesians 3:12—You may approach God with *freedom* and *confidence.*
Ephesians 5:8—You were formerly darkness, but now you are *light.*
(Fruit of the light is goodness, righteousness, and truth.)
Ephesians 5:30—We are a *member* of His body.

Philippians 4:7—Your heart and mind are *guarded* by the peace of God.
(Peace comes from *knowing* something; it is not necessarily a feeling.)
Philippians 4:19—Your *needs* are supplied.
Colossians 2:10—You are *complete.*
Colossians 3:1—You are *raised* up with Christ.

I pray that these verses come alive to you and shed light on who you are in Christ. Our spiritual enemy would love to pull a heist on our spiritual identity and keep us from ever knowing who we truly are. We are a new creation in Christ Jesus. We are loved and cherished by Him. We have been born anew. We have every spiritual blessing listed above and many more. Although we have been spiritually adopted, we must not forget that we are children of the Most High. We have been given a birthright and have been given a new heart. Our identity is written in the Book of Life (Revelation 3:5).

●●●

The LORD does not look at the things man looks at. Man looks at the outward appearance, but the LORD looks at the heart.

1 Samuel 16:7—NIV

For the word of God is living and active. Sharper than any double-edged sword, it penetrates even to dividing soul and spirit, joints and marrow; it judges the thoughts and attitudes of the heart.

Hebrews 4:12—NIV

This verse says the Word of God is *"living and active."* I love it!

102 • Dr. George Goodman

I love thinking about the Word of God as a living thing. It may not have a pulse, but believe me, it is truly alive. It brings life out of death ... light out of darkness ... joy out of sadness ... hope out of hopelessness. The list goes on and on. God's Word is our sustenance. It is the bread of life. It is our living water. It is life to our bones. It gives us a heart transplant!

> Wisdom is supreme; therefore get wisdom. Though it cost all you have, get understanding.
>
> Proverbs 4:7—NIV

John Stott, a Christian author wrote: "Knowledge is indispensable to Christian life and service." He went on to say, "If we do not use the mind which God has given us, we condemn ourselves to spiritual superficiality."

Many Christians may mean well, but many are like a ship without a compass—they have absolutely no idea where they are going. They have run up the Christian flag, but their ship is just sailing around in circles, not aiming for God's port.

> We have much to say about this, but it is hard to explain because you are slow to learn. In fact, though by this time you ought to be teachers, you need someone to teach you the elementary truths of God's word all over again. You need milk, not solid food! Anyone who lives on milk, being still an infant, is not acquainted with the teaching about righteousness. But solid food is for the mature, who by constant use have trained themselves to distinguish good from evil.
>
> Hebrews 5:11–14—NIV

Spiritual Superficiality

This is sadly true of the majority of Christians that I have met in my life. Their knowledge and understanding of God's word is superficial at best. They profess faith and live a life with a Christian label, but where is the substance? Too many believers are still spiritual infants who rely solely upon a diet of spiritual milk, while other believers are still spiritual vegetarians—they are ingesting some solids, but they are lacking in the meat of the Word. When we really dig in and chew on the meat of the Word, we will take in more complete, well-balanced spiritual nutrition and we will really begin to grow and mature in our spiritual lives. Through His Word, God has provided a spiritual all-you-can-eat buffet. For us, as believers, His Word is a veritable smorgasbord. It's time to quit nursing, develop a healthy appetite, and start eating (chewing and digesting) real spiritual food.

 It is impossible for a new believer to grasp the depth and richness of the Bible, but they have an excuse—they were just born into their faith. The rest of us, who have been Christians for a while now, are without excuse. We should be more spiritually mature by now. We should be more than just a "Christian"; we should be true "disciples of Christ." We should be learning about Him and truly following Him. It is sad to me that more Christians don't desire to know more of God's Word and apply it to their life, but like I have said it many times before—so many Christians just want to conform the Bible to their life, instead of conforming their life to God's Word. It is as if no desire to mature exists at all. We really need a change of heart.

I have hidden your word in my heart that I might not sin against you.

Psalms 119.11—NIV

At all costs, we must get in the Word of God and really learn what it says about everything in life. We need to hide it in our hearts. We need to store it and meditate on it regularly. The Word of God is so vitally important. We need to act like it is important. How can we communicate our faith to others if we don't even know what we believe? How can we defend our faith when it comes under attack? We need to know what God says about something in order to stand on His Word with a godly conviction.

As I previously mentioned, in my experience, the vast majority of "Christians" have no clue what the Bible says about much of anything, so how can we be convicted about something when we haven't even learned the basic facts? Many of us are truly sincere, but the problem is that we are often sincerely wrong! As Christians, we often fail miserably at so many basic things that are essential to our faith. We don't pray enough. We don't study God's Word enough. We don't tithe. We don't regularly fellowship with other believers. We don't witness to others about the life-changing message of the Gospel. Why is this? Forgive my boldness, but do we believe that all this stuff about God is true, or not?

Why do we not do a better job of being a good example of what it means to be a Christian? To be honest, if I were not a Christian today, I would have little desire to become one based upon the example of the vast majority of so-called "Christians" that I see. When I get into conversations with professing Christians, it amazes me how people who profess faith in Christ are so oblivious to what the Bible says about so many things! Where is the basic understanding? Where is the conviction? Where is the desire to learn what the Bible says and then live out the faith that Christ teaches us? Do we really love Him or are we just interested in knowing Him casually? None of us want

to spend eternity in hell, but is that the only reason that we profess faith in Christ … for "fire insurance"? Give me a break! How
completely insulting that must be to our LORD!

> "You are the salt of the earth. But if the salt loses its
> saltiness, how can it be made salty again? It is no longer
> good for anything, except to be thrown out and trampled
> by men. "You are the light of the world. A city on a hill
> cannot be hidden. Neither do people light a lamp and put
> it under a bowl. Instead they put it on its stand, and it gives
> light to everyone in the house. In the same way, let your
> light shine before men, that they may see your good deeds
> and praise your Father in heaven.
>
> Matthew 5:13–16—NIV

Question:

Why are we not the "salt and light" that the Bible speaks of?

Have we lost our "saltiness?" Does our "light" shine for anyone
to see? These things are so important and they are a part of our
knowing, believing, and trusting in God and the truth of His
Word. We need to ask Him to renew our sense of purpose and
reveal to us what His will is for our lives. I promise, if you will
do this, these things will return. Another thing; think about the
term "faith in Christ." What does that mean to you? Do you
have faith that a relationship with Christ will secure your place
in heaven? Does this relationship go any deeper than that for
you? Do you know Christ? Do you *really* know Christ? Do you

Belief & trust in God

really *want* to know Christ? I pray that you do. What I really
want to do is lead you into a more meaningful relationship with
Him. In order to have this real relationship, you must personally
decide to grow in your knowledge of Him. This means ...

• You must converse with Him (*pray*).
• You must trust Him for your every need (*believe*).
• You must learn what it means to be a Christian (*read* the
  Bible and *apply* it to your life).

Last year, I read a few books written by John Eldredge. I read
Wild at Heart, Captivating, and *Waking the Dead.* I really enjoy
his writing style. By the way, as a man, if you have not read
Wild at Heart, you are missing out on a huge blessing. That book
squarely hit me at the right time; it really *blessed* me because
it spoke to me as a man. It helped me understand how I am
designed—as a masculine man, as God intended. I really needed
to hear what it had to say at the time I read it. In a day where
men are emasculated every time you turn around, *Wild at Heart*
helped reveal more about my godly manhood than any other
book I have ever read.

(For the benefit of better understanding my wife, I also read
Captivating. It was written by John Eldredge and his wife, Stacy.
I believe that if you are a woman, *Captivating* will speak to you
and bless you as a woman, the same way that *Wild at Heart* spoke
to me and blessed me as a man.)

Waking the Dead is a great book as well. In it, one of the major
themes is the thought: *"The glory of God is man's heart fully alive."*
Sadly, today I think most of us are just walking around "dead."
We are numb. We are "saved" but seem "lost." We have no spiritual maturity. No passion for the things of God. No desire for
growth, especially if it costs us something. Until recently, I was
in this crowd. I knew enough about the Bible to feel secure in my

faith, but in reality, this just showed my lack of real faith. Thanks to God for getting my attention and allowing me to come to the end of myself. My eyes were opened. When we become fully alive, that is to say, when we really see "God's big picture," we realize that we have purpose. We get the vision. When we realize what we were created for, it gives meaning and purpose to our lives. How is it that so many countless millions of people live out their entire lives with no real sense of purpose? What a tragic waste of time and potential!

I have heard it said many times that when we stop dreaming, we stop living. Maybe we don't die a physical death, but inside, a major part of us dies. We must never allow this tragedy to happen in our lives. If we could only find a way to "plug in" to God's *"good, pleasing, and perfect will"* for our lives, things would be so much better. I believe that if we could see more clearly or get more of a glimpse of the plans that God has for us, it would make all the difference in the world.

It all starts with a change of heart!

> Create in me a pure heart, O God, and renew a steadfast
> spirit within me.

> Psalms 51:10—NIV

Steadfast. Hmmm ... "steadfast"... what a great word. To me, steadfast simply means consistency. Steadfast is defined as *firm in belief,* determination, or adherence. It is an unwavering devotion (to your calling). Wouldn't it be great if we could have this kind of consistent, stable relationship with God? I want you to pray that God would bring about in your life a pure heart and a renewed and steadfast spirit within you. Imagine a life of constant communication with God and consistency in your faith.

What a blessing it would be to have this in your life. If you ask Him for it, He will give it to you, but you have to do your part.

> Until now you have not asked for anything in my name.
> Ask and you will receive, and your joy will be complete.

John 16:24—NIV

Key Thought:

We don't have ... because we don't ask.

I thank God that He will provide these things for us if we will just seek Him and ask Him for them. (Remember—*ask, seek,* and *knock?*) This verse says to *ask.* It also says that when we *ask,* we *will* receive. Don't get me wrong about this point! This is *not* a recipe for getting everything in life that we don't need just to satisfy our selfish desires. It is an opportunity to ask God for what really matters.

Still confused about what to ask for? So many people ask for things that have nothing to do with godliness. It is selfish, and frankly stupid, to ask for something that will cause you to have a lesser dependence upon God. We need to ask God to change our hearts. Give us pure hearts. Give us a steadfast spirit. Give us an unquenchable desire to love Him and devote ourselves to Him. I suggest that you pray this prayer, or one like it:

> *Father, in Jesus' name, I ask for a pure heart. Change me from the inside out. Create in me a renewed and steadfast spirit so that I may serve You with unwavering consistency.* LORD,

it is my desire to come into a closer, deeper relationship with You. I want to sense Your loving hand protecting me. I want to draw strength from You. I want to need You like a helpless child needs a loving Father. Guide me along the narrow road that leads me home to You. Help me to never stray off the path. Allow me to clearly see the lessons in life that You would have me to learn without having to stumble and fall along the way. Reveal Yourself to me in ways that I never imagined. Make my faith in You more real than ever before. Humble me. Allow me to see my own limitations in order that I may more completely understand my need for You. I ask You for wisdom. Please give me the answers to the questions that I don't even know to ask. Help me to live a life that would cause You to smile upon me. Fill me with Your endless love and show me what it means to be truly faithful.

I confess that when I have tried to do life on my own, without You, my life has been a series of failures. I recognize my need for You in my life. LORD, I want to know what Your "good, pleasing, and perfect will" is for my life. I ask You to reveal it to me. I want to know what You created me to be. Lead me to a place where I can begin to see Your will for me. Help me to know what You would have me to do with this life that You have given me. Give me a desire to live out Your will and make a difference in the lives of those that You put on my path. I profess my love for You. I profess my need for You. I praise Your name because You are worthy to be praised. Bless my life. Help me to be a blessing in the lives of others. Help me to learn that You can use someone as seemingly "unlikely" as me to change the world in some meaningful way. Give me a hunger for Your Word. Help me to read it and understand it. Help me to hide Your Word in my heart. Give me discernment. Help me to have deep conviction about Your revealed truths. Help me to want to live according to Your Word more than anything else. Tug at my heart and correct me when I begin to live a life that serves my purpose at the expense of Your purpose. Help my will and my desires to be crucified daily. Help me to live a life of purpose beginning with the knowledge of Your plan for me. I want to live a life of conviction. I want to serve You when it is not convenient to do so. I want to stand for something. I don't want to take the easy way out. I want to grow in my faith and knowledge of You. I seek Your face. LORD, there are so many things that I need to learn. Make me receptive to the leading of Your Spirit. Teach me what being a disciple really means. Thank You, LORD that I can come to You with my burdens and give them to You for You to carry for me. Help me to fully give my cares to You. Make me whole and complete in You. In Jesus Christ's holy name—Amen.

I hope that you prayed that prayer and that you will continue to pray for a pure heart and a renewed spirit. Personalize your communication with God. When we pray, I believe that God wants to hear what is on our hearts. I think that when we pray memorized, regurgitated prayers, God hears our words, but He doesn't get to hear what is in our hearts. Open yourself up. Free yourself to pray to Him in your own words. He doesn't want to hear our eloquent, memorized words. Our prayers need to be less from our heads and more from our hearts.

Stop sometime and listen to the prayer of a child. They have an amazing ability to say anything they have on their hearts without any reservation or fear. Some of my greatest blessings come when I just listen to my children talk to God. We don't need to feel the pressure of lifting up a lofty, impressive prayer. Don't be deceived. Don't let Satan steal your joy by leading you into thinking that your prayers have to "measure up" to be worthwhile. God just wants to hear our hearts ... pure and simple. Don't hold back. Talk openly with Him. Talk a while, and then stop and listen. Make prayer a two-way conversation. When we pray and say "Amen," what we are really saying is "So be it." I like to think of it as ending my prayer with the thought, *Please, LORD, hear and answer my prayer.*

My pastor said something simple and yet profound about prayer. He said, *"If we really believed in prayer, we would do more of it."* (Let that sink in.)

We need to go to God in prayer.
Look at the following verses.

> Rejoice always, pray without ceasing, in everything give thanks; for this is the will of God in Christ Jesus for you.
>
> 1 Thessalonians 5:16–18—NKJV

Pray without ceasing. How is that possible? Well, I guess it is an attitude. When something good happens, thank God for it. When you have a need, ask God for it. Bottom line: we need to go to God *first*, before we try to figure things out on our own. Notice in verse 18 it says, *"the will of God in Christ Jesus for you."* God's will ... for you. You! Every time we get a glimpse of God's will for us we need to embrace it and internalize it and allow it to change us and transform us.

Key Thought:

The degree to which you pray is proportionate to the degree that you believe that you need God's advice or intervention.

For some people, prayer is their last resort, when in reality, prayer needs to be our front-line defense. To me, praying without ceasing is like an attitude of constant worship and recognition that

God is really in control of our lives and that we acknowledge our dependence upon Him.

> I refresh the humble and give new courage to those with repentant hearts.
>
> Isaiah 57:15—TLB

We all have times that we need to be refreshed. You could call it "recharging your batteries." Notice it says that God will refresh the humble. Sometimes I don't feel very humble, but it is at those times that I ask God to humble me and purify my heart and help me draw closer to Him. The verse goes on to speak of repentant hearts. Merriam-Webster defines the word "repent" as *to turn from sin and dedicate oneself to the amendment of one's life.* Are we regularly confessing our sins to God and seeking His forgiveness? When we do this, we are humbling ourselves in the sight of the LORD. When we are weak, He is strong! We need to humble ourselves more often and lean on His strength.

> For we walk by faith, not by sight.
>
> 2 Corinthians 5:7—NKJV

This is such an amazing concept! To walk by faith and not by sight means that we walk by what we *know* and *believe* to be true, not by what we *see* or *perceive* to be true. We need to trust God. God will create circumstances in our lives that require us to have faith. I think that tithing is a great example of this. Most people will say that they can accomplish more with 100 percent of their income rather than with 90 percent of what is left after tithing 10 percent. In human terms, this is true, but in God's economy, this is not true. When we tithe 10 percent of our income, as we are instructed to do, we say by our actions that we are trusting God to do something that we cannot do. It opens the door and invites God to supernaturally work in our lives. Read the following verse:

> "Bring the whole tithe into the storehouse, that there may be food in my house. Test me in this," says the LORD Almighty, "and see if I will not throw open the floodgates of heaven and pour out so much blessing that you will not have room enough for it."
>
> Malachi 3:10—NIV

Nowhere else in the Bible does God say, "Test Me." Wow! Think about that. If we will just let go and really trust God, especially in the area of our finances, He will shower us with blessings beyond our imagination. Let me be very clear. I really hate it when people use this verse as a means of saying that God will shower us with *financial* blessings if we give. Think about it. Is God our cosmic vending machine? Absolutely not! What is our motivation here? Are we giving to get something in return, *or* are we giving back to God what is really His in the first place so that He will bless us as *He* sees fit? This blessing may come in the form of many things, but to say that we give money to get money, really disgusts me. I think that it is a perversion of the spirit of giving.

I Want the Blessings That God Thinks I Need!

If He chooses to bless me financially, that's great. If He chooses to bless me with an amazing ministry, with health or wisdom or whatever, that's great too. I just want to live a life that is blessed. Who am I to tell God what blessing is best for me? How completely ridiculous and selfish can some of us be? Don't offend God. Get your heart right. Give because you are supposed to. Give God what's right; not what's left. Then sit back and watch God work. Believe me—what He chooses to bless you with will be what you really need. God is always on time and always on target!

> Keep your lives free from the love of money and be content with what you have, because God has said, "Never will I leave you; never will I forsake you."
>
> Hebrews 13:5—NIV

> But godliness with contentment is great gain.
>
> 1 Timothy 6:6—NIV

Let's break this verse down. *Godliness.* To be godly means that we have a reverence for God and that we live a life of holiness. *Contentment.* From a Christian perspective, *contentment* is a real satisfaction or sufficiency that comes only from God. From my perspective, learning to be content in all things communicates a satisfaction in God's plan.

There is a big difference between *holiness* and *happiness.* To me, holiness is the horse and happiness is the cart. (Note that happiness is the cart—happiness doesn't drive the cart! Happiness goes nowhere without being led by/driven by holiness.) If we place happiness in front of holiness, we get into trouble. Instead, if we will put holiness in front of happiness, God will create in us a contentment that causes us to find a "happiness" that we have never known. This is known as joy. Joy is like happiness on steroids. We need to put our focus and our efforts into becoming holy if we are to find the joy we hope for. God designed us and

He knows how we work. He knows that we need to concentrate on holiness, but we don't see it sometimes. We need to get this truth down and pursue it. Pray that God would show you the path to holiness.

> Then Jesus said to his disciples, "If anyone would come after me, he must deny himself and take up his cross and follow me. For whoever wants to save his life will lose it, but whoever loses his life for me will find it.
>
> Matthew 16:24–25—NIV

> And he died for all, that those who live should no longer live for themselves but for him who died for them and was raised again.
>
> 2 Corinthians 5:15—NIV

Speaking of a change of heart, let's read about Simon Peter.

> "Simon, Simon, Satan has asked to sift you as wheat. But I have prayed for you, Simon, that your faith may not fail. And when you have turned back, strengthen your brothers." But he replied, "LORD, I am ready to go with you to prison and to death." Jesus answered, "I tell you, Peter, before the rooster crows today, you will deny three times that you know me."
>
> Luke 22:31–34—NIV

Trust me. If there is one thing I know about, it's being "sifted." To sift something out means to separate out something to be discarded. The process requires shaking things up and filtering through a sieve to remove lumps or large particles. I know what it feels like to be turned upside-down and be shaken. God has shaken my foundation on numerous occasions (mostly because of my tendency to be stubborn and prideful).

Question:

What are the "lumps" in your life that need to be sifted out? What are the "large particles" that pollute the purity of your character?

Although the process of "sifting" is a painful one, it is necessary to smooth out our character and help us be "refined." Just like a child, we all have to learn our boundaries. Sometimes God has to shake us up to show us His boundaries for our lives.

> Simon Peter and another disciple were following Jesus. Because this disciple was known to the high priest, he went with Jesus into the high priest's courtyard, but Peter had to wait outside at the door. The other disciple, who was known to the high priest, came back, spoke to the girl on duty there and brought Peter in. "You are not one of his disciples, are you?" the girl at the door asked Peter. He replied, "I am not."
>
> John 18:15–17—NIV

> As Simon Peter stood warming himself, he was asked, "You are not one of his disciples, are you?" He denied it, saying, "I am not." One of the high priest's servants, a relative of the man whose ear Peter had cut off, challenged him, "Didn't I

see you with him in the olive grove?" Again Peter denied it,
and at that moment a rooster began to crow.

John 18.:25–27—NIV

I can only imagine the sinking feeling that Peter must have
felt as the reality of the moment was allowed to sink in. That
rooster crowing must have been the most heart-breaking sound
to Peter. What an immediate, overwhelming sense of failure!
Peter's prideful arrogance and over-confidence were so blinding
that he never once even considered that he would fail Christ so
miserably. Think about Peter's state of mind that followed. He
had denied knowing Jesus three times after so boldly professing
his love and devotion to Him. It must have been devastating.
Peter's foundation had been violently shaken. Not only had Peter
been wrestling with his own failures, but next, he had to watch
his LORD and Rabbi be crucified on the cross and die a horrible,
painful death. Talk about a dark time in the life of Peter. He was
grieving the death of his beloved Rabbi and LORD.

After the social unrest that led to the crucifixion of Jesus, I
imagine that it was an extremely unpopular thing to be a disciple
of Jesus at that moment in time. Peter was scared for his life
because of his association with Jesus. People wanted him dead.
Talk about a full plate. He denied Christ, watched Him die, and
was then hiding out of fear of his own death.

We know that after the resurrection, Jesus appeared to His
disciples. I want you to pay attention to what Jesus had to say
specifically to Peter on this special occasion. And now, as Paul
Harvey would say, "And now let's hear the rest of the story."

When they had finished eating, Jesus said to Simon Peter,
"Simon son of John, do you truly love me more than these?"
"Yes, LORD," he said, "you know that I love you." Jesus said,

"Feed my lambs." Again Jesus said, "Simon son of John, do you truly love me?" He answered, "Yes, LORD, you know that I love you." Jesus said, "Take care of my sheep." The third time he said to him, "Simon son of John, do you love me?" Peter was hurt because Jesus asked him the third time, "Do you love me?" He said, "LORD, you know all things; you know that I love you." Jesus said, "Feed my sheep."

John 21:15–17—NIV

Just like Peter denied Christ three times, Christ restored Peter in a loving way by asking him to "feed my sheep" *three times*! What a beautiful illustration of God's love for us. What an amazing example of the fact that we serve a God who extends loving grace to His children by giving them a "second" chance—over and over again.

Another awesome example of this can be found in Mark 16. In this passage, which occurs prior to Christ's appearing to His disciples after His resurrection, Mary Magdalene and Mary (the mother of James) went to the tomb of Jesus to anoint His body, and they discovered that the stone had been rolled away and the tomb was empty. An angel of the LORD appeared to them and said:

"Don't be alarmed," he said. "You are looking for Jesus the Nazarene, who was crucified. He has risen! He is not here. See the place where they laid him. But go, tell his disciples and Peter, 'He is going ahead of you into Galilee. There you will see him, just as he told you.'"

Mark 16:6–7—NIV

How amazing that this heavenly messenger would specifically call out Peter's name (verse 7). God knew how bad Peter was hurting and He sent a messenger with a message that would strengthen him. God is Love, and God is so good.

Let's take a departure and examine the life of Peter. I am amazed at some of the extraordinary things about Peter that I have recently learned.

> As Jesus was walking beside the Sea of Galilee, he saw two brothers, Simon called Peter and his brother Andrew. They were casting a net into the lake, for they were fishermen. "Come, follow me," Jesus said, "and I will make you fishers of men." At once they left their nets and followed him.
>
> Matthew 4:18–20—NIV

[This story is also repeated in the Gospel of Mark (Mark 1:16–18).]

I have read the story of Jesus calling Peter to follow him and be His disciple, but until recently, I didn't completely understand the conversation or the reasons behind why someone would just drop what they were doing and walk away from their family business to follow a rabbi who walked up to them on a beach and said, *"Come, follow me."*

I want you to know that I truly believe that God wants me to include this information in this book. The reason that I believe this so strongly is because, within a ten-day period of time, I had three different people tell me specific things about the life of Peter. None of them knew each other and none of them knew that I was writing about Peter or that I even wanted to write about Peter, yet all three people had the same information to share with me. The very next week, my pastor preached on the same information. Wow! Ever get that feeling that God is trying to tell you something or teach you something? After the third person communicated the following truths to me and I heard it from the pulpit, I was convinced that I needed to be obedient to God's leading and include this information in this book.

Before I go into a long discourse, I want to explain where I gathered my information. I researched Jewish encyclopedias and dictionaries for the proper terminology and concepts, but one of the greatest sources came from a DVD video named Dust that I was given by my friend John (my accountability partner). He gave me this video after I had communicated to him what God had done by bringing all this information to my attention about the life of Peter.

If we could go back to the days that Christ walked this earth and study some of the societal traditions of that time, it helps us to better understand the story of Peter's calling. At that time, the only aspect of the Bible that was in existence was what we now know as the Old Testament. The first five books of the Old Testament were called the *Torah* (pronounced: toe RAH). "*Torah*" is a Hebrew word that means "instruction" or "law." It is God's instruction and law given to His people. These books are commonly referred to as the "Books of the Law," the "Books of Moses," and the "Pentateuch." Moses told the people,

Command your children to obey carefully all the words of this law.

Deuteronomy 32:46—NIV.

Key Thought:

In the Jewish faith, observing the teachings of the Torah is a way of life that is based upon the covenant that God made with His people. It requires complete dedication because it is seen as God's direction for living the covenant relationship.

I like the fact that the word *"testament"* is best translated to mean *"covenant."* In the Old Testament, God made a covenant with the nation of Israel. In the New Testament, Jesus came to make a new covenant with us! When you think about it, this is a wonderful truth! I personally like the concept of calling each testament by the names *"Older Testament"* and *"Newer Testament"* because so many Christians today just want to know about the New Testament—they forget about the history behind Christianity—they forget about our Jewish roots. We, as Christians, need to acknowledge (or be reminded) that Jesus was Jewish. Jesus quoted from the Old Testament on a regular basis. The main difference between who we are to be as Christians and who Jews are is the difference that we, as Christians, believe that the Messiah (the Christ) has already come in the person of Jesus. Jews believe everything that we believe about the Old Testament, but they believe that the Messiah has yet to come. The difference is Jesus. To us, He is the Christ.

Fact:
Historically, during the time of Peter's childhood, children would memorize (word for word) all five books of the Torah (Genesis, Exodus, Leviticus, Numbers, and Deuteronomy).

I have heard it said that in the Jewish view, study is the highest form of worship. With this thought in mind, I would like to explain in more detail, the Jewish educational system during the time of Peter's childhood.

Bet ha-Sefer is the name of the school that children under thirteen attended to learn the Torah. Upon completion of Bet ha-Sefer (essentially primary school), children would then go to *Bet ha-Talmud*. The Hebrew word *"Talmud"* means "study" or "learning." Attending the Bet ha-Talmud was basically like attending middle school today. At this level of education, students would memorize all the books of the Old Testament. (In case you are wondering, there are thirty-nine books in the Old Testament—Genesis through Malachi. The Old Testament makes up about 8/13 of the content of the whole Bible as it exists today with the New Testament included.) Only the best and brightest students completed this level! Those that completed Bet ha-Talmud then went on to *Bet ha-Midrash*. Bet ha-Midrash was sort of like high school. The Hebrew word *"Midrash"* means "to search out." Bet ha-Midrash literally means "house of study." It was a place where the students of the Jewish law gathered to listen to the discourse or exposition of the law (also known as the Midrash). Only the very best of the best and brightest completed this level of study. Those that did successfully complete the Bet ha-Midrash, often went on to become a disciple of an individual rabbi.

Now that we understand more about the education of Jewish children in Old Testament times, it is also important to know more about their society. With so much emphasis on knowing the Word of God, the Jewish society placed great respect in their rabbis. To be a rabbi meant that you were very knowledgeable about the things of God because you dedicated your life to knowing all that you could know about God as revealed in His

Word. Every Rabbi would interview prospective disciples and take on one or more of them to teach. A disciple can be defined as "a student, learner, or pupil." To become a disciple of a rabbi, you take on the rabbi's "yoke." The rabbi's yoke was that particular rabbi's understanding and interpretation of God's Word. A disciple of a rabbi takes on his rabbi's yoke because he desires to be like his rabbi. He wants to know what his rabbi knows and do what his rabbi does.

Key Thought:

As disciples of Christ, we should have a hunger to know what our Rabbi teaches because our Rabbi is our LORD and Savior.

Look at the following verse where Jesus speaks of His "yoke."

> "Come to me, all you who are weary and burdened, and I will give you rest. Take my yoke upon you and learn from me, for I am gentle and humble in heart, and you will find rest for your souls. For my yoke is easy and my burden is light."
>
> Matthew 11:28–30—NIV

In this verse when Jesus speaks of His yoke by saying "my yoke," it can be understood to mean that he is saying "the service of God as I teach it." If you take verse 29 where it says "my yoke" and replace it with "the service of God as I teach it" and re-read it, it takes on a clearer meaning.

Take [the service of God as I teach it] upon you and learn from me, for I am gentle and humble in heart, and you will find rest for your souls.

Matthew 11:29—NIV

Now let's look at the scene where Jesus walks up to Peter and says, "Come, follow me."

Now that we understand more about Peter's educational background, it makes more sense. If Peter was a fisherman, he obviously wasn't a disciple of a particular rabbi. This meant that he wasn't one of the best and brightest (or, like some of us, he hadn't yet come to recognize the significance of what it meant to fully serve God). No rabbi had taken him on to train, therefore, Peter was left to work and run the family business. Now imagine that you are Peter and the rabbi of all rabbis walks up to you and says, *"Come, follow me."* Of course, as a devout Jewish young man, you are going to jump at the chance to be the disciple of a well-respected rabbi, even if it means leaving everything behind. If you remember, Jesus had been astounding the other rabbis with his knowledge of the Word of God from a very young age. No doubt that He had developed a reputation as a respected rabbi. The fact that Jesus would call someone who was *"unlikely"* should not surprise us. Thank God that He sees the heart and not the résumé, otherwise, most of us would be in trouble—we wouldn't make the cut.

There are some other interesting facts about the life of Peter that I want to draw attention to. Not only did he drop everything to follow Jesus, but he also was the only disciple to get out of the boat and go to Jesus on the water.

"LORD, if it's you," Peter replied, "tell me to come to you on the water." "Come," he said. Then Peter got down out of the boat, walked on the water and came toward Jesus. But when he saw the wind, he was afraid and, beginning to sink, cried out, "LORD, save me!" Immediately Jesus reached out his hand and caught him. "You of little faith," he said, "why did you doubt?"

Matthew 14:28–31—NIV

Peter wanted to be like his Rabbi and do what He did, so much so, that he got out of the boat and headed out to meet Jesus. Only after he stepped out to meet his Rabbi, and began to walk to Him, did he begin to sink. So many people look at this story and say that Peter had so little faith. On the contrary, I believe that it took a lot of faith in his Rabbi to even step out of the boat and begin to walk toward Him. Although Peter's faith wasn't sufficient enough to keep him standing on the water, he displayed more faith than the rest of the disciples in the boat by even attempting to go out and meet Jesus. The fact that his faith began to falter and that he began to sink isn't what stands out to me ... it is the fact that he was the only disciple to get out and attempt to walk to Jesus on the water. I think it is the experiences like this that Peter drew upon in his later life. I think these things shaped his character and made him a better disciple and witness for Christ.

Another thing that stands out to me in this verse is that as soon as Peter began to sink, Jesus reached out His hand and caught him. That is just like our LORD. He is always there when we need Him. Sometimes we can't see Him or can't feel His presence, but we know that He is there ready to catch us. A saying that I love is, *"When you can't see His hand ... trust His heart."* God tells us in His Word that He will never leave us or forsake us (Hebrews 13:5). We need to know that we know that we know that He is always there, every single time. We just need to lift our hands to Him knowing that He is there, whether we see Him or not, ready to take our hand and raise us up.

I love it that Peter seems to be the kind of disciple that operates in "full-throttle" mode. It seems that if you look at his life, he was the kind of guy that would soar high or crash hard. He wasn't afraid of jumping in and embracing the teachings and instruction of his Rabbi. I also love the fact that after Christ restored Peter (after asking him to "feed my sheep" three times), Peter went on to do some amazing things for the kingdom of God. Look at Acts 2, on the day of Pentecost. God allowed Peter to be a part of one the greatest moments in the New Testament. On the day of Pentecost, approximately 3,000 people came into a relationship with Jesus as their LORD and Savior and were baptized.

I think that you can boil down Peter's attitude to a single comment that we find in Luke 5. Look specifically at verse 5. My pastor recently spoke about this comment by Peter and it really resonated with me. One more proof that having the right attitude is so important.

> When he had finished speaking, he said to Simon, "Put out into deep water, and let down the nets for a catch." Simon answered, "Master, we've worked hard all night and haven't caught anything. But [because you say so], I will let down the nets." When they had done so, they caught such a large number of fish that their nets began to break. So they signaled their partners in the other boat to come and help them, and they came and filled both boats so full that they began to sink. When Simon Peter saw this, he fell at Jesus' knees and said, "Go away from me, LORD; I am a sinful man!"
>
> Luke 5:4–8—NIV

"But because you say so ... "

As Christians, and even more importantly, as disciples of Christ, we need to have this attitude. We need to stop and say to our LORD and Rabbi, like Peter did, *"But because you say so"* (verse 5), I will do it. If we expect to find God's will and purpose for our lives, we must change our perspective to line up with His Word. *wow!* If it says it, we must obey it. We need to be doers, not hearers (James 1:22). We need to be the real-deal and not just posers.

Recently, I have come to see a lot of myself in Peter. I relate to Peter so well. I seem to share some of his personality traits. Although now I am more calm than in years past, I was the one to rush in without thinking it through, open my mouth too wide and stick my foot in it, start strong and then fade, deny my faith (by my apathy), etc. It took finding the end of myself and the beginning of God to truly have my change of heart.

Good Question:

How do we find the end of ourselves?

Better Question:

Do we actually find ourselves or do we really lose ourselves?

The problem is we find ourselves early in life and, in our fleshly selfishness, we never give up our control until our lives spin out of control. I believe that when we lose ourselves (come to the end of our self) and truly "die to self," we really begin to understand why we need God so desperately. When we begin to see ourselves as God sees us and we learn of our true identity in our relationship with Christ, we come to terms with our need to crucify the flesh daily and depend upon God to sustain us.

We need to ask that God would replace our heart of stone with a heart of flesh. The problem is that our heart of stone thinks it is in charge. It doesn't see the need for God. That's why we need radical (spiritual) heart surgery. In order to experience this transforming change in our hearts, we must first have a desire to change. Behind this desire, there is a motive, a reason for wanting to change. Our motive to change should be our need for godliness.

What is "godliness," and what does it look like? Before we answer that, let's find out who is in charge.

very important

Chapter 4

who's in charge here?

"For my thoughts are not your thoughts, neither are your ways my ways," declares the LORD. "As the heavens are higher than the earth, so are my ways higher than your ways and my thoughts than your thoughts."

Isaiah 55:8–9—NIV

The fear of the LORD is the beginning of wisdom

Proverbs 9:10—NIV

So many people in this world live their life as if there is no God. All I can say is that if you choose to live that way, you had better be right, because a lot is riding on that decision. One must consider that in all decisions, there are eternal consequences. Although I personally know that God exists (for reasons we have discussed and will discuss later), I would rather be wrong and live a life according to biblical principles and simply die having led a meaningful life, rather than live a life devoid of any morality, and realize, when it was too late, that God *is* real and I wasted my life and gave up my chance to spend eternity with Him. I have heard it said that the road to hell is paved with good intentions. Well, in contrast, finding the "narrow road" that leads to heaven is as simple as putting your faith in Jesus Christ.

Key Concepts:
- Religion won't save you.
- Good intentions won't save you.
- Good works won't save you.
- Christ, and Christ alone, will save you—if you put your faith in Him.

Key Thought:

Being a disciple of Christ is all about having a relationship with Jesus—not a religion about Jesus.

Question:

What causes us to come to a point where we are ready to relinquish control of our lives?

Some of us, and I would argue that it is most of us, have to fight the tendency to live life our way. We like control. Our culture puts us in control. We have controls for everything. We have universal remote controls, cell phones, cordless phones, high speed wireless internet access, satellite and HDTV, keyless entry, air conditioners and heaters that obey our precise range of comfort, doors that open up as we walk up to them ... the list goes on. We mostly do what we want, when we want and how we want. If you don't think so, go to a third world country and see the poverty and living conditions and overall quality of life. We are, without question, among the wealthiest, most materially blessed people of the world, yet we don't recognize it or allow that to permeate how we choose to live our lives.

> So because you are lukewarm, and neither hot nor cold, I will spit you out of My mouth.
>
> Revelation 3:16—NAS

It would seem that our culture is progressively becoming more godless, or perhaps, less God-fearing, which, I would argue, is much worse. I was raised to have a reverential fear of God. There is a level of respect that we should have for God that most people, even some Christians, just don't seem to grasp. For example, for me, the concept of taking the LORD's name in vain by saying (and I hate to even type it out) *"God damn!"* is just awful and totally disrespectful to God and is directly addressed and spoken to in the Ten Commandments ...

> You shall not misuse the name of the LORD your God, for the LORD will not hold anyone guiltless who misuses his name.
>
> Exodus 20:7—NIV

... yet I hear professing Christians say this phrase all the time. Once, by accident, I said "God da ..." and I caught myself before I let it rip. I knew what I was about to say, but I caught it. I had tears well up and I immediately asked for forgiveness for having even uttered it. Other than that one occurrence, I have never, to my knowledge, ever taken the LORD's name in vain. I don't say this to sound pious; rather, I say this to say that I am so thankful that my father instilled in me, during my childhood, the concept of having a reverential fear of God. It makes my skin crawl that we, as believers, can be so callous and indifferent to something so important and so elementary and allow ourselves to tolerate this. This example may seem extreme, but even for those of you who don't speak the LORD's name in vain, you still may be living a life that doesn't honor Him.

Question:

Which is worse? A blasphemous statement blurted out or a life wasted?

Forgive my boldness, but we need to think like this more often. What we say and what we think and how we live our lives *does* matter. It matters to God; therefore, it should matter to us.

Let's go back and discuss this non-God-fearing society for a moment. For those individuals, organizations, special interest groups, etc., that oppose the church and constantly speak out against it, why is it that their voice seems to be heard the loudest? Because most of people in the church are idly standing by letting our religious freedoms be challenged and the church dragged through the mud without raising our voices in defense. Do we believe this stuff or not? Where is our conviction?

Maybe the world thinks badly of Christianity because so many of us give the church a bad name by the way we have been living our lives. We can be so hypocritical. We preach this and that, and then we go do this and that and destroy our witness to those around us. I have said it before, if I were currently a non-believer and all I had to go by was the world's perception of the church (the body of Christ), you would have a hard time convincing me that this whole church thing was worth my time. I mean, who wants to join what others say is a cult and be bad-mouthed by the majority and be looked down upon because of my association with a group of judgmental, lukewarm, non-committed pacifists? What a sad commentary on the church ... or at least the world's *perspective* on the church.

My perspective is a little different. I believe that Christians need to rise up and be more like Christ if we expect to change this world we live in. We have been called to a higher standard than what we have accepted as the *status quo*. We have a God-given purpose! It's about time the real body of Christ recognized and began to live up to that purpose! We need to discover (or re-discover) God's *"good, pleasing, and perfect will"* for our lives, and it all starts with you and me. What are *we* doing for the kingdom of God? What are *we* doing to change our world and show the world the depth of God's *love?* The world is sick of hearing about things like *"God hates queers!"* or *"You're going to hell!"* It is about time that the world got a taste of God's love. God is love, but the world hears the message that *"God hates _____!"* (use your imagination and fill in the blank like everyone else does).

> For God so loved the world that he gave his one and only Son, that whoever believes in him shall not perish but have eternal life.
>
> John 3:16—NIV

Why don't we hear more about this loving part of God's character? God made the ultimate sacrifice to allow our sins to be forgiven so that we could truly be forgiven and made righteous. He has offered us the gift of eternal life. This is the message about God that the world needs to hear. We are not representing our LORD like we are supposed to be. We need God's help!

Key Thought:

It is time that we give up our plans and our control and offer ourselves to God.

We need to remember: God is in control, not us! It is His job to judge, not ours. It is our job to be a beacon to a dark and dying world. We need to be instruments of love and instruments of spiritual revival. Some people get hung up on the word "revival," but think about its meaning. We live our Christian life as if our "spiritual man" was dying and on life-support, all the while our "fleshly man" is healthy, strong, and actively running our lives and the decisions we make as a person. Our spiritual man needs to be awoken and "revived" and given authority over our fleshly man so that we can begin to live like we were created to live—at peace with God. Imagine if the world got a glimpse of how God sees His children, all living up to their calling, living out their passionate faith for the entire world to see. This world would be a completely different place.

Key Thought:

If you want to see a positive change in the world, then be a catalyst for that change—Be the necessary ingredient for starting the change.

Take that first step on your journey to holiness. The first step is the hardest because inertia (and Satan) is holding you back. Break the silence. Break the stillness. Take that first step (which is actually a kneel). When we get on our knees and humble ourselves before God, we need to ask God for the following things:
- Forgive us for being control freaks.
- Take our control away from us.
- Give us strength and guidance.
- Reveal to us Your "good, pleasing, and perfect will" for our lives.

Early this morning, I was taking my wife to the airport. While we were driving, we were listening to one of our Clay Crosse CDs. I have listened to this album many times, but this morning, it was as if I really heard the message of the song *"I Surrender All"* more clearly than I ever had before. I love it when God opens up my eyes and ears to see and hear His truths with crystal clarity. Once you see and hear the message that He wants you to receive, you sit there and wonder why it wasn't that clear to you before. When it happens, it is as if the blinders have been removed. This morning, for me, I guess God's plan was that I be given this wonderful truth when I needed it most. When it happened, I couldn't wait to get home and start writing about it.

Read some of the lyrics to the following song and see if God doesn't grab your heart and speak clearly to you, as He did to me this morning.

I Surrender All[7]

I have wrestled in the darkness of this lonely pilgrim land
Raising strong and mighty fortresses that I alone command
But these castles I've constructed by the strength of my own hand
Are just temporary kingdoms on foundations made of sand
In the middle of the battle I believe I've finally found
I'll never know the thrill of victory 'til I'm willing to lay down
All my weapons of defense and earthly strategies of war
So I'm laying down my arms and running helplessly to Yours

If the source of my ambition is the treasure I obtain
If I measure my successes on a scale of earthly gain
If the focus of my vision is the status I attain
My accomplishments are worthless and my efforts are in vain
So I lay aside these trophies to pursue a higher crown
And should You choose somehow to use the life I willingly lay down

I surrender all the triumph for it's only by Your grace
I relinquish all the glory, I surrender all the praise

As I personally sit here and read the words to this song, I am acutely aware that this song sums up what I am trying to communicate in this book. These words are so powerful. The truth of the message is enormous. As hard as it is to wrap our minds around what it means to surrender all, it is even harder to do it. This is where the rubber meets the road.

If you're ready to surrender all and have the truth of this song be evident in your life, then bookmark this page, put the book down, and spend some time with God. Come out of your fortress and surrender your life. Lay everything down. Talk to Him and build your relationship with Him. Get in His Word. That is more important. This book will be here when you get back.

Being in control is in our very nature. In the book of Genesis, we read that Satan wanted "to be like God," so he waged war in heaven and tried to overthrow God. Satan failed and was subsequently banished from heaven, along with all of those who chose to fight alongside him. Later, we read about Satan deceiving Adam and Eve in the Garden of Eden. He convinced them that they could "be like God." He told them that if they would only eat the forbidden fruit, their eyes would be opened. Despite the fact that God previously and specifically commanded them not to eat the fruit, they did it anyway because they bought into the lie Satan told them. In doing so, Adam and Eve sinned against God and were banished from the Garden of Eden (just like Satan and his fallen angels had been banished from heaven).

Today, just as in Genesis, we are tempted to believe the lies of our spiritual enemy. It is because of our fallen nature (the sin of

Adam that created separation from God) that we seek to be in control. We are broken people, incomplete and separated from our Creator because of the consequence of original sin.

Question:

What does it mean to be broken?

Brokenness is when we finally realize that we are not able to go on without God's intervention. After struggling in our own strength, we realize that our obstacles are all insurmountable without God, yet something in our heart has to change in order for us to go on.

Brokenness can be summed up in so many ways. Despair. Devastation. Faintness of heart. Hopelessness. With brokenness comes the realization that we are truly hopeless without God in control of our heart and lives. No matter how hard we try to do things on our own, our best efforts fall short and will eventually lead to less than what God has for us. We need to have the desire to give it *all* to God, knowing that His plan is far better than ours. With Him in charge, our brokenness is turned into joy. God can take a shattered life and put it back together and make something beautiful out of it.

During my darkest times, I thank God that I had an insatiable hunger for knowledge. I read book after book trying to gain understanding into how and why God does what He does in our lives. This was a wonderful time of growth for me. I came to the realization that everything meaningful in my life that I had tried to create on my own was laid in waste. My control led to failure. Only God can successfully manage our lives.

As Christians, do we have a willingness to allow God to change our hearts? Do we see the need for a change of heart? Do we even want to change? Are we ready for this change to occur? If so, what are we willing to give up to be changed and placed into a position to be used by God? What is it that is holding us back from letting go and letting God ... ? We just need to seek Him and confess our sins and turn to Him.

Every day of our lives, we have choices concerning how to spend our time. Although reading is enjoyable, I previously had no passion for it. For some unknown reason, other than my abounding pridefulness, I previously refused to read books about anything that could be construed as self-help, because I thought I had it all in control and I didn't need to hear anyone else tell me things weren't great in my life. I thought I had it all together, but as the Bible says, *"Pride goes before a fall."* And I eventually fell hard and my life shattered into pieces.

When God allows us to be broken, He creates in us the realization that we cannot possibly make it through life on our own, without Him. Until we learn to trust Him, He will allow us to run away from Him and fall on our faces. When we do fall, He is right there to pick us back up and love us anyway, despite our foolishness.

I know that some Christians come to God through simply being drawn to God's love and truth and the conscious realization of the need for a Savior. For the rest of us, it seems to take something violent. Tragedy is a powerful motivator because the pain of tragedy forces us helplessly to our knees.

Question:

Is tragedy in our lives necessary to cause us to cry out to God?

For some of us, tragedy seems necessary. Some of us are very hard-headed, and for us, God allows tragedy to shake our foundations to get our attention back on Him. Does this mean God is cruel because He would allow His children to suffer? Absolutely not! If we are suffering, it is generally because of our own choices and the mess that those choices have created for us. When we seek God's opinion on any subject and we have faith in Him to care for us, we may still experience hard times, but the difference is, when we are in the middle of a trial or tribulation in life, we know that He is in the middle of the trial with us, helping us, guiding us, teaching us, and conforming us into His image in the process.

Key Thought:

Tragedy reveals to us our weakness, while it also reveals to us God's strength.

God uses the *"unlikely"* people of the world to accomplish some amazing things. In the Old Testament, Moses experienced tragedy and then fled to the desert in fear. It was there in the desert that God chose to reveal Himself to Moses in the form of a burning bush. It was in this place that God first revealed to Moses what His *"good, pleasing, and perfect will"* was going to be. God showed Moses that He was going to use him to free the nation of Israel from their Egyptian slavery under Pharaoh. God then led the Hebrew nation to the land that He had promised to them. It was through Moses' tragedy that God revealed His will for Moses' life, and it was also through this tragedy that God brought about freedom and a wonderful new life for the nation of Israel.

Throughout the remainder of Moses' life, God would often speak to him.

> The LORD would speak to Moses face to face, as a man speaks with his friend.
>
> Exodus 33:11—NIV

Reminder:
We serve a relational God!

In the New Testament, in the book of Acts, we read about Saul (later known as the Apostle Paul) and his journey and encounter with God while on the road to Damascus. To say that Saul was zealous was an understatement. Saul zealously persecuted Christians. Eventually God met up with Saul in a powerful way.

> As he neared Damascus on his journey, suddenly a light from heaven flashed around him. He fell to the ground and heard a voice say to him, "Saul, Saul, why do you persecute me?" "Who are you, LORD?" Saul asked. "I am Jesus, whom you are persecuting," he replied.
>
> Acts 9:3–5—NIV

Wow! Jesus—the very person whose teachings Saul had refuted and tried to silence by persecuting believers. God allowed tragedy in Saul's life to get his attention. What is amazing about this story is that Saul was the most *"unlikely"* person to champion the teachings of Jesus, yet despite the fact that Saul actively hunted down and persecuted Christians prior to his conversion, God went on to use him in a mighty way. He was once opposed to Christianity until God got his attention, then Saul (the Apostle Paul), with all his zealousness, went on to be one of the most influential believers in the entire New Testament.

I imagine that if you look back on your life, you can see the hand of God at work. For some reason, some Christians believe that after salvation, everything is going to be great and that they are going to live a life of "victory." I am personally more concerned about whether God is doing a work through me than I am about trying to sell my faith to others under the guise of "living in victory." I am sorry to those who believe differently than this, but I believe that God wants to have a relationship that is meaningful with us, not just give us everything that our selfish hearts desire (wealth, material possessions, and "victory"). Don't get me wrong, we have victory in our lives because we have assurance that the grave is not the end. We will ultimately have victory over death, but why are we duped into thinking that the Christian experience is so easy, esoteric, cheesy, etc., as to believe that we will never have troubles or trials? A life of constant "victory" is a life with faith that is not challenged or allowed to grow and mature. God wants more than this for us.

As I sit here and write this, I am reminded of a sermon that I heard at my church a few months ago. The message was about stepping into the pain rather than running from it. It was a powerful message that moved me. When we face our fears and step into our pain, God meets us in that place and gives us the grace we need to get through it.

Think of the story of Shadrach, Meshach, and Abednego in the fiery furnace. This is a common Sunday school story, but there is more here than a message for children. These men had a choice to make in a time of crisis—they could stand up for what they believed in and be persecuted for it, or give in and deny their faith. While most trials in our lives don't come at us in such a clear and distinct fashion, we all have similar chances to make decisions that communicate to others what we believe in and what we hold dear. Do we make our decisions based upon our faith or based on our wants and desires? In other words, do our decisions reflect that we believe that God will provide and protect us, or do our decisions reflect something else entirely?

The Bible says that where our treasure is, there our heart will be also. What is it that we treasure? Do we treasure a deeper relationship and faith in God than we have ever known?

Key Thought:

If you want something you have never had, you must do something that you have never done.

Sayings like this seem so simple, so why can't we find the courage to give up our control and trust God? For the more stubborn, it may take a crisis or stress to get us to the point where we say, "I can't do this alone. I need God's help."

It all seems so simple. When we are sick, we go to the doctor. When we need legal advice, we go to an attorney. When we need counseling, we go to a counselor. When all else fails in our lives, why don't we run to God? The better question is: Why don't we run to God *before* everything fails? If we would just accept our limitations and our weaknesses and turn to God first, we would not have to wait until we are coming unraveled before we finally decide we need Him. We can be so dumb sometimes!

One of my favorite "dumb people" stories is the one about the prodigal son.

"There was a man who had two sons. The younger one said to his father, 'Father, give me my share of the estate.' So he divided his property between them. Not long after that, the younger son got together all he had, set off for a distant country and there squandered his wealth in wild living. After he had spent everything, there was a severe famine in that whole country, and he began to be in need. So he went and hired himself out to a citizen of that country, who sent him to his fields to feed pigs. He longed to fill his stomach with the pods that the pigs were eating, but no one gave him anything. When he came to his senses, he said, 'How many of my father's hired men have food to spare, and here I am starving to death! I will set out and go back to my father and say to him: Father, I have sinned against heaven and against you. I am no longer worthy to be called your son; make me like one of your hired men.' So he got up and went to his father. But while he was still a long way off, his father saw him and was filled with compassion for him; he ran to his son, threw his arms around him and kissed him. The son said to him, 'Father, I have sinned against heaven and against you. I am no longer worthy to be called your son.' But the father said to his servants, 'Quick! Bring the best robe and put it on him. Put a ring on his finger and sandals on his feet. Bring the fattened calf and kill it. Let's have a feast and celebrate. For this son of mine was dead and is alive again; he was lost and is found.' So they began to celebrate."

Luke 15:11–24—NIV

The thing that I love most about this parable is that the "prodigal" child was allowed to leave home and live life "his way," free from his father's influence. His father loved him enough to let him go. In verse 14, we see that the prodigal came to the end of his resources, but not the end of the road. It isn't until verse 17, that the prodigal realizes the severity of his circumstances and "came to his senses." He experienced real brokenness—the kind of brokenness where all you want to do is go home and be loved unconditionally, regardless of all the bad decisions that you made. In his time of brokenness, he recognized that he really needed his father. Isn't that a beautiful representation of how we treat our Heavenly Father? We don't want to hear His advice or live by His rules, until, of course, we fail on our own and have no other alternative but to turn to Him. We are too busy trying to live out our own selfish life. Who needs God? Somehow we justify our actions and, the next thing we know, we are miles away from God and we are living a life that is in absolute shambles. Suddenly, we come to our senses and realize that we need to "go home."

The fact that the father in this story sees his son from far off suggests that he was patiently and eagerly looking for him to return. When he saw his son, he was instantly forgiving and joyful to have his son safe at home. The part about a ring on his finger, a robe, shoes, and the fattened calf is very symbolic. The ring symbolizes favor, wealth, dignity, and family ties. The robe symbolizes to me: covering, protection, and the righteousness of Christ. The shoes symbolize belonging to the family (servants did not wear shoes). The calf symbolizes the perfect sacrifice, Christ's death on the cross as atonement for our sins. There are so many more beautiful illustrations in this story that we could discuss. To put it simply: the father restored his son to his rightful place of honor, despite the fact that the son had come to a point that he would have been happy to even be a servant in his father's house.

The wayward son humbled himself, and his father lifted him up. Sound familiar? It should. This is a summary of our own conversion experience. We humbled ourselves, called out to our Father, confessed our faults, and asked Him for forgiveness. He forgave us our sins, He cleansed us from our unrighteousness, He raised us up as a new creation, He set us apart, and He bestowed upon us a new heritage.

When we were born into God's family, we received His
- *Grace*—He gave us what we didn't deserve (forgiveness and eternal life), and
- *Mercy*—He didn't give us what we did deserve (punishment and death).

Glory be to God! Maybe it's time we thanked Him again and rediscovered the joy of our salvation.

> Better is one day in your courts than a thousand elsewhere;
> I would rather be a doorkeeper in the house of my God
> than dwell in the tents of the wicked.
>
> Psalms 84:10—NIV

We are all prodigal children at times. Even though we have been selfish, wandered away, gotten into trouble, and cried out to God to rescue us, we have a patient and loving Heavenly Father who is waiting for us to grow up and recognize our need for Him. Coming home to Him means getting on our knees and humbling ourselves before Him. When we get to the place where we realize that the least in God's house is better than anything else outside God's house, we begin to understand the big picture. Coming home to our Father (God), as a child with a broken spirit, and being willing to live any kind of life that He has for us (because we know that His plan for our lives would be better than the life we have created for ourselves) is the ultimate sign of wisdom and understanding beginning to develop in our lives.

> Am I now trying to win the approval of men, or of God? Or am I trying to please men? If I were still trying to please men, I would not be a servant of Christ.

Galatians 1:10—NIV

[handwritten margin note: Pastor Preaches this]

We all have a choice. Does our life show that we are trying to please God? If not, we should meditate as to why. As Christians, we don't always live up to our potential. Sometimes we are too focused on what other people think instead of what God thinks. If we really wanted to know what God thinks, we would spend more time in His Word discovering His truths. When we aren't in the Word, we can't possibly understand who we are and how we are supposed to live. When will we decide to learn what made the relationships that God had with His people in the Bible so great?

A great example of a close relationship between a man and his creator is found in the Bible where it says that David was *"a man after God's own heart."* What an incredible thing to say about somebody! What was it about David's life that would make God say that about him? What did David do that we don't do? If you want to know, then read about David and discover for yourself what attributes he had that drew him back to God after each mistake that he made in his life. You could start with a beautiful, well-known passage:

Psalm 23—A psalm of David.

> The LORD is my shepherd, I shall not be in want. He makes me lie down in green pastures, he leads me beside quiet waters, he restores my soul. He guides me in paths of righteousness for his name's sake. Even though I walk through the valley of the shadow of death, I will fear no evil, for you are with me; your rod and your staff, they comfort me. You prepare a table before me in the presence of my enemies. You anoint my head with oil; my cup overflows. Surely goodness and love will follow me all the days of my life, and I will dwell in the house of the LORD forever.
>
> Psalms 23:1–6—NIV

As you read this psalm, you get a sense of the love, hope, and trust that David had in his relationship with God. David knew without a doubt that God loved him and that God was in charge and had everything under control. He also knew that God would protect him and deliver him from danger. He had personally experienced the realities of this psalm and seen God provide for him many times before. Despite David's occasional failures, he loved God, served Him, and trusted Him with a commitment and passion that won the heart of God.

> The highway of the upright avoids evil; he who guards his way guards his life.
>
> Proverbs 16:17—NIV

"He who guards his way ..." What a cool thought. If we would consciously guard our way, we would become champions for our faith. If we led a life that was more "upright," we would ultimately be guarding our life and its spiritual integrity. Spiritual integrity is something that more of us need to strive for and possess. I believe that non-believers have a tendency to view Christians as weak minded or hypocritical. This is possibly due to the lack of conviction that many Christians convey. Again, I will remind you that it is easier to live the life of a non-Christian than to live the life of a true disciple of Christ. It is hard to be who we are supposed to be; that's why we need God's help to become who we were meant to be. A life of conviction and passion for the things of God looks totally different from a life of no conviction or a life of just superficial understanding. When will we want to impress God more than man? When will we strive for integrity in our walk with God?

> Young man, do not resent it when God chastens and corrects you, for his punishment is proof of his love. Just as a father punishes a son he delights in to make him better, so the LORD corrects you.
>
> Proverbs 3:11-12—TLB

(This same thought can be found in Hebrews 12:5–8.)

Just as I shared in my personal testimony, God has always allowed me to take my own path and subsequently fall on my face because I wasn't leaning on Him, but when I confess my sins to Him, He has always been there to restore me and remind me that I belong to Him. Most of the time these lessons are painful, but one thing is for sure: they are always educational. Take this next thought and let it sink in. If there is no chastisement for our actions, we should be very, very concerned. This is a matter of great importance. It is a matter of who we belong to. It is an example for us to see who we serve. Do we serve God, or do we serve ourselves?

I hear a lot of Christians speak of others that they know who seem to live ungodly lives and get away with everything and never seem to face any consequences. Well, all I have to say about that is, in that situation, one of two things is most likely true. Either those people *do not* truly know God and have that Father-child relationship with Him, or they *do* know Him and have yet to face the music and deal with the consequences of their actions. Either in this life or in the one to come, there will be a reckoning. There will be an accounting for our deeds and actions. If we face hardships in this life, we should thank God that He is allowing us to be conformed into the image of His son, Jesus.

I want to arrive in heaven with my lessons having been already learned. I want to arrive already knowing the rules of His kingdom, and I want to know my way around. This life is supposed to be a dress rehearsal for eternity. Therefore, I want to hit the stage of eternity ready to meet my LORD, having been already conformed to His image before my arrival. I want to look like His child. I want to be recognized as His child. I want to know that at our first face-to-face meeting, the expression on His face will be that of a smiling, proud, and loving Father welcoming His beloved son to his real home.

Who's in charge here? God is! God is in charge. He is in complete control. The sooner we accept this truth and live for Him, the better we will be. If we resist His discipline and ignore His truths, we will never grow in maturity. Consequently, if we are not being disciplined, then we should immediately stop, get on our knees, and pray to God, confess faith in His son Jesus, accept Him as our LORD and Savior, and be born into God's family.

Key Thought:

God is only going to discipline you if you belong to Him.

If you belong to Him, then rest assured. Graciously accept His discipline and grow from it. As you grow, you will learn more about Him and His nature and character. As you learn more about Him, He will reveal to you His *"good, pleasing, and perfect will"* for your life. Get ready!

Chapter 5

what's my purpose?

Then Jesus came to them and said, "All authority in heaven and on earth has been given to me. Therefore go and make disciples of all nations, baptizing them in the name of the Father and of the Son and of the Holy Spirit, and teaching them to obey everything I have commanded you. And surely I am with you always, to the very end of the age."

Matthew 28:18–20—NIV

Simply put, our primary purpose is to love God with all our hearts and love our neighbors as ourselves. Once we begin to understand these two commandments, then we begin to grasp the seriousness of sharing the Gospel message. If you have been a Christian for any length of time, you have surely heard Matthew 28:18–20, commonly referred to as *"The Great Commission."* As disciples, in the Great Commission, we are charged by Jesus to *"go and make disciples of all nations ..."*

I would imagine that the thought of sharing your testimony and the gospel message is terrifying to most Christians. Most people I talk to are very apprehensive when it comes to sharing their faith with others. I personally understand this aversion. For some reason, I can talk to believers all day long about Jesus, but I have always been much more uncomfortable when I am sharing the Gospel with someone who is not a believer. The rejection, the uneasiness, etc., is tough to get past for me. I mean, who really wants to share our faith and be shunned or ridiculed for it? It takes a renewed mind to want to share our faith. I am gaining a greater comfort level with this, as I will now explain.

Lately, when it comes to sharing our faith with non-believers, I sense God conveying to me that we would all do a better job, as a whole, if we would just get a glimpse of the big picture. We need to have an eternal perspective and not get hung up on the present. Every day there are people that God puts on our path, who we have the opportunity to share with them the message of the Gospel. Maybe they have heard it but not believed it because they have failed to see a good example of someone living out their faith and convictions (this is another reason why you need to live right). Maybe they haven't heard it. Who knows? It is only our job to share Jesus with others. God will take the seeds that we have sown along the path and cause some of them to grow.

I love the following saying:

Give a man a fish and you will feed him for a day.

Teach a man to fish and you will feed him for a lifetime.

Now think about this saying in spiritual terms. Allow me to paraphrase: If we give to meet the "physical needs of someone, we have helped "feed" them in the here-and-now, but if we teach someone about Jesus and they come to know Him, you have helped "feed" them with life everlasting. Once again, here is the temporal *vs.* eternal perspective. Living in the present and being so focused on our surroundings and situations, often distracts us

from the goal, the prize. We are to share our faith. As we begin
to share, we will discover that we all have a higher calling on our
lives than we realize.

> And we know that in all things God works for the good
> of those who love him, who have been called according to
> his purpose.

Romans 8:28—NIV

Do you remember in Chapter 2 when we discussed the word
"Chazown" (*dream, revelation, or vision*)? At that point, I told you
that in Chapter 5 we would revisit the following question:

What is God's *"good, pleasing, and perfect will"* for your life?

I hope that God has been revealing to you what your *"Chazown"*
really is. But first, let's look at someone who God blessed with
an amazing *"Chazown."*

Recently, I received an email from a friend of mine that contained an interview done by CNN's Paul Bradshaw with Rick
Warren, the author of the bestselling book *The Purpose Driven
Life*. If you haven't read this phenomenal book, I suggest that
you get it and read it. It has sold countless millions of copies and
has been a major Christian literary success story. Who better to
quote on the subject of finding your purpose than Rick Warren
himself? In the interview, Rick had some wonderful insights that
I want to share with you. He said:

> People ask me, *"What is the purpose of life?"* And I respond:
> In a nutshell, life is preparation for eternity. We were made
> to last forever, and God wants us to be with Him in heaven.
> One day my heart is going to stop, and that will be the end
> of my body—but not the end of me. I may live 60 to 100

years on earth, but I am going to spend trillions of years in eternity. This is the warm-up act—the dress rehearsal. God wants us to practice on earth what we will do forever in eternity. We were made by God and for God, and until you figure that out, life isn't going to make sense. Life is a series of problems: either you are in one now, you're just coming out of one, or you're getting ready to go into another one. The reason for this is that God is more interested in your character than your comfort. God is more interested in making your life holy than He is in making your life happy. We can be reasonably happy here on earth, but that's not the goal of life: The goal is to grow in character, in Christ-likeness. This past year has been the greatest year of my life but also the toughest, with my wife, Kay, getting cancer. I used to think that life was hills and valleys—you go through a dark time, then you go to the mountaintop, back and forth. I don't believe that anymore. Rather than life being hills and valleys, I believe that it's kind of like two rails on a railroad track, and at all times you have something good and something bad in your life. No matter how good things are in your life, there is always something bad that needs to be worked on. And no matter how bad things are in your life, there is always something good you can thank God for. You can focus on your purposes, or you can focus on your problems. If you focus on your problems, you're going into self-centeredness, *"which is my problem, my issues, my pain."* But one of the easiest ways to get rid of pain is to get your focus off yourself and onto God and others. We discovered quickly that in spite of the prayers of hundreds of thousands of people, God was not going to heal Kay or make it easy for her. It has been very difficult for her, and yet God has strengthened her character, given her a ministry of helping other people, given her a testimony, drawn her closer to Him and to people. You have to learn to deal with both the good and the bad of life. Actually, sometimes learning to deal with the good is harder. For instance, this past year, all of a sudden, when the book sold 15 million copies, it made me instantly very wealthy. It also brought a lot of notoriety that I had never had to deal with before. I don't think God gives you money or notoriety for your own ego or for you to live a life of ease. So I began to ask God what He wanted me to do with this money, notoriety and influence. He gave me two different passages that helped me decide what to do, 2 Corinthians 9 and Psalm 72. First, in spite of all the money coming in, we would not change our lifestyle one bit. We made no major purchases. Second, about midway through last year, I stopped taking a salary from the church. Third, we set up foundations to fund an initiative we call The Peace Plan to plant churches, equip leaders, assist the poor, care for the sick, and educate the next generation. Fourth, I added up all that the church had paid me in the 24 years since I started the church, and I gave it all back. It was liberating to be able to serve God for free. We need to ask ourselves: Am I going to live for: Possessions? Popularity? Am I going to be driven by: Pressures? Guilt? Bitterness? Materialism? Or am I going to be driven by God's purposes (for my life)? When I get up in the morning, I sit on the side of my bed and say, God, if I don't get anything else done today, I want to know You more and love You better. God didn't put me on earth just to fulfill a to-do list. He's more interested in what I am than what I do. That's why we're called human beings, not human doings.

Happy moments—Praise God
Difficult moments—Seek God
Quiet moments—Worship God
Painful moments—Trust God
Every moment—Thank God

●●●

Wow! What an amazing viewpoint. Personally, I want to know that my character is in the likeness of Christ and that my integrity is intact. Frankly, sometimes it's hard to be a follower of Christ. It takes determination and courage to attempt to live out the high ideals of the Christian life. Anytime that I hear someone criticize someone else who is trying to walk the straight and narrow, I think about this powerful thought:

Key Thought:

Credibility and integrity are very difficult to obtain, but they can be lost so very easily.

True character comes from living a life that honors God. In other words, true character is developed over time through living a life with purpose and passion. That is not an easy task, and we all fail to live up to that perfect ideal. We must remember while we are striving for perfection, that there has only been one man who has ever walked on this earth and lived a perfect, sinless life, and that is Jesus Christ. Thank God for His *grace* and *mercy*—we would be hopeless without it!

I love the thought of God working in our lives to bring about holiness, rather than concentrating on our happiness. When we really see how much we need God and that we were created in Christ's image, how can we deny God the love and respect that He deserves?

Ask Yourself These Questions:
• Would you rather be conformed to the image of Christ

and be in fellowship with our LORD, and share in His sufferings, knowing that you are growing in your faith?
—or—
- Would you rather seek Him only out of getting your needs met for your personal happiness and personal gratification?

Let that sink in. Maybe you should read the questions again. This time, read them slowly and meditate on their meaning.

- Would you rather be conformed to the image of Christ and be in fellowship with our LORD, and share in His sufferings, knowing that you are growing in your faith?
—or—
- Would you rather seek Him only out of getting your needs met for your personal happiness and personal gratification?

These are tough questions to ask. Are we real about what we believe and why we believe it, or are we just posers? I will admit that most of my Christian life, I was a poser. I trusted only when I had no other alternative. I would rationalize and say things like, *"God, I am in a bind, if you will get me out of this situation, I will serve you forever ..."* Blah, blah, blah! How nauseating when I look back on it now. How childish and selfish I was. As soon as God would rescue me from my situation, I would turn away from Him and rely on my own strength and knowledge to get me through the next battle in my life, until once again, like a spoiled child, I would fall on my face and cry out to my Heavenly Father to come and rescue me, again and again. God wants our complete devotion. I am sure that He doesn't want our relationship to be reduced to a 9-1-1 call to Him when we are in trouble and need to be bailed out.

Key Thought:

Faith is believing in things that are not seen.

For we walk by faith, not by sight.

2 Corinthians 5:7—NKJV

Many are the plans in a man's heart, but it is the LORD's purpose that prevails.

Proverbs 19:21—NIV

The last few months of my life, God has made Himself known to me in many powerful ways. It all started with a time of personal turmoil. As I shared in my testimony in Chapter 1, I went through many difficult and painful situations. Through bankruptcy, divorce, loss of custody of my children, tax problems, etc., I lost almost everything that was important to me in a very short period of time. (I felt like Job, except for the fact that Job had been leading a truly devoted life to God before his trials and tribulations occurred ... unlike me.)

It's funny how God works so potently through tragedy in our lives! He used situations and turmoil in my life to finally break me and show me that without Him, I was continuously failing and that I would continue to fail miserably, until I learned to lay everything at His feet and let Him carry my burdens. He showed

me that I needed to trust Him in every area of my life if I wanted
to live a God-centered, God-honoring existence. When we learn
to trust God and truly believe that He knows what is best for us,
we will begin to grow in our faith exponentially. I have spent so
much of my Christian walk trying to lead, rather than purposely
trying to stop, pray, listen, and respond to His instruction. It is
a lesson in patience like no other that I have ever experienced,
but it is unbelievably rewarding (the completion and publication
of this book is living proof of my obedience to God's instruction
and His honoring of that obedience). I have sought God and
surrendered to Him my willingness to serve Him by whatever
means He sees fit.

For years, I had known that God had placed a calling on my
life, but, sadly, I had ignored His urgings because I was too busy
doing things "my way." Deep down, I have believed for years that
I was supposed to be involved in some form of ministry. I could
always picture myself preaching, because I have always loved
good preaching. Seeing myself standing and delivering the gospel message in a loving, but non-compromising way, has always
appealed to me. The problem was that I wasn't ready (or willing)
to submit to His authority. After falling down hard (again!) and
losing almost everything dear to me, I cried out to Him and He
was right there. The fact is that He had been there all along, but
He was waiting for me to come to the end of myself so that I
could then clearly see my need for Him and begin that difficult
journey of trusting Him to provide for me, rather than the other
way around. It is like that holiness *vs.* happiness thing (cart *vs.*
horse thing) that we spoke of previously. I had put my happiness
(as I saw it) in front of my holiness, and the cart jack-knifed
and spilled all its contents in complete disarray. Through confession and humbling, God has picked up the pieces of my life, put

everything into its proper place, and is now leading me down the narrow path that He has set before me.

> Do not conform any longer to the pattern of this world, but be transformed by the renewing of your mind. Then you will be able to test and approve what God's will is—his good, pleasing and perfect will.
>
> Romans 12:2—NIV

As I mentioned previously, God began to reconstruct my thoughts and my will through the process of renewing my mind. I began to pray and believe that He would show me an area of ministry where I could serve Him and find the purpose for my life that I had been missing all along. Though I envisioned myself in full-time ministry, and had begun taking steps in that direction, God had other plans for me. Through all my searching, praying, reading, fasting, etc., I began to see what His plans were for me.

God had given me the recurring thought that I should make a list of all the topics that I believed I could speak on with some degree of knowledge, authority, or experience. Finally, after days of His urging, I sat down and began to compile a list. I was truly blown away at everything that I was able to write down. It was at that moment that I began to see that God had brought me through some pretty amazing experiences and that it was through the difficulties in my life, that He had caused me to grow and mature.

I am painfully aware that in my own strength, there is no way that I could sit down and write a book about anything that would be pleasing to God. I am just as aware that I need His guidance to complete this journey. My prayer is that God will work through this book, by the power of His Holy Spirit, to speak life into the hearts of my readers. I want *everyone* who picks this book up to get from it the passion that I have for my LORD and for what He has taught me during this phase of my life.

Answer to Prayer:
Little did I know that God was going to answer this prayer in a most unexpected and unusual way.

Prior to submitting the final manuscript for this book, my good friend Josh repeatedly asked me if he could read it. Josh is Jewish. I was initially hesitant to give him the manuscript because this is a book written by a Christian and intended for Christians. I stalled him and tried to tell him that he was not my target audience and I was concerned that he wouldn't fully appreciate it. Also, as a good friend, I didn't want to offend him and make him feel that I was trying to proselytize him (he knows I deeply respect the Jewish faith because I view it as the foundation of Christianity). Josh was insistent, so I reluctantly gave it to him. I figured he wouldn't like it and that it would create some very uncomfortable moments in our relationship, but hey, I warned him, right?

Well, once again, I was wrong. Not only did Josh read it, he called me and was raving about it. He loved it! He was so complementary. To my amazement, within a week, he read it again. He told me, "The first time I read it, I read it for emotion. The second time I read it, I read it for logic." After reading the manuscript for the second time, Josh said that he understood me as a friend much better. Next, he said something to me that was so meaningful. He said he could tell I had a real *relationship* with God, whereas he had a *religion* about God. Wow! What an amazing perspective! I was completely shocked at his bluntness

and honesty. It was a great observation and tremendous comple-
ment to me regarding my faith. It made me smile to hear it, but
it also made me realize how empty I would feel if the God I
served wasn't real to me. As much as I love tradition, I want and
need substance.

I can't get my friend's comment out of my mind. Whether or
not he and I agree as to whom the Messiah is, we share the same
Father in heaven (the God of Abraham, Isaac, and Jacob), and
regardless of whether we are Jewish or Christian, we are to love
and serve our Father and have a meaningful relationship with
Him. My prayer is that my friend can eventually lose his *religion*
and develop a meaningful *relationship* with our Father and find
new meaning in his Jewish heritage (the substance behind the
tradition).

> Oh, the depth of the riches of the wisdom and knowledge
> of God! How unsearchable his judgments, and his paths
> beyond tracing out!
>
> Romans 11:33—NIV

To sum up what I am trying to communicate, I am so blessed
and amazed that God would use my book to cause someone outside my Christian faith to question their own spirituality. Only
God could cause a non-Christian to be blessed and touched by
a Christian book. We serve an amazing God! His wisdom is
unfathomable. After this experience, I can't wait to see what
kind of impact this book has on the Christian people to whom
I am writing it.

Key Thought:

We were created to love Him and be loved by Him (relationship).

Bottom Line: When we learn to really trust God and really seek His face, He will draw near to us and cause us to grow into the image of His son. What follower of Christ doesn't want to get to heaven and hear His creator and LORD say to them, *"Well done, good and faithful servant!"*

> We are therefore Christ's ambassadors, as though God were making his appeal through us. We implore you on Christ's behalf: Be reconciled to God.

> 2 Corinthians 5:20—NIV

When I think of an ambassador, I think of a leader who is a mature statesman. I envision a polished diplomat, in a suit and tie, who represents his country with absolute dignity and unquestionable credibility. Webster's Dictionary defines "ambassador" as *a representative of the highest rank*. As an "ambassador for Christ," we have the awesome privilege of being used by God to make His appeal to the world.

From the moment of our salvation, we became God's ambassadors to the world. This sounds so intimidating, because we think that we have to look the part, or play a certain role, in order to perform as an "ambassador." Not true! The truth is it is our job to represent Jesus with the testimony that we live out every day. The title of "ambassador" sounds weighty and carries with it a sense of authority; however, we need to view it as an awesome privilege and not a role that we are incapable of living up to. It is our job to live a life that is pleasing to God. It doesn't matter what we have done in the past. It doesn't matter what our age, gender, race, denomination, or educational background is. All that matters is that we have a heart that is sold out to God and that we share the "Good News" of the saving grace of our LORD Jesus.

> Whatever happens, conduct yourselves in a manner worthy of the gospel of Christ.
>
> Philippians 1:27—NIV

Ask Yourself These Questions:
- How well are you serving as an ambassador for Christ?
- Are you living a life worthy of your calling?
- Do the people around you see God's greatness and power through your life?

> As a prisoner for the LORD, then, I urge you to live a life worthy of the calling you have received.
>
> Ephesians 4:1—NIV

I want to share a story with you about God's greatness and power. There are many examples throughout the New Testament of well-known biblical figures who literally were, at one point or another, "prisoners for the LORD." One of my favorites is in Acts 16. Here we find Paul and Silas on one of their missionary journeys. While they were ministering in the city of Philippi, they were arrested, beaten, and thrown into prison. They were taken to the most secure place within the center of the prison and their feet were shackled. What a seemingly bad day they were having.

To be serving God and to be singled out, beaten and ridiculed, would cause most of us to question God's purpose (or His very existence).

It is what happens next in this story that I am so amazed by.

> About midnight Paul and Silas were praying and singing hymns to God, and the other prisoners were listening to them. Suddenly there was such a violent earthquake that the foundations of the prison were shaken. At once all the prison doors flew open, and everybody's chains came loose.

> Acts 16:25–26—NIV

Can you imagine the faith that it takes to travel as a missionary, witness to the lost, be arrested, stand trial, be falsely convicted, endure flogging and imprisonment, and then have the love of God so deeply rooted in your heart that you can begin to pray to Him and sing hymns to Him? Most of us would be looking around saying *"Why me, LORD? What have I done to deserve this? It's not fair!"* (We will discuss these particular types of questions in the next chapter, but for now, let's continue to look at this incredible story.)

Paul and Silas had absolute confidence that they were serving God and living out His will for their lives. I believe that it is from this vantage point that they were able to have peace about what God was allowing to happen to them. It was this peace and assurance that allowed them to have joy in their hearts during a time of extreme physical and emotional hardship. For us to not question God during trials in our lives, but rather to pray to Him and praise Him, is so difficult for most of us to do. I am gradually learning to trust God like this, because, like Paul and Silas,

I have seen God's hand at work in my life and I know that He knows, better than I do, what is best for me.

> But in your hearts set apart Christ as LORD. Always be prepared to give an answer to everyone who asks you to give the reason for the hope that you have. But do this with gentleness and respect.

> 1 Peter 3:15—NIV

In the story of Paul and Silas, after the walls began to shake and the prisoner's chains fell off, we get to see the life-changing power of God at work, in the heart of the jailer.

> The jailer called for lights, rushed in and fell trembling before Paul and Silas. He then brought them out and asked, "Sirs, what must I do to be saved?" They replied, "Believe in the LORD Jesus, and you will be saved—you and your household." Then they spoke the word of the LORD to him and to all the others in his house. At that hour of the night the jailer took them and washed their wounds; then immediately he and all his family were baptized. The jailer brought them into his house and set a meal before them; he was filled with joy because he had come to believe in God—he and his whole family.

> Acts 16:29–34—NIV

Instead of Paul and Silas focusing on what had happened to them, they focused on serving God when it wasn't easy for them to do so. What a miraculous story! Through praying and praising God through their weakness and pain, God showed up in a mighty way and used Paul and Silas to bring the jailor and his household into a relationship with Jesus. Think of the countless lives affected through that jailor's descendants, as well as through those who have heard this story through God's Word. Yes, Paul and Silas suffered for the Gospel, but they share in the glory for every life changed through God's amazing hand at work.

Question:

How do we find our purpose?

Like Paul and Silas, I think we should start by submitting to God and seeking His will through prayer. Next, we should maintain an attitude of praise. In Psalm 22:3, King David tells us that God inhabits the praises of His people. In other words, God makes His presence known to us as we praise Him by living in the midst of our praise or dwelling in the atmosphere of our praise.

Question:

What is the purpose of trials and tribulations in our life?

First of all, trials and tribulations create a dependence upon God! Secondly, these times of hardship accomplish many things in our lives. They give us first-hand experience, opportunity for growth and maturity, as well as development of character. They also make us humble and allow for transparency in our lives through a free and open spirit.

Key Thought:

God's character doesn't change with our circumstances.

It is when we are at our weakest point that God seems to reveal Himself to us in the most amazing ways. If we will stop, pray, praise, and look for God's hand at work during our personal trials and tribulations, we would learn a lot about the character and nature of God (God is good all the time). If we could also focus on the fact that God is more concerned about our *holiness* than our *happiness*, we would learn to accept difficulties with more grace and understanding.

> We do not know what we ought to pray for, but the Spirit himself intercedes for us with groans that words cannot express. And he who searches our hearts knows the mind of the Spirit, because the Spirit intercedes for the saints in accordance with God's will.
>
> Romans 8:26–27—NIV

Pray without ceasing.

1 Thessalonians 5:17—NKJV

Key Thought:

If we really believed in the power of prayer, we would do more of it.

That is a truly profound statement! Think about it: our actions speak to what we really believe. Do we pray enough? Likely, the answer is that we don't. How does someone pray without ceasing? Honestly, I don't really know. My best guess is that it is more of an attitude. Kind of like a frame of mind where everything that happens around us, we recognize that God is in control. It is in this frame of mind that we are able to better communicate with God because we are giving Him constant acknowledgement. If our faith is a relationship, not a religion, then we need to be ever mindful of who God is. I believe this helps us recognize our need for Him, or more specifically, our dependence upon Him.

We serve a relational God!

Question:

Does God want your best imitation of faith (religion) or do you think He wants your heart and mind to be in constant communication with Him (relationship)?

Why would God create us unless He wanted a relationship with us? Think about it. Jesus came to this earth to redeem us. Look at the life of Jesus. Every fiber of His being is relational. The time

He spent on this earth during His ministry, He spent destroying the *religious* perspective and building/creating *relationships*.

For many years, I have heard Hank Hanegraaff (a.k.a. *"The Bible Answer Man"*) of the Christian Research Institute on various Christian radio stations. I have never listened to anyone who I believe knows more about the Bible as a whole, and who has the gift to spontaneously recall scripture in an instant, as it applies to the subject at hand. I personally respect Hank a great deal because I believe he wants to equip every Christian to be able to defend their faith when it comes under attack. As Christians, we need to be able to give an account, to anyone who asks, for the hope that we have within us. Hank teaches Christian apologetics.

Apologetics is defined as *reasoned arguments or writings in justification of something, typically a theory or religious doctrine.*

Hank's teachings also include:
- You need to know what you believe and why you believe it (be able to back it up with scripture).
- You need to be able to communicate what you believe to others with gentleness and respect.

On the subject of prayer, I have heard Hank say countless times that prayer is like *"firing the winning shot."* I agree with this statement ... mostly. I believe that our consistent prayers will help us win battles in our lives (through the power of the Holy Spirit), but I like to think of prayer as so much more than just *"firing the winning shot."* When I think of prayer in this way, I think of a few analogies:
- *Basketball*—the last second on the clock, shoot a three-pointer at the buzzer to win the game.

- *Football*—the last play of the game, throw a "Hail Mary" pass for a touchdown to win the game.
- *War*—drop the "mother of all bombs" on an enemy to cripple them and force surrender.

Instead of "firing the winning shot" at the end of the battle, if we would stop and pray *first* and not put prayer at the end of our plans, or at the bottom of our lists, after everything has started to unravel, we would have a stronger faith, a stronger prayer life, and a stronger relationship with our LORD.

The Bible refers to the church as a "house of prayer" in Isaiah 56:7. The New Testament also references this phrase in Matthew 21:13, Mark 11:17, and Luke 19:46.

I must admit, it has always annoyed me when I hear people say, "Well, I guess all I can do now is pray." *What?!* Is that a Christian response? Absolutely not! We should be praying long before we get to a point of feeling hopelessness where we would consider making such a ludicrous, faithless sounding statement.

Let everything that has breath praise the LORD.

Psalms 150:6—NKJV

The area of praise has been a major stumbling block for me for most of my Christian life. To fully explain what I mean by this, I feel that I should explain my background a little better; this will help you appreciate my struggle. As I have said before, I grew up in the church. As far back as I can remember, I have loved good preaching. I especially liked hearing it bold, direct, and not watered down. I really like it when it is *expositional* (straight from the Word, verse by verse, and not esoteric). I always hungered for the Word because I could remember it (head knowledge). How does this fit into my difficulty with praise? Well, you see, I always looked at praise as the appetizer, or the salad, and the sermon as the main course. It is not that I didn't think that praise was important; it just didn't seem as important as hearing the Word of God.

To sit here now and read my prior thoughts on praise makes me realize just how far off the mark I was. I really didn't understand the true significance of praise back then. I was raised in a church that sang hymns and was very subdued. The only instrument was a piano. Today, I attend a church that has very contemporary worship style. For the longest time, I just could not relax and praise God to this kind of music. Hearing drums, guitars, keyboards, etc., just didn't fit into my perceived vision of what praise is all about. I felt I was at a rock concert; not standing in God's presence giving Him glory. If I wanted to lift my hands, I felt weird, almost restrained. It was as if I felt spiritually shackled and unable to freely praise Him.

As God was dealing with my heart on the issue of praise, He led me to have a conversation with my friend Trent about my feelings. Trent is the worship pastor at my former church. He is an amazing, talented, yet remarkably humble musician. He does an outstanding job in leading worship. God has put the right person in the right position when it comes to Trent's worship ministry. Trent and I sat down one night, and I explained my "position" on the matter and then listened to everything that he had to say about it. After our conversation ended, I continued to reflect on what he had said to me and I knew that God was dealing with me and renewing my mind on the subject.

After a few days, God gave me a new outlook (He renewed my mind). Praise isn't about me. It is about Him. It isn't about my comfort level. It is about recognizing who God is and giving Him the worship that He deserves. Whether you are beating two sticks together to make a joyful noise, or singing hymns, or

dancing in the aisles, as long as you are lifting Him up and glo-
rifying Him, you are doing it right. It is an attitude of the heart
and a freedom to love God in a manner that pleases Him.

Recently, my wife and I were in the car driving between
Oklahoma City and Chicago. It is a greater than twelve-hour
trip (about 800 miles), so needless to say, we had plenty of time
on our hands. We were traveling on a Sunday morning (without
the kids), so since we weren't at our church, we were listening to
our favorite Christian music, singing and having our own version
of church while on the road. We really had a great time together.
After we had listened to a couple hours of assorted Christian
music, as the radio reception would allow, we started listening to
various preachers on the Christian radio stations that we found
along the way. We listened to hours of good preaching. It was a
wonderful day.

Before we started listening to preaching, my wife and I had
the most interesting conversation. We were listening to some
praise music and I stopped the music to comment that the song
that we were playing was very repetitive and just kept saying
the same thing over and over and over. I explained to her that I
like songs that tell more of a story. My wife said that there are
times when she wants to hear regular Christian music, but there
are other times that she just wants to hear praise music. What
came out of her mouth next was straight from the heart of God;
I know, because it convicted me instantly. She said that most
Christian music communicates to us truth about God, but praise
music gives us the opportunity to sing to God from our hearts. It
was like she hit me in the head with a brick. Wow! A ridiculously
simple distinction, but for a guy who loves to hear good preaching, be it spoken or sung, I found it hard to enjoy praise music
because it wasn't giving me anything intellectually. For me, the
sad thing is that outside the church walls, I seldom wanted to

hear praise music because I generally want to hear (receive) the message of the song. In her own sweet, concise way, my wife taught me that I need to let go and praise God more than I do. I know that I need to get just as excited about singing *to* God as I do about singing *about* God. The difference is huge! For me, it is the age-old struggle that I have between head knowledge and heart knowledge.

I am such a creature of habit. I have always had to fight the tendency to want to receive the message, rather than lift up my praise to Him. For that, I have been dead wrong! I love it when God reveals truth to me about myself. Praise be to God that He has allowed me to recognize that I have been wrong and that He has given me the desire to change. We serve a patient, loving, and relational God!

Here are a few biblical examples of how to express praise that I want to share:

By Declaring Thanks

> Therefore by Him let us continually offer the sacrifice of praise to God, that is, the fruit of our lips, giving thanks to His name.
>
> Hebrews 13:15—NKJV

By Clapping Hands and Shouting

> Clap your hands, all you nations; shout to God with cries of joy.
>
> Psalms 47:1—NIV

By Musical Instruments and Dancing

> Praise him with the sounding of the trumpet, praise him with the harp and lyre, praise him with tambourine and dancing, praise him with the strings and flute, praise him with the clash of cymbals, praise him with resounding cymbals.

> Psalms 150:3–5—NIV

By Singing Praise Songs

> Sing praises to the LORD, enthroned in Zion; proclaim among the nations what he has done.

> Psalms 9:11—NIV

By Psalms, Hymns, and Spiritual Songs

> Speak to one another with psalms, hymns and spiritual songs. Sing and make music in your heart to the LORD, always giving thanks to God the Father for everything, in the name of our LORD Jesus Christ.

> Ephesians 5:19–20—NIV

By Making a Joyful Noise

> Shout for joy to the LORD, all the earth, burst into jubilant song with music.

> Psalms 98:4—NIV

By Lifting Our Hands

> Lift up your hands in the sanctuary and praise the LORD.

Psalms 134:2—NIV

By Being Silent and Still

Know that the LORD has set apart the godly for himself; the LORD will hear when I call to him. In your anger do not sin; when you are on your beds, search your hearts and be silent. Offer right sacrifices and trust in the LORD.

Psalms 4:3–5—NIV

"Be still, and know that I am God; I will be exalted among the nations, I will be exalted in the earth."

Psalms 46:10—NIV

By Being Loud

Sing to him a new song; play skillfully, and shout for joy.

Psalms 33:3—NIV

Come, let us sing for joy to the LORD; let us shout aloud to the Rock of our salvation. Let us come before him with thanksgiving and extol him with music and song.

Psalms 95:1–2—NIV

There is no single right way to praise God. He gives us plenty of examples, but what is really important is that we give Him our praise. Out of a heart that overflows with thanksgiving for all that He has done for us, we owe it to Him to praise His name.

There is a time for everything, and a season for every
activity under heaven.

Ecclesiastes 3:1—NIV

Although we are told to pray without ceasing (maintain an attitude of prayer), we are also to continuously praise God. There is
a time to be loud, a time to be still, a time to lift your hands and
a time for every other way to praise Him. Just keep your eyes
on Him and your heart inclined toward Him, and He will lead
you in the manner in which you are to praise Him. Don't let our
enemy steal our desire to praise God and rob us of the blessing
that comes from being in close fellowship with our LORD. Stay
focused on God. Continuously communicate with Him. Praise
Him through the way you live your life (by your actions and the
attitude of your heart). Make Him the object of your worship.

Key Thought:

God inhabits the praises of His people.

Let your heart go. Allow yourself to get excited about worship.
Close your eyes. Lift your voice. Make a joyful noise. Raise your
hands. Fall in love with God. Shower Him with your affection.
Tell Him you love Him and that you need Him. He is your
everything. Praise Him for your life. Praise Him for salvation
and the gift of eternal life. Praise Him for breath. Praise Him for
everything. Thank Him for every experience that He allows you
to live through because He is in the process of conforming you
into the image of Christ. All things (every good thing and every

bad thing) work together for good, for those who love God and are called according to His purpose (Romans 8:28).

Remember, God wants all of you. Give Him your all. Be free to praise Him without reservation or hindrance. Cast your cares on Him. Be a blessing to Him. Open the lines of communication and establish a relationship with Him. This is part of losing your *religion* and finding your *relationship*. This is also part of finding God's *"good, pleasing, and perfect will"* for your life.

You were born to praise Him. This is your purpose and this is part of your identity as a follower of Christ.

Chapter 6

why me?

1/4/16

Brothers, think of what you were when you were called. Not many of you were wise by human standards; not many were influential; not many were of noble birth. But God chose the foolish things of the world to shame the wise; God chose the weak things of the world to shame the strong.

1 Corinthians 1:26–27—NIV

There are many verses, like this one, that speak to the *"unlikely."* In verse 26, this passage reminds us of what we were when God called us (we were broken and hopeless). This passage implies that we are something more after His calling on our lives. Think of the language and the use of the words *"you were"* in verse 26. Prior to our conversion, we were not wise; we were not influential; we were not of noble birth. After we were drawn to God and born again by accepting Jesus as our LORD, we were changed. Now we have God's Word for our wisdom. Now we have God on our side—that *is* very influential! Now we are born into the noblest family of all. We are children of the Most High. We belong to God, the King of kings, the LORD of all, and if you haven't figured it out yet, it doesn't get any more influential than that!

In verse 27, God sheds some light on how He operates. Remember, we are not reading this passage and learning about conventional wisdom. We are being taught God's way of doing things—God's wisdom. The wisdom of the world is foolishness to God, whereas God's wisdom is foolishness to the world (unregenerate people). How can we possibly understand how God works if our mind hasn't been renewed? Before we are saved and born into the family of God, we are all *"unlikely."* For many Christians, we keep going forward with this notion that we are somehow unworthy of being used by God to do anything for His kingdom. The whole point of this book is to get you to see that you have a God-given purpose and because of that, you are *not* "unlikely" at all. You were born, you were called, and you were saved into a purpose.

> "So now, go. I am sending you to Pharaoh to bring my people the Israelites out of Egypt." But Moses said to God, "Who am I, that I should go to Pharaoh and bring the Israelites out of Egypt?" And God said, "I will be with you ..."
>
> Exodus 3:10–12—NIV

In these verses, we read about God's discussion with Moses at the burning bush in the desert. Moses questions God by saying, *"Who am I, that I should ... ?"* Don't we all think this way of ourselves to some extent? I mean, if we heard God's voice in an audible tone telling us to *"Go,"* would we be more likely to think and say the same thing as Moses ..."*Who am I?"*

We must remember that God did call out to Moses and Moses was reluctant, to say the least, but God had a specific plan and a specific purpose for him. Most of us are reluctant too. We must remember that God has a specific plan and a specific purpose for all of us as well. We may not be called to lead a nation, but we may be called to lead a family, an office, a group, or even a single person in some specific way. Regardless of how big or how small the task may be, we each have a specific plan and purpose in God's will. The important distinction is whether or not we care to seek God to discover what His plan and purpose is for ourselves.

Many of us wonder what we have to offer in the way of significance. We ask ourselves very quietly, *"What is so special about me? I am ordinary. I lead an ordinary life. I have no special talents or gifts. I have no unique value. I have nothing special to offer."* These statements are made by those who still see themselves as *"unlikely."*

> Before I formed you in the womb I knew you, before you were born I set you apart.
>
> Jeremiah 1:5—NIV

> For you created my inmost being; you knit me together in my mother's womb. I praise you because I am fearfully and wonderfully made; your works are wonderful, I know that full well.
>
> Psalm 139:13–14—NIV

God told Jeremiah that He knew him and set him apart before he was ever in his mother's womb. God has the same thing to say to us. The psalmist wrote that he praised God because he was *"fearfully and wonderfully made."* God has given each of us a purpose. Imagine God telling you personally that He *"set you apart."* When we grasp this idea and get it into our thoughts (the fact that He has set us apart), we will begin to open our minds to the awesome possibilities that God has for us. If we would only live up to our Christian potential and seek Him for the answers to all of life's questions, we would each discover this truth for ourselves.

Let me contrast for you the difference in the prophet Isaiah's life from the last part of the book of Isaiah to the early part. In the end, Isaiah recognizes who he is compared to who God is. At the beginning of the book, he had not yet experienced this difference. Look at the comparison:

Later ...

> Yet, O LORD, you are our Father. We are the clay, you are the potter; we are all the work of your hand.
>
> Isaiah 64:8—NIV

Earlier ...

> "Woe to me!" I cried. "I am ruined! For I am a man of unclean lips, and I live among a people of unclean lips, and my eyes have seen the King, the LORD Almighty."
>
> Isaiah 6:5—NIV

In this "earlier" verse, Isaiah had just gotten a glimpse of God's majesty and all he could do was cry out to Him and profess the inadequacy that he felt. This may seem absurd to some of us, but imagine that God decided to show each of us His majesty. First of all, we would be blinded instantly, that is, if we could even live through this exposure. We couldn't begin to grasp the fullness of His physical presence, but let's say, for sake of the argument, that our finite minds could, for a moment, grasp the greatness of God without mortal danger. What would we do in His presence? Would we just shrug and say nothing? Hardly!

Believe it. If God chose to show us even a glimpse of His Majesty, it would violently shake our foundation. We would realize, in an instant, our unworthiness in His presence. More than that, we would see His greatness and then everything in us would cry out to Him out of our absolute, desperate need for Him. It would be like having the rug pulled out from under us. We would fall flat on our faces before Him.

Before I go any further into a discussion about majesty, I think that we need to discuss the basics of a monarchy. It occurs to me that most of us don't have the first clue about what it is like living in a land that is ruled by a monarch (a king or queen). So maybe we should break this down so we can better understand the point I am trying to make. Let's define the following words: monarch, monarchy, and majesty.[8]

Definitions:

> Monarch—*A sovereign head of state, especially a king, queen, or emperor.*
> Origin: late Middle English: from late Latin monarcha, from Greek monarckhēs, from monos (alone) + arkhein (to rule).

> Monarchy—*A form of government with a monarch at the head.*
> Origin: late Middle English: from Old French monarchie via late Latin from Greek monarkhia, the rule of one.

> Majesty—*Royal power.*

Origin: Middle English (in the sense greatness of God): from Old French majeste, from Latin majestas, from a variant of majus, major.

Simply put, a monarchy is "the rule of one." If God (the "One") is in His proper place in our lives, serving as our Monarch, our Sovereign Head of State, then we have given all of our power and control of our lives over to Him and we are serving Him; we are His loyal subjects. In contrast, think of the word *"anarchy."* The prefix *"an-"* means without, and as we just learned, the suffix *"-archy"* (in the sense of a monarchy) means, *"the rule of one."* So, in a Christian sense, based on the prior definitions, anarchy means *"without + the rule of one."* Think about that! If we haven't given control of our lives over to God (the "One"), then, literally, we are living in a state of *anarchy*. Interesting thought, isn't it?

If we will think back to the moment when we first accepted Christ as our LORD and Savior, at that point, we had a glimpse of just how awesome God is and we knew then how much we needed God to come into our lives and radically change us. We needed the "One" to come into our lives and adopt us into His Kingdom. If we could go forward from that point of accepting Christ and continue to keep focused on who He is and why we need Him so desperately, we would be light years ahead of where most of us are now in our understanding. We would come to realize how our prior lack of understanding has held us back in the past. God wants great things to occur in our lives as we honor Him. He will bless us in areas of ministry and allow us to be involved in leading other people into a relationship with Him.

In Isaiah 6, we read about Isaiah's realization ...

186 • Dr. George Goodman

Then I heard the voice of the LORD saying, "Whom shall
I send? And who will go for us?" And I said, "Here am I.
Send me!"

Isaiah 6:8—NIV

I sit here contemplating the reality of God calling out to Isaiah
and Isaiah responding to God by saying *"Here am I. Send me!"*
Once Isaiah got a glimpse of God's majesty, he realized who he
was (a sinner) and who God was (the LORD Almighty). When
Isaiah saw the big picture, he responded as he should have.
Without further hesitation, He said with enthusiasm, *"Here am
I. Send me!"*

Still, some of you might ask, *"Why would God want to use
me?"* If you haven't figured that one out yet, then keep reading.
I will remind you again. God wants to use you because you are
uniquely special to Him and you are gifted in ways that no one
else is. The combination of your talents and your life experiences
makes you completely unique. There is not one soul out there
like you.

The fullness of God's *"good, pleasing, and perfect will"* for your
life has yet to be revealed to you. Think about that for a minute. God's will for our lives is "good." It is "pleasing." Better yet,
it's "perfect"! I don't know about you, but I could stand a little
more presence of a perfect God in my life. God knows my flaws,
my failures, my weaknesses, and my fears; yet, miraculously, He
still chooses to do His work through me. Let's face it; we are
included in God's big plan because He loves us so much. In case
you forgot, we serve a relational God who loves His children,
watches over them, provides for them, and protects them.

"Does God need me?" Need you? No. Not really. *"Then why
does God bother with me?"* Because He wants to teach us about
Himself while conforming us into the image of His son, our

LORD, Jesus Christ. This process can bring about some amazing transformation in who we are. The new creation that we become at the moment of salvation is followed by periods of personal spiritual growth; sometimes intense growth. These periods of growth will occasionally shake our foundation and will always make us stronger.

Imagine a fruit tree. What a perfect analogy for the Christian life. As the tree grows, its roots reach deeper into the soil as its branches reach upward toward the light. With every passing day, the trunk grows thicker, the branches grow stronger and the leaves and fruit multiply. The bigger the tree grows, the more fruit it can bear. The stronger the tree grows, the more fruit it can support on its branches, and the more others begin to depend on the tree to help feed them.

Key Thought:

God wants you to grow where you are planted.

He put you where He wants you. He chose your soil and your surroundings. He gave you the nutrients that He knows you need to flourish.

You need to get grounded in Him and develop a deep relationship with Him that grows with time. You need to reach out to others as you are stretching out to receive His light. You need to be constantly watered with the Word of God so that you may continue to grow through the years and weather the droughts of life. When storms come, the maturity and depth of your relationship with God will protect you and keep you from cracking under pressure.

> He will be like a tree planted by the water that sends out its roots by the stream. It does not fear when heat comes; its leaves are always green. It has no worries in a year of drought and never fails to bear fruit.
>
> Jeremiah 17:8—NIV

> I can do all things through Christ who strengthens me.
>
> Philippians 4:13—NKJV

A few years ago, at my former church, I knew someone named Michael who lost his wife to cancer. Right after her death, Michael sang a solo in church that profoundly touched me. As long as I live, I will never forget hearing the words of that powerful song and how touching it was considering the circumstances of Michael's life at that particular moment. God used that moment to speak to me of His amazing, immeasurable grace.

As you read some of the words to the following song, I want you to personalize it and picture yourself in a similar painful situation.

The Anchor Holds[9]

I have journeyed
Through the long, dark night
Out on the open sea
By faith alone
Sight unknown
And yet His eyes were watching me
The anchor holds

Though the ship is battered
The anchor holds
Though the sails are torn
I have fallen on my knees
As I faced the raging seas
The anchor holds
In spite of the storm

It is so powerful to me that the memory of this event still lingers on in my mind. There are a few defining moments in all our lives where we can look back and say that we really absorbed the message of the moment. That was one of those times for me. I still get goose bumps when I think of my brother in Christ standing there on that stage, in front of his church family, singing about the greatness of God through the storm that he was experiencing at that moment. He could have cried to his friends and family and asked, *"Why me?"* but he didn't. Instead, he chose to stand up in front of his church family and sing a song that testified of God's faithfulness and immeasurable grace, despite his situation.

Key Thought:

Real faith is never more visible to others than when demonstrated during our times of greatest hardships.

"The LORD lives!
Blessed be my Rock!
Let God be exalted,
The Rock of my salvation!

2 Samuel 22:47—NKJV

God is the rock of our salvation and the anchor that keeps us from being ripped apart by the storms in our lives. No matter what rages on around us, we are safe and secure and wrapped in His loving protection, whether we realize it at the time or not. There are times in our lives that remind us of this simple fact with absolute crystal clarity.

> He will sit as a refiner and purifier of silver.
>
> Malachi 3:3—NIV

If you look around in your everyday life, there are a myriad of simple details around us that can teach us more about our LORD and how He operates. The most obvious details are found in nature. We have the beauties and intricacies of nature that show us God's handiwork.

A perfect example of one of these simple details came by me recently in the form of a story. The story was about the process of refining and purifying raw silver. As in any good story, there is a superficial meaning that is obvious, and a deeper meaning that is woven beneath it all. It is this meaning that I love to meditate on as I read the story.

Before we get to the story, I think it is interesting how, when you look at the process of how silver is refined, you don't have to look too deeply into the process to see spiritual truths about the character and nature of God. These simple truths shed light on who He is and what He wants for us in our relationship with Him. As simple as this story is, it is always nice to be reminded again about the obvious, yet seldom recognized, truths in life because we all have a tendency to complicate things and over-look what is truly important. I am sure that most of you can relate with what I am trying to say, but let's get to the point and quit beating around the bush.

The story goes something like this ...

> Once upon a time, a silversmith wanted to purify some raw silver. He carefully took the unrefined, impure silver and placed it into the fire and let it heat up. As it got hotter, he placed it in the hottest part of the flame to burn away all the impurities. This process required him to stay and keep a constant, watchful eye on the silver. He knew that if he looked away and ignored the silver, it would be destroyed. As the heat burned away all the impurities, the silversmith began to see his own reflection appearing in the purified silver, and with time, he was able to clearly see his own image in the reflection. Once he could see his reflection clearly, the silversmith removed the newly purified silver from the fire.

Now, imagine God holding us in such a hot spot. As Malachi 3:3 says, He (God) sits as a refiner and purifier of silver. We are His silver. We are His workmanship. If you are feeling the heat of the fire, thank God and remember that God Himself placed you there and He has His watchful eye on you.

Our purification is a process. We want it to be over in a flash, but it doesn't work that way. God will keep watching you until all your impurities burn away and He sees His image in you. It may seem harsh, but He wants you to be made pure. He wants you to be made whole. No matter what you are going through in your life, when God refines you, you will be a better person for it in the end. He constantly watches over us and allows us to face trials so that we may be made complete, lacking nothing.

If we had jumped out of the fire and started asking questions like, *"Why me?"* or *"Why do bad things always happen to me?"* or *"What did I do to deserve this?"* we would have missed out on one of God's most valuable life lessons. If we are going to be conformed into the image of Christ, we need to be purified. God may apply heat or pressure to you, but be patient—remember this simple, obvious, but overlooked truth:

Key Thoughts:

Intense heat purifies precious metals.

Intense pressure turns coal into diamonds.

Precious metals and precious stones? Sounds like not only the material to form a crown, but the jewels to go in it!

Question:

Do you ever think about the reception you will receive upon arrival in heaven?

In 2 Timothy 4:8, the Bible speaks of our "crown of righteousness." In James 1:12, it speaks of our "crown of life." The imagery of us receiving a crown is beautiful. Our heavenly crown is a symbol of our eternal hope, as well as the righteousness that we have as a gift from God.

Key Thought:

Christ's righteousness is imputed to us, and the gift of His righteousness is imparted to us.

It is through the sacrificial death, burial, and resurrection of our Savior that we have this gift made available to us. We must remember that every day of our lives, by the way we choose to live our lives, we are all laying up our "treasure" in heaven.

Think about a heavenly treasury ("First Bank of God & Trust") that you make deposits into. What is it that you depositing into your account? Are you depositing things of eternal value, or are you depositing things of temporal value? Think of it this way: Are you building your house on a solid foundation, or are you building it on an unstable foundation?

> By the grace God has given me, I laid a foundation as an expert builder, and someone else is building on it. But each one should be careful how he builds. For no one can lay any foundation other than the one already laid, which is Jesus Christ. If any man builds on this foundation using gold, silver, costly stones, wood, hay or straw, his work will be shown for what it is, because the Day will bring it to light. It will be revealed with fire, and the fire will test the quality of each man's work. If what he has built survives, he will receive his reward. If it is burned up, he will suffer loss; he himself will be saved, but only as one escaping through the flames.

> 1 Corinthians 3:10–15—NIV

Good Question:

What does your "treasure" in heaven consist of?

Better Question:

Will your "treasure" stand up to the purifying fire, or will it burn up?

Is your treasure "gold, silver, costly stones" or is it "wood, hay, or straw"? Of course these are metaphors, but think about it. Are you laying up "treasure" in heaven, or are you just accumulating a bunch of "junk" down here?

So many Christians don't want to discuss things like judgment, yet they all seem to want to talk about "streets of gold" and living forever. Why is this? I guess, in part, it is human nature to long for the good things in life, while trying to ignore the uncomfortable things. We should be mindful of these biblical truths and not just let them pass us by. There is so much of the Bible that people overlook, probably because it makes them uncomfortable. God has a way of using discomfort to help shape us, while He is refining us and building up our character as we get to know Him more intimately. As the heat gets turned up in our lives, the impurities get burned away and the purest, most precious aspects remain. You could call it "trial by fire."

What does our *"work,"* as described by verse 13, consist of? What is it that we are doing, or have done in the past, that will stand and survive this *"revelation by fire"*? If we look at this question with the mindset of eternal *vs.* temporal, we may find our answer.

Question:

What are we doing to further God's kingdom?

I saw heaven standing open and there before me was a white

> horse, whose rider is called Faithful and True. With justice
> he judges and makes war. His eyes are like blazing fire, and
> on his head are many crowns. He has a name written on
> him that no one knows but he himself. He is dressed in a
> robe dipped in blood, and his name is the Word of God.

> Revelation 19.11–13—NIV

Many believers avoid reading the book of Revelation for various reasons. Some say that they just cannot understand all of its meaning. Others are scared by its vivid imagery. Regardless of what we think or feel, the book of Revelation is an essential part of the Bible that God saw fit to include in His Word.

The verses listed above from the book of Revelation have always resonated with me. It is a powerful picture of the return of Christ in all His power and majesty. Verse 12 describes Christ's eyes *"like blazing fire."* I imagine that when we see Christ face to face, His eyes will gaze upon us and, just like a refiner's fire, our impurities will burn away and we will stand there before our LORD, pure, refined, and redeemed. For the first time in our lives, we will know, in the fullest sense, our true identity.

As I reflect on this chapter, I am left asking the question, "Did I adequately explain the title of this chapter, 'Why Me'?" Yes, in part I think I did, but not quite as completely as I would have liked. I think, at this point, it is important to think about the concept of *"unlikely"* a little bit more to complete the thought and finish this chapter as I intended.

"Why me?" Well, God called you to live up to His standard and follow His plan and rules. He chose you. You probably seem *"unlikely"* to anyone who knows you, but thankfully, God sees you differently than they do. The Bible is rich with examples that prove the point that I am trying to make. There are so many *"unlikely"* characters in the Bible that God used to do amazing things.

This is just an observation on my part, but it seems to me that people who have a humble opinion of themselves are more likely to be used by God to do miraculous things. God gives strength to the humble, yet, in complete contrast, He allows the prideful to take a fall. This is just one more mystery in God's worldview that we need to learn.

Key Thought:

Working with God is much better than working against Him.

God is glorified when things happen in our lives that couldn't possibly have happened in our own strength. In these instances, He gets the full credit that He deserves and wants. If you have someone who is arrogant or cocky about their gifts, talents, or abilities, they seem to be less likely to be used by God to do miraculous things. These people tend to be humbled by God, rather than be humbled by their own choice. As one of these "wonderful" people, I can attest to the fact that God had to humble me before I got the message. The process of my humbling was painful to say the least, but I survived it and came out the other side of my dark valley with a new perspective that could only come from God. He is in charge, not me. Now that I have had what seems like a lifetime supply of humble pie, I am being used by God to do something worthwhile and deeply meaningful. I now have focus about what is truly important in my life. Prior to my humbling, I just didn't get it. I couldn't see why things in my life were falling apart. God turned my *"Why me?"* into *"Thanks,* LORD.*"*

Key Thought:

God has the answers if we want to know them.

Again, you ask, *"Why me?"* Well, I must ask, *"Why not you?"* Do you see yourself as someone that God can use to change the world? If you don't, then open your eyes to everything that has been revealed to you thus far! You may be used to change the world *of someone* you know by being who you were called to be and serving as a role model of God's grace to that person. You may change the world *for someone* by making the world a better place by being who God called you to be on a larger scale and to a bigger audience. Who knows what God has in store for you? (The answer to the question: *He* does.)

If we are seeking to make a real difference in someone's world, or in the world in general, we must learn to make God's love, power, and attributes known to a world that desperately needs to learn about our LORD. Whether you are a part of leading one soul to the LORD or a thousand souls, we know that heaven celebrates each and every child who comes to know God. We are all part of the body of Christ and we are to function in the capacity that we are able and never trivialize any accomplishment for the kingdom of God. God's accounting is different than our accounting!

We must remember that Jesus Christ was hung on a cross and died for our sins, and never did He ask the question: *"Why me?"* He knew the job that He had to do, and He did it. It wasn't easy for Him at all. In fact, it was incredibly, unbelievably difficult!

It cost Him absolutely everything: His status, His family, His friendships, and ultimately, His life.

The good news is that Jesus' death and burial was only the beginning of a new chapter for all of humanity. When Jesus was resurrected, He gained everything back and much more. He now sits at the right hand of our Father in heaven. He is eternal. Not only did He gain everything; as a result, we gained everything as well. We now have direct access to God through Jesus. God sees us as cleansed from our sins because of Jesus' sacrifice. The veil of the Temple has been torn from top to bottom. The Holy of Holies is now open. We have full access to our LORD.

If you don't understand what I am talking about, just know that before Jesus' time, in the Old Testament, there was a design for a Tabernacle that included a Holy of Holies—a sacred place where God would dwell. Only the high priest could enter beyond the dividing veil, and only under specific conditions and only once a year. I suggest that you read about the Tabernacle of God in the wilderness of Sinai if you want to understand more about why, after Jesus' death, burial and resurrection, the veil in the Temple was torn from top to bottom giving all Christians the gift of open fellowship with our Creator.

After everything that we have discussed so far, if you are still asking, *"Why me?"* all I know to say to you is that we will end this chapter at this point by saying to you that it is your responsibility to seek God for the answers yourself. Pray about it. Ask God for guidance. Ask God for wisdom. Be patient. The understanding will come. This will all come into focus.

Next we will discuss *"Finding Your Way."*

Chapter 7

finding your way

But small is the gate and narrow the road that leads to life, and only a few find it.

Matthew 7:14—NIV

Recently, my wife and I went on a trip to Tortola (British Virgin Islands) with her family. One day we all took the ferry to the remote island of Anegada because we heard the scuba diving there was amazing. Anegada is not like any of the islands in the region. It is mostly flat and arid. It has a very large barrier reef that makes for incredible scuba diving, but the island itself has a population of less than 200 people. After a couple of incredible dives, swimming through valleys and tunnels made out of massive coral that was teeming with God's amazingly beautiful creation, then carrying all the scuba gear out of the water, off the beach, and hiking to the road, I was completely physically exhausted. My wife's family wanted to walk along the beach to a restaurant that was fifteen minutes away. My wife and I decided to stay out of the sun because I had too much sun the day before and I was rather sunburned, so we waited in the shade for a taxi to take us to the restaurant. We waited for almost an hour for a taxi to arrive; and it never did. So, after a long hot wait, we decided to walk the road that led toward the restaurant because we thought this would be less tiring than a fifteen minute walk on sand and logically, it seemed like a shorter distance. Let's just say that our walk was a long miserable journey. We felt like we were lost in the desert, all alone. The path wasn't paved and it seemed to meander aimlessly through the country side. It split off in different directions. After about an hour of wandering, we came to the conclusion that we were lost.

When we thought we couldn't go any further, a carload of people pulled up, and I waived to the driver to stop so I could ask directions. I will never forget what he said. In his strong island accent he said to me, *"Follow the straight path ahead of you. Don't turn to the left or to the right, but stay on the straight path and you will find your way."*

My wife and I looked at each other and smiled. I said to her that those were the best directions that I had ever heard. They were not only directions ... they were words to live by. I immediately told her that when we got home, I was going to add that to this book. I love it when God creates situations or puts people on our path that reaffirms to us that He is in charge and that He will provide for us. We just have to believe and trust that He knows the way.

As I asked you at the beginning of Chapter 1—*"Are you on the path?"* If not, are you "finding your way" to the path? Are you seeking His direction to find the path or stay on the path?

> As a prisoner for the LORD, then, I urge you to live a life worthy of the calling you have received.
>
> Ephesians 4:1—NIV

Part of finding your way is knowing where you are going. If you plan to go from point A to point B, then you generally get a map or obtain directions and then head out to get to your destination. What about the journey that God wants us to embark on? For all believers, the way is mapped out, the transportation is provided, the fare is paid, yet, for some of us, we won't take the trip. What is keeping us from departing? He has called out to us and changed us. We are new creations, thanks to His saving grace and free gift of salvation. So why is it that so many of us, being called to do good works and live according to a new code, won't get going? The bus has pulled up, the cab is waiting, the ship is docked, and the plane is fueled and ready. It's time to go!

> Being confident of this, that He who began a good work in you will carry it on to completion until the day of Christ Jesus.
>
> Philippians 1:6—NIV

From the moment of our salvation, we have the assurance that we will spend eternity with God. This is a wonderful reality to a Christian. It is our blessed assurance. However, if we never proceed forward in our relationship with God, from our original introduction to Him, how will we become who He called us to be? We need to actively participate in the process. He began a good work in us when He saved us—let's grow in our spiritual maturity and live a life worthy of our calling.

> Whatever happens, conduct yourselves in a manner worthy of the gospel of Christ.
>
> Philippians 1:27—NIV

Key Thought:

A moral compass can point you in the right direction, but it can't make you go there.

Life definitely has its difficulties and challenges. At times, I have thought to myself that life would be so much easier if I didn't have a moral compass. Although I know that is not true; when you find yourself being persecuted for your faith, you may spend time wondering why God would allow you to experience the pain and rejection that comes when you share the love of God with someone else, only to have them ridicule you to your face or behind your back. This experience can leave you feeling trampled, especially when you just opened up and poured yourself out to someone, only to be ridiculed for it.

I can only imagine the pain and heartache that our Savior endured as He made His way through His earthly ministry. His journey to the cross cost Him everything, including His life. When I take an insult for sharing my faith, I try to remember that I am only enduring verbal abuse, not being physically beaten and nailed to a cross. Although my emotional pain is very real, I have not given up my life and suffered a brutal death for my faith. So I guess that enduring some criticism or condemnation for my faith is safer than dying for it. It is all a matter of perspective.

As Christians, specifically as disciples of Christ, we need to behave like we belong to God and not behave as the rest of the world does. The Gospel of Jesus spells out clearly how we should behave. The Bible is the best moral compass you could ever ask for. Most of it is not easy to live up to and all of us fail to live up to the standard, but we need to strive to be who we are created and called to be. As I have said before, anyone can live the life of a non-Christian, but to live as a disciple of Christ is much more challenging. I dare anyone to try. It is easy to pick on people who fail when they are trying to live right, but what about the masses of people who just don't care to try to live up to any standard of decency? No one can live up to God's standards, but, by faith, along with forgiveness, as His disciples, we try, and hopefully, we are trying to the best of our ability.

> Do your best to present yourself to God as one approved, a workman who does not need to be ashamed and who correctly handles the word of truth.
>
> 2 Timothy 2:15—NIV

Living right is one thing; knowing, understanding, and properly handling the Word of God is another thing altogether. Many people speak the Word of God boldly, but do so unlovingly. They use the Word of God to destroy others, as if the Bible was their personal attack weapon. People don't want to be hit on the head with a sledgehammer. We should read it, learn it, memorize it, and impart it with loving grace to others. The Bible is "alive and active" and is everything to a true disciple. If we would pray for discernment and pray for opportunities to share the message of the Gospel, we would be much more effective in winning souls.

> "Everything is permissible for me"—but not everything is beneficial. "Everything is permissible for me"—but I will not be mastered by anything.
>
> 1 Corinthians 6:12—NIV

Just because God will forgive us, doesn't mean that we should keep on intentionally sinning. We have freedom in Christ, but how we use that freedom matters. We benefit from staying in the lines and operating under our established code of conduct. When we stray from the truth and begin to indulge ourselves in ungodly behaviors, we hurt ourselves, weaken (or destroy) our testimony to others, and grieve the heart of God. God has given to us the power of Christ to overcome. Whether you are addicted to cigarettes, alcohol, drugs, pornography, or anything else, God can deliver you from these addictions. Christians are called to be overcomers.

Key Thought:

You cannot overcome anything that you are willing to tolerate.

Conviction *vs.* Convenience

If we operated on our convictions instead of what is convenient, we would be different people. We would be the salt and light that the Bible speaks of. We would change the world in the name of Jesus. Human nature wants to take the path of least resistance, but when we are operating on our convictions, we are doing the things that we know are right, even though they are difficult or seemingly impossible (nothing is impossible with God). Conviction is a deeper sense of right and wrong, regardless of the circumstances. That which seems most convenient is seldom the right thing. Living a life of conviction is the best way to "find our way."

Key Thought:

God works best in our weakness and our willingness.

We must be willing to lose our will and accept the higher calling of God for our lives. We seem to forget that His plan is bigger and better than our plan. We need to be available and living out our convictions daily. As Christ followers, there are a few specific things that we should do *every single day*, if we expect to find God's best and His specific will for our lives. How can we possibly miss the mark if we will do the following things?

Read His Word
Study His Word
Pray to Him
Meditate on Him
Live for Him

If we will consistently "plug-in" and incline our hearts and minds toward Him, we will hear from Him and find the guidance that we so desperately need. This is what I personally like to call the "Higher Way" (FYI—*Higher Way* was the original title that I wanted to give to this book, but over time, as this book came together, the name *Unlikely* just seemed to be the right choice). If we really want to find God's best for our lives, we must be in a right relationship with Him.

Key Thought:

What part of your body could survive if it was detached (separated from its nutrient source) for an extended period of time?

What makes us think that if we detach ourselves from God (and only try to reattach when we think that we need Him) that we can maintain a healthy degree of holiness? The truth is that we need Him to nurture us every single day. We will truly grow in our relationship with Him once we realize this truth.

Basic Spiritual Needs
• Daily connection with God.
• Daily spiritual nutrition.
• Daily growth.
• Daily maturity.

It is essential that you grasp and internalize this point:

The depth of your future spiritual relationship and the degree of holiness that you develop over your lifetime is in direct proportion to the degree of communication, connection, and "nutrition" that you feed your spirit.

We are taught that our bodies are the temple of the Holy Spirit, and we are to take care of our earthly body as an act of worship to our LORD. What about the importance of creating an atmosphere of holiness where we can commune with God and stay close to Him and feed off His loving truth and guidance?

As the deer pants for streams of water, so my soul pants for you, O God.

Psalms 42:1—NIV

Today, I heard a Christian radio broadcast by Dr. David Jeremiah (Turning Point Ministries) that totally blew me away. I was in my car driving to work, and I almost had to pull over because the message was truly that powerful. It was the type of preaching that gets me excited. He was right on the money with me today. He was saying what I was feeling in my spirit. It was like he was talking to me as if I were the only one in the audience. He was talking about having spiritual hunger and thirst and seeking God with your whole heart.

Key Thought:

If we lack spiritual hunger, we will fail to know God.

Hunger and thirst are facts of life. We all experience hunger when we go without food, and we all experience thirst when we go without water. The longer we go without food and water, the greater our hunger and thirst grows. To deprive our bodies these essentials, will only lead to weakness. So it is with our spirit. Hungering and thirsting after God is required for spiritual growth. Are we hungry to know Him?

Blessed are those who hunger and thirst for righteousness, for they will be filled.

Matthew 5:6—NIV

Ask yourself this question:
"Am I where I should be spiritually?"

The answer to that question should shed some light on where you are on your Christian journey. It is also a good judge of your Christian maturity. In a spiritual sense, there are giants among us, and there are those who are starving and emaciated. There are those who seek after God with their whole heart, and there are those who are half-heartedly seeking Him, just enough to barely maintain the title of "believer." To be around a person who half-heartedly does things is frustrating at times, whereas being around a person who puts their whole heart into everything, is much more pleasant and rewarding because we can see the passion which drives that person to excel.

Question:

What are you hungry for?

Key Thought:

We all have about as much of God as we really want.

Ouch! That hurt me to hear. This was the statement that Dr. Jeremiah made on his radio broadcast. It hurt to hear, but that is how truth works. When people speak of the painful truth, this is what they mean. We either accept it as truth, or we dismiss it because we don't want to face it, or consider that it might be truth. Dr. Jeremiah's statement really made me think about things like my own hungering and thirsting for God, and question the quality of my relationship with Him. Like I received this message today, I wish I could create in you a desire to receive the message that I am trying to send out right now and have you receive it with a receptive heart and an open spirit. If you have ever received a truth and wrestled it and accepted it into your heart and let it change who you are, then you know what I am talking about here. During times like these, you know that the power of the Holy Spirit is at work in you. Thank God for it.

Question:

How much God do we have?

Do we have enough to make us feel eternally secure, but no more? Do we have a raging fire that consumes us and creates in us an unquenchable hunger and thirst for the things of God? Most of us are somewhere in the middle. We get occasionally excited about God—mostly when we need Him to do something for us. We need to lose our apathy and lukewarmness and find our fervor. We need to get hungry! We need to find our way to God's table and eat and drink to our heart's content.

The Apostle Paul had an insatiable appetite for God (read Philippians 3). In this chapter, Paul expresses how he wishes to know Christ in a more complete way. I have heard it said that, next to Jesus, Paul is one of the most influential men in all of scripture. He had passion. He had a hunger and a thirst for the things of God. Even though Paul is a biblical icon, he never felt as if he had fully attained the depth of relationship possible with our LORD. His hunger to know the LORD was intense. He lived an amazing life that was totally and utterly sold out to God.

I think that we could all stand to develop an insatiable hunger. When we are passionate, we tend to rub off on those around us. People are attracted to others who display happiness, contentment, and peace. These are all things that should ooze from our pores as disciples of Christ. If people around us see in our lives a deep joy and passion, they can't help but be attracted to it. When the people around you sense your excitement and enthusiasm, they feed off it. They want to know what it is that makes us so different. It will make them want to know this peace for themselves. It is an awesome way of sharing the message of the Gospel with them. Just as sharks are attracted to the scent of blood in the water, people around us are drawn to want what we have. The difference is that the blood that they are attracted to is the redeeming, cleansing, freeing blood of our LORD and Savior, Jesus Christ.

Question:

How is God going to use me?

Before I go into how God brought me into submission, I want to tell you about my past personal financial woes and explain how God has carried me through some tough times and helped me find my way.

On a personal note, my primary goal at this point in my life is to get completely, 100 percent debt free. I want to owe nobody anything. Why am I so passionate about this? First of all, the

Bible says that the borrower is servant to the lender (Proverbs 22:7). Well, I feel like I am a servant, a slave to my expenses. It is not that I am obsessed with money, far from it; I just want to be free of the burden of debt. For various reasons, mostly previous stupidity (bad spending patterns, failed business, failed marriage, tax problems, etc.), like most Americans, I have debt that forces me to work to be able to service that debt. I know that if I continue to work hard, be smart with my finances, and pay off these debts, I will be in a financial position to immediately respond to whatever God calls me to in the future without having to think about it or plan for it. Then I can be even more available to God in any area of ministry. Don't get me wrong, I will respond to what God calls me to right now, because where God guides, God provides, but I just don't want to be in a financial position that would hinder me from dedicating myself to His calling fully, without hesitation.

In the past two years, I have made some tough financial decisions to achieve my goal. I have downsized my home considerably by cutting square footage in half, parted with a larger luxury SUV, and purchased a used minivan. I even got rid of my motorcycle. I started working a second job. My regular job, I work Monday through Friday. My second job, I work every Saturday and every other Sunday. This allows for one day off every two weeks. This feverish pace has gone on now for almost two years. Yes, I am tired because I work all the time (which has left little time to sit and write a book), but when I look back over the last two years, I am amazed at how many thousands of dollars of debt that I have been able to pay off. I see my freedom in the distance, so I keep pushing on. I also started paying my bills like Dave Ramsey would have me do it. If you don't know who Dave Ramsey is, you are missing out on a huge blessing. Dave Ramsey has helped countless thousands of people achieve their financial independence through biblical money managing principles. If you don't have one of his books, put it on your shopping list. It is a must have. The "debt snowball" method of paying bills is worth your time and worth the purchase of the book on its own merits.

Why did I let you get a glimpse of what has gone on in my world? Because I want you to see what is in my heart. I just want to be free. I want to live a life that is not imprisoned to anything, but instead is free to respond to God's purpose as He continually communicates His plans to me for my life. I recognize that I am severely limited in my ability to respond to a position of full-time ministry or whatever else God would later call me to do as long as I am a slave (servant) to my debt. The good news is someday I will no longer be a "servant to the lender." I will be free. Ultimately, I want my only debt to be the one I owe my LORD.

There is another way that I look at this situation. First of all, I am writing this book because I feel that it is my calling at this point in time. It is what God has led me to and provided for me. I also look at my work as a mission field. I can pour myself into people that I come in contact with and share with them what God has done and is doing in my life. In this way, we are all in some form of ministry. I suggest that you make the most out of what you have and where you are.

Key Thought:

Bloom where you are planted.

If we will look at our lives as a mission field and make our life and our work our ministry, we can change our little piece of the world. Remember the parable of the sower? The job of the sower is to sow (throw out) seed. If we are all out there sowing seeds, we will all take part in changing lives. As we walk through this life (our Christian journey), we are to continuously throw out seed along the way. Do we know the quality of the soil that our seed will fall on? No we don't. It is our job to just be obedient and throw the seed out.

Key Thought:

It is not your job to be the judge of the soil (the hearts of others). Just throw the seed and let God bring the harvest.

Here is the first part of the Parable of the Sower:

> "A farmer went out to sow his seed. As he was scattering the seed, some fell along the path, and the birds came and ate it up. Some fell on rocky places, where it did not have much soil. It sprang up quickly, because the soil was shallow. But when the sun came up, the plants were scorched, and they withered because they had no root. Other seed fell among thorns, which grew up and choked the plants. Still other seed fell on good soil, where it produced a crop—a hundred, sixty or thirty times what was sown."

> Matthew 13:3–8—NIV

(This parable can also be found in Mark 4 and Luke 8.)

Notice that in this parable, the seed was scattered in various places. In each instance, something happened that was out of the sower's control. (Let that sink in.) Some seed was devoured before it could grow. Some seed grew too quickly and died in the heat before roots could develop. Some seed grew but was choked out. Some seed fell on good soil and produced a large crop.

> Ask the LORD of the harvest, therefore, to send out workers into his harvest field.
>
> Matthew 9:38—NIV

As disciples, somehow we all found our way to God. How did this happen exactly? God puts people and circumstances into our lives that cause us to call out to Him. Someone in our lives had thrown the seed of God's Word onto the soil of our hearts. Next, the seed was watered and nurtured, helping it to grow. In the end, someone was there to harvest the seed when it had grown to maturity. What a beautiful example of the life that God gives us and the provision that He has made for each of us.

Here is the second part of the Parable of the Sower:

> "Listen then to what the parable of the sower means: When anyone hears the message about the kingdom and does not understand it, the evil one comes and snatches away what was sown in his heart. This is the seed sown along the path. The one who received the seed that fell on rocky places is the man who hears the word and at once receives it with joy. But since he has no root, he lasts only a short time. When trouble or persecution comes because of the word, he quickly falls away. The one who received the seed that fell among the thorns is the man who hears the word, but the worries of this life and the deceitfulness of wealth choke it, making it unfruitful. But the one who received

the seed that fell on good soil is the man who hears the word and understands it. He produces a crop, yielding a hundred, sixty or thirty times what was sown."

Matthew 13:18–23—NIV

Never forget that it is God who brings the harvest. Think about that. We, as disciples, don't save people. God saves people. God uses us to help bring in His harvest, but we are only His instruments. It is His saving power that transforms us and brings us to life spiritually. We are so blessed to be a part of His plan of salvation.

Do not be deceived: God cannot be mocked. A man reaps what he sows. The one who sows to please his sinful nature, from that nature will reap destruction; the one who sows to please the Spirit, from the Spirit will reap eternal life.

Galatians 6:7–8—NIV

While we are on the subject of throwing seeds, think about the following.

Question:

What kind of seeds are you sowing?

Are you sowing seeds that will grow into something beautiful, or are you throwing out seeds that will grow into weeds? My old pastor used to say that as Christians, we should *"just do right"*! We should be living right and we should *"just do right"* in whatever situations we find ourselves in. Sow seeds that will grow into something that you want to be in and around. I would rather be in a field of beautiful wildflowers instead of being in a field of prickly weeds.

The Bible tells us that we reap what we sow. If we are sowing seeds of strife, anger, bitterness, etc., then our crop is going to consist of, you guessed it, strife, anger, bitterness, etc. We have the ability to speak life into those around us because of the power of our tongues. If our lives display an inner peace that only can come from a right relationship with God, we will begin to see the crops around us turn into beautiful fields of wildflowers (changed lives with the sweet fragrance of godly character).

When you become a follower of Christ, you become a leader as well, in the sense of leading by example. We are called unto good works. What are "good works"? Well, in my opinion, good works consist of anything that you do to further the kingdom of God. We can serve God in the local church by greeting people at the door and making them feel welcome; by working in the nursery so parents can have some time without their infants so they can sit through service uninterrupted and focus on God; by volunteering in the youth department and mentoring kids by example, and so on. There are countless things that you can volunteer to do and use your talents for God's glory.

Outside the church, we can serve by visiting widows, mowing yards for the elderly or handicapped, working in a mission or soup kitchen, and so on. The fun of it is opening your mind to how God can use your given talents to bring Him glory and honor. Remember what Jesus said about "the least of these" (Matthew 25:40)? What we do to and for others is a form of worship and it can bring glory to His name, but if we are not living out our calling, it can bring disgrace to His name. How we live and behave is so important. We are ambassadors for Christ. We are His hands and feet. We are the church—His bride. We should be encouraging each other to live out our calling, and we should be a light unto the world.

> Let us hold unswervingly to the hope we profess, for he who promised is faithful. And let us consider how we may spur one another on toward love and good deeds. Let us not give up meeting together, as some are in the habit of doing, but let us encourage one another—and all the more as you see the Day approaching.
>
> Hebrews 10:23–25—NIV

We serve a relational God. He created us to be social beings, and He desires for us to be in fellowship with one another as a means of both encouragement and accountability. In Chapter 10, we will discuss the importance of personal accountability, and it is at that point that we will take accountability to the next level. We cannot be everything that God wants us to be outside of the local church. Just as Christ is the head of the church, we all comprise its body. We all serve to make the body complete. Every one of us has special traits and talents that are God given and unique. Personally, I sit here writing a book and I marvel at the very thought of it. Through hardships, trials, accountability, fellowship, prayer, fasting, and reading, God impressed upon me that I needed to be doing this specific work at this specific time in my life. During this time, I have not allowed myself to drift out of fellowship or church attendance, because I understand the importance of being around God's people and being in the presence of shared faith.

There are some great verses that drive this point home.
- Psalm 22:3 tells us that God inhabits the praises of His people.

- Matthew 18:20 says that where two or three are gathered in His name, God is right there in the midst of them.

If His people aren't getting together to praise Him, they are missing out on His presence and His blessings for their lives. If we really want to get to know God more intimately, then we need to seek His face and make time to go where His people are gathered in His name.

If you are not currently attending a local church, I suggest that you find a local body of believers and get connected. We all need to hear the Word of God preached with boldness and authority in a loving way, and we can't very well do that if we are not going to God's house to fellowship with other believers. This is an important aspect of "finding your way."

Chapter 8

2/21/16

facing opposition

Be self-controlled and alert. Your enemy the devil prowls
around like a roaring lion looking for someone to devour.
Resist him, standing firm in the faith, because you know
that your brothers throughout the world are undergoing
the same kind of sufferings.

1 Peter 5:8–9—NIV

We have an enemy! He has many different names, but he is generally referred to as the devil or Satan. He is very real and he
would just as soon you not know his true identity. He would love
it even more if you doubted his very existence. If we doubt his
existence, then he is able to operate in secret and silently attack
our faith. He wants to deceive us (preferably covertly) and distract us from focusing on God and living a godly lifestyle.

Here are some verses that communicate what the Bible has to
say about him:

He is a *thief*!

> The thief comes only to steal and kill and destroy; I have come that they may have life, and have it to the full.
>
> John 10:10—NIV

He is a *liar*!

> You belong to your father, the devil, and you want to carry out your father's desire. He was a murderer from the beginning, not holding to the truth, for there is no truth in him. When he lies, he speaks his native language, for he is a liar and the father of lies.
>
> John 8:44—NIV

He is *rebellious*!

> And there was war in heaven. Michael and his angels fought against the dragon, and the dragon and his angels fought back. But he was not strong enough, and they lost their place in heaven. The great dragon was hurled down—that ancient serpent called the devil, or Satan, who leads the whole world astray. He was hurled to the earth, and his angels with him.
>
> Revelation 12:7–9—NIV

He is *angry*!

> He is filled with fury, because he knows that his time is short.
>
> Revelation 12:12—NIV

As you look over this short list of Satan's attributes, I want to draw your attention to the fact that these traits are the polar opposite of what Christ stands for.

Satan
- Steals Life
- Father of Lies
- Rebellious
- Angry

Christ
- Gives Abundant Life
- The Way, The Truth, and The Life
- Prince of Peace
- Peace That Passes Understanding

Another attribute of Satan is that he is a *counterfeiter*. As you learn more about his nature, you will see that he tries to give us substitutes for everything so that we will be distracted from God's best. He wants to pervert our thoughts towards things like relationships, intimacy, and love. If he can get us to settle for less than God's best, he has succeeded. We must be ever watchful and not allow ourselves to become so desensitized that we become calloused and indifferent toward God's *"good, pleasing, and perfect will"* for our lives. The renewing of our minds by the Holy Spirit gives us fresh perspective and helps us to be spiritually on-guard and not lulled to sleep.

Fact:
We will face opposition as we live our lives for Christ.

We need to get that fact in our minds right now, before we go any further. We must realize that we live in enemy territory because we are born into this world. Because we are strangers in a foreign land, we will be persecuted for our faith.

> Consider it pure joy, my brothers, whenever you face trials of many kinds, because you know that the testing of your faith develops perseverance.
>
> James 1:2–3—NIV

The mind that exists apart from Christ (our former nature prior to our salvation) does not comprehend what this passage is saying. It would seem like nonsense to the unregenerate mind.

If we were not Christians:
- Why would we want to have our faith tested anyway?
- Why would we find joy in the face of a trial?

As Christians, the answer is simple—we endure trials for the development of *perseverance*. In Chapter 11, we will discuss perseverance in more detail. For now, I want you to understand and accept that we need to develop perseverance because, the development of perseverance leads to the development of something wonderful, which we should all desire as disciples of Christ.

> To keep me from becoming conceited because of these surpassingly great revelations, there was given me a thorn in my flesh, a messenger of Satan, to torment me. Three times I pleaded with the LORD to take it away from me. But he said to me, "My grace is sufficient for you, for my power is made perfect in weakness." Therefore I will boast all the more gladly about my weaknesses, so that Christ's power may rest on me. That is why, for Christ's sake, I delight in weaknesses, in insults, in hardships, in persecutions, in difficulties. For when I am weak, then I am strong.
>
> 2 Corinthians 12:7–10—NIV

This passage fascinates me. When I think of Paul, I imagine a spiritual giant, yet here we get to see his humanity. It is a beautiful picture. We all struggle in our Christian journey, yet I think it is helpful, and even encouraging, to know that our spiritual heroes were humans like us, and dealt with real-life challenges too. We tend to imagine them to be like Charlton Heston when he played Moses in the movie *The Ten Commandments* (steadfast, confident, and fearless) and often forget that they were sinners saved by the grace of God, just like the rest of us. One distinct difference is that they knew their purpose. Once they got a glimpse of God's plan for their lives, they did not continue to see themselves as *"unlikely."*

There are at least two reasons that God allowed Paul to have a "thorn" in his flesh. The purpose of Paul's thorn was to serve as a reminder that:

- God's grace is sufficient.
- God's power is made perfect in weakness.

Now imagine for a moment that you are Paul. You have seen God do miraculous things in the lives of those around you, yet through it all, God has allowed you to be tormented, even though you have begged Him to take the thorn away from you. Imagine the frustration. Now get this point straight: to keep Paul from becoming conceited, God *allowed* this "thorn" to persist. God wanted Paul to never lose sight of the fact that He was in complete control. Our depraved nature causes us to want to begin to take credit for things that are accomplished in our lives. The more "we" accomplish, the more empowered we feel and the less we perceive the need for God in our lives. In our fleshly nature, if we had seen some of the things that Paul had seen, we might become conceited ourselves (we might tend to forget that it was

God doing those things through us and not just ourselves). We must never forget that God's grace is sufficient (more than just adequate) for us. Also, His power is best seen displayed through our weakness. It is in this state of weakness that Christ's life-changing power "rests" on you and is most apparent to those around you.

Key Thought:

When we are tested, we get to see what we are made of.

Theory vs. Reality

Think of it this way: Imagine that you designed an airplane and built it, but you never allowed it to fly. The purpose of a maiden flight is so that you can test whether or not the design and construction of the aircraft are aeronautically sound. Until the test (trial) comes along, who knows if the plane will even fly? If you don't like that analogy, try this one on for size: consider that you designed and built a boat. If your boat is never put in the water for its maiden voyage, how would you know if it is nautically sound? Will it float? Who knows until you put it to the test (trial).

The beauty behind these analogies is this: God is our designer. He knows that we will fly when tested. He knows that we will float when tested. He knows that when we put our hope and trust in Him, we can "soar on wings like eagles" (Isaiah 40:31) and draw our strength from Him. He built us this way. We are closest to Him when we live according to His design for us.

When we face trials in our lives, we should be happy because we know that our faith is tested. When we get to see our faith in

God produce results in our lives, such as the development of per-severance, character, hope, etc., we grow closer to God because we learn to trust Him more to guide us and protect us along our journey.

I am reminded of a great country music song entitled *"You've Got to Stand for Something"*[10] sung by Aaron Tippin that says:

> "You've got to stand for somethin' or you'll fall for anything. You've got to be your own man, not a puppet on a string. Never compromise what's right, and uphold your family name. You've got to stand for somethin' or you'll fall for anything."

Well, my friend, you do stand for something. The moment you confessed Jesus Christ as your LORD and Savior, whether you know it or not, you took a stand. As for your family name, when you accepted Christ as LORD and Savior, you were born into the family of God. That is now your spiritual heritage. Are you facing opposition because of this profession? If you are living a life of a disciple, you probably are enduring spiritual opposition. But remember this: If you could see a picture of your eternal family crest, you would see God on it. You belong to His family. You were permanently adopted to be conformed into the image of Christ.

There is an enemy who stands against us, but we must keep in mind what 1 John 4:4 tells us: *"Greater is He that is in us* [Jesus], *than he that is in the world* [Satan]*"* (KJV). Satan has already been defeated in heaven, but now his main objective is to defeat any-one who stands up for Christ and bears Christ's image. You are now an enemy of the prince of this world (Satan).

> For though we live in the world, we do not wage war as the world does. The weapons we fight with are not the weapons

of the world. On the contrary, they have divine power to demolish strongholds. We demolish arguments and every pretension that sets itself up against the knowledge of God, and we take captive every thought to make it obedient to Christ.

2 Corinthians 10:3–5—NIV

Our thought life is so important. This verse suggests that our thoughts can run free and get us into trouble. We need to capture our runaway thoughts and make them obedient to Christ. For some, and probably most of us, the mind is the devil's playground. We entertain thoughts sometimes that are ungodly and depraved because we have certain desires, lusts, etc., that entice us and cause us to continuously stumble. I could go into detail about our culture, morality, television, etc., but regardless of the source that we choose to blame for our impure thoughts, we, as fallen human beings, are inherently sinful and we fall short of the glory of God. We need to regularly give our thoughts to God. Lay our burdens down at His feet. Ask Him again for a continuous renewing of our minds.

Question:

What is it that we spend our time thinking about, wishing for, looking at, etc., that is not in line with God's will for our lives?

Proverbs 23:7 says that as a man thinks in his heart, so is he. If you were honest with yourself, there is probably an area that you know that you haven't surrendered to God and asked Him to "take captive." We prolong this silent behavior because we have the perceived luxury that we are alone with our thoughts. We tell ourselves, "Nobody really knows what goes on in the silence of my thought life, right?" Wrong! God knows. When we have impure thoughts, that is, thoughts that have not been taken captive and made obedient to Christ, we are not living a life with a renewed mind (Romans 12:2). Imagine if your thoughts could be projected onto a screen that everyone could see. Scary, huh? Maybe that thought will convince you how important it is that we ask God to renew our minds regularly.

When I reflect on the idea of our thoughts holding us captive, instead of the other way around, I think about being in chains. We live so much of our lives in bondage to those areas that have not been given over to the Lordship of Jesus Christ. We need to recognize this. We need to let go of what has been handicapping our walk with God. I have this mental picture (from one of my favorite Christmas movies) of the character Jacob Marley in the 1951 version of *A Christmas Carol* (based on the book by Charles Dickens) starring Alistair Sim. I picture Ebenezer Scrooge being visited by the ghost of Jacob Marley, his former cutthroat business partner. The ghost of Mr. Marley was in bondage and was in constant torture because of the way in which he chose to live his life while he was alive on this earth. His prior misdeeds, indifference, obsessive hoarding of money, selfishness, and complete lack of concern for anything other than his accumulation of wealth, at the expense of others, had destined him to an eternity of wandering through the afterlife, dragging chains behind him that were connected to his eternal baggage of burden.

Although this is not a biblical story, it gets us thinking about the consequences of our sins. We should spend a little more time thinking about sin's consequences and not be so indifferent to the concept. Whether you like it or not, there are consequences for our sins. God may forgive us and cleanse us, but He still allows us to live through the consequences of our decisions. So you could say that forgiveness of our sins will get us to heaven, but the consequences of our sins can create a hellish life for us on earth. When will we learn?

Are you dragging your own chains and old baggage through this life? As the story of Ebenezer Scrooge points out, we have a chance in this life to make things right. We need to recognize this awesome opportunity and not waste it, like he did. Eventually, he finally realized what was really important in life. My prayer is that every one of us would come to this realization sooner, rather than later.

Someday, scripture tells us, every knee shall bow and every tongue will confess that Jesus Christ is LORD. Face it, someday we will be judged by God. We will be judged by our deeds, but I believe that we will also be judged by our thoughts and the attitude of our hearts. Therefore, we can clean up our outside image by doing good deeds, but if our inside is not constantly renewed, we may just be a rotten apple with a sweet caramel coating. It looks great from the outside, but just wait until the first bite from life comes along. Not a pretty picture.

Question:

If God allowed you to be squeezed right now, what would come out of you (spiritually)?

Would it be sweet or sour?

We need to regularly evaluate our Christian life by spiritually stepping up to God's mirror and looking into it to see our reflection. In God's mirror, you can see the thoughts and attitudes of the heart. What do you see when you look in this mirror? Do you see the image of Christ? Do you see a beautiful life based on Christian values, a life bearing the fruit of the Spirit? Or do you see a life that is full of compromise? A life whose faith has been sold out for convenience or comfort?

Question:

What do we need to do to be able to look in God's mirror and see the appropriate image?

God wants us to have renewed minds. He wants us to meditate on good things. He wants us to be pure and focused on Him.

> Finally, brothers, whatever is true, whatever is noble, whatever is right, whatever is pure, whatever is lovely, whatever is admirable—if anything is excellent or praiseworthy—think about such things.
>
> Philippians 4:8—NIV

We should spend more time concentrating on these types of things. The problem is that our minds are often weak because we are not having them renewed through a connected relationship with our LORD. Our minds are one of Satan's favorite playgrounds (if we ignore him and give him free reign) or battlegrounds (if we stand up to him). If we are not guarding our thoughts and asking God to continuously renew our minds, we are opening the door for Satan to abuse us, and he will abuse us if we let him.

Think of a spirited horse with a bridal in its mouth. With the least amount of pressure on the reins, we can cause this strong, massive creature to turn in whatever direction we so desire. Also consider a large fish with a hook in its mouth. With just a little constant force, we can wear down this giant and then mount him on our wall (if you are into that sort of thing).

Key Thought:

Turn the head and you will turn the beast.

These beasts may fight us, but we will ultimately win. Thank God that we are more intelligent than horses and fish (most of the time). Satan may try to get in our heads and turn us away from God by putting a bit in our mouths or baiting us with his disguised hooks, but we don't have to give in to him or take his bait. Unlike the analogy of the horse or the fish, we, as Christians, have the Holy Spirit residing in us. Through the power of the Holy Spirit, we can defeat Satan and refuse to be led astray, no matter how he tries to "reign" over us or "hook" us and reel us in.

We cannot forget that we have a spiritual enemy and that he will try to overtake us by any means necessary.

Key Thought:

Satan has no authority over us, except what we give him by living outside God's plan.

Do not be afraid or discouraged because of this vast army.
For the battle is not yours, but God's.

2 Chronicles 20:15—NIV

We need to fight our enemy using the spiritual tools that God
gave us. We need to suit up and prepare to defend our hearts.
The Bible is rich with illustrations of spiritual warfare, weapons
of our warfare and spiritual armor. Why would God bother to
reveal to us these things if there were not an ongoing battle to
fight? Read the following passage and think about what it is trying to communicate to us:

> Finally, be strong in the LORD and in his mighty power.
> Put on the full armor of God so that you can take your
> stand against the devil's schemes. For our struggle is not
> against flesh and blood, but against the rulers, against
> the authorities, against the powers of this dark world and
> against the spiritual forces of evil in the heavenly realms.
> Therefore put on the full armor of God, so that when the
> day of evil comes, you may be able to stand your ground,
> and after you have done everything, to stand. Stand firm
> then, with the belt of truth buckled around your waist, with
> the breastplate of righteousness in place, and with your feet
> fitted with the readiness that comes from the gospel of
> peace. In addition to all this, take up the shield of faith,
> with which you can extinguish all the flaming arrows of the
> evil one. Take the helmet of salvation and the sword of the
> Spirit, which is the word of God. And pray in the Spirit on
> all occasions with all kinds of prayers and requests. With
> this in mind, be alert and always keep on praying for all
> the saints.

Ephesians 6:10–18—NIV

What an awesome picture of the Christian warrior!

When I was a kid, I attended a church that only played hymns. One of my favorite old hymns is *"Onward Christian Soldiers."*[11] I can still hear my dad's voice singing the bass part. If you closed your eyes, it really sounded like marching soldiers. To this day, that hymn sticks out in my mind. Some of the words to this great old hymn are as follows:

> Onward, Christian soldiers, marching as to war,
> With the cross of Jesus going on before.
> Christ, the royal Master, leads against the foe;
> Forward into battle see His banners go!
>
> *Refrain*:
> Onward, Christian soldiers, marching as to war,
> With the cross of Jesus going on before.
>
> Like a mighty army moves the church of God;
> Brothers, we are treading where the saints have trod.
> We are not divided, all one body we,
> One in hope and doctrine, one in charity.
>
> Onward then, ye people, join our happy throng,
> Blend with ours your voices in the triumph song.
> Glory, laud and honor unto Christ the King,
> This through countless ages men and angels sing.

Awesome song. Awesome message.

Key Thought:

The problem with the Christian army is that we often shoot
our own wounded.

Let me explain what I mean by this.
Consider the verse of the hymn that says,

> We are not divided, all one body we;
> one in hope and doctrine, one in charity.

We are not supposed to be divided. We have ... One body. One
hope. One doctrine. One charity (love). If you ask me, we have
missed the point. We don't seem to have much "oneness" (unity)
at all. I believe that this is a major flaw within the church today.
We have so much division within the body of Christ. We have
division that comes in the form of denominational quarrels,
church splits because of internal power struggles, pastors who
are afraid to speak the real and sometimes harsh truths of the
Word because they fear that they will be removed from the pulpit by people in the congregation who don't want to follow their
shepherd, but instead try to lead, and the list goes on and on.

We need more pastors to stand up and teach the Word of God
boldly, and we need more disciples that will place themselves
under the authority of these great men of God. Conversely, we
need fewer disgruntled church members, especially those who
seem to exist only to create division and discord. (If you are one
of those people, then I pray that you will be open as you read this

book and take this message to heart and begin to see your reflection in God's mirror and change.)

Where is the unity? We are all supposed to be in the same army, yet we take shots at each other and seldom miss the opportunity to step on our comrade (brother in Christ) when he falls on the battlefield of life. Instead of fighting for the same cause, the cause of Christ, we fight amongst ourselves and bring the glorious name of our LORD into shame. Our prayer for our local church (and the body of Christ at large) should be that we can be *united*. There is too much division already. Don't be the catalyst that brings more division to the body. Instead, I encourage you to read John 17. In this chapter, Jesus prays for Himself, His disciples, and all believers. Understand that Christ's prayer for us was for *unity*.

Proceed with Extreme Caution:

Before I delineate and elaborate on the next concept, I want to be extremely careful and cautious in my approach. I want to preface these next comments by saying that I know that I am approaching a potentially sensitive topic and I feel, with a reasonable degree of certainty, that a part of my audience will be offended *before* they even hear the point of what I am trying to say. My sincerest prayer is that God, through the power of the Holy Spirit, would filter my words as they enter your mind in such a way that you would be able to receive the truth of my message and not feel offended by my words in any way. Please keep this prayer in mind as you read on.

With that being said, here it is, as straight as I know how to say it. An example of this lack of unity within the body of Christ is no more evident than when we are introducing ourselves to other believers. Instead of introducing ourselves as "Christians," we often, maybe subconsciously, feel the need to be labeled by our denomination. For example, at one time I attended a Baptist church, and as a member of a Baptist church, I might introduce myself to you by saying, "I'm a Baptist" (I picked Baptist at random. I could have said, "I'm a Presbyterian" or I could have chosen any other denomination to make my point. My choice of denominations here is not what is relevant.). What bothers me is that when we attend any given denomination, we tend to introduce ourselves under this *label*, as if the *label* was our spiritual identity. This is completely not true! We are *Christians* first and foremost. We are all children of the same God—the God of Abraham, Isaac, and Jacob; the King of kings; the LORD of lords; the Alpha and Omega; the Beginning and the End. The reality is, if we believe and have faith in Christ as our LORD, we are all Christians—who happen to attend various denominations.

Do you understand what I am trying to say? We have drawn lines in the sand, fought amongst ourselves about who is doctrinally "right," and argued over what is the only denomination that is going to heaven, and other such topics. Don't you understand that Jesus came to this earth to do away with this sort of division? (Again, the message of John 17 is *unity*!)

In our Bibles, we can read about the organized religions that were upset by Jesus' teachings and, as we read about these ancient people, we should think about how these people were missing the point. Yet, for some reason, we get so embedded in our own differences (often denominational differences) that we forget that we are all in the same spiritual family. Are we, like some people of Jesus' day, missing the point too? We need to be reminded that we all pray to the same God and we are all His children.

Key Thought:

"United we stand; divided we fall."

We should be united by our faith, not divided by it!

This, in my opinion, is the one of the greatest attacks by Satan on the church today. We really need to love and support each other no matter where we choose to worship. As long as we know God, confess Jesus as our LORD, serve Him with our whole heart, while consistently reading and studying God's Word so that we can continuously learn about our faith, we have assurance that we will be with Him in heaven. The rest is worth discussing, but not fighting about and certainly not worth dividing over. To quote a familiar cliché, *"Why can't we all just get along?"*

In the world we live in, many people have no respect for Christians. Sadly, this is partly our own fault. If you listen to the news, listen to other people interacting, or even read the newspaper, you will see that the way the world views Christianity has changed a lot in the last few decades. Christians have lost a lot of credibility in the world's eyes. Why does the general, non-Christian population feel this way?

As Christians, we should be the salt and light of this planet, but instead, we waste our time, energy and resources debating and dividing amongst ourselves. We don't spend our time seeking ways to be *united* in our belief and faith in God and in His son, our Savior, Jesus Christ. Don't get me wrong. I am a firm believer of knowing what you believe and why you believe it, and I especially like the Word of God presented in a direct, bold, and unashamed way.

> But in your hearts set apart Christ as LORD. Always be prepared to give an answer to everyone who asks you to give the reason for the hope that you have. But do this with gentleness and respect,
>
> 1 Peter 3:15—NIV

It is our duty to be ready to give an answer to anyone who asks us about our faith. We are instructed to be able to provide the reason for the hope that we have, but we are told to do so with *gentleness* and *respect*. I know there are some of you who are reading along, wondering where my gentleness and respect have gone. Believe me; I am doing the best I know how to present this idea in an honest and sincere way without stepping on everyone's toes.

When it comes to explaining to others what we believe and why we believe it, it is beyond important to have a grasp on what the Bible says. I have attended various denominations over my life, but I have come to this realization: My faith in God, my relationship with Him, my adherence to His Word as the governing law of my life, is more important than whether I am a member of any particular denomination. Again, let me stress that I mean no disrespect to any given denomination, but I have to ask the burning question: what is the most important thing?

What is it that we are most concerned about?
- Living a life sold out to God and living according to His will for our lives,

  —*or*—
- Proclaiming to belong to a denomination but not loving our Christian brothers or "neighbors" as we should

I am not implying that just because we are in a denomination that we have missed the mark. Far from it! What I am saying is this: Are we living for Christ, or are we missing Him somehow?

Key Thought:

Are we devout Christians, or are we staunch partisans?

Are we following the Word of God first and foremost, above all else, or are we more concerned about promoting our denominational affiliation? Who are we and what is our true identity? God knows the answer. I believe part of His *"good, pleasing, and perfect will"* for us is for us to discover our true identity. I personally believe our identity is in Him and in Him alone. Our identity should not be defined by our affiliations, but instead by our relationship with our LORD. There is nothing wrong with belonging to a denomination, as long as it doesn't interfere with your relationship to the LORD and to other believers.

My faith in God and my profession of faith in His son Jesus Christ as my personal Savior is the only thing that will save me. I am sorry to say it if it offends you, but your denominational affiliation will not save your soul. Only God can save you. This is a definitive, undeniable biblical truth. We need to have more faith in God and less faith in the institutions we have created for ourselves.

This is a subject that I am extremely passionate about. So much so, I am seriously considering writing another book just about this subject. To put it simply, I believe that one of greatest, if not the greatest, satanic attacks on the church (the Body of Christ) is the fact that Christians can't even agree as to what they believe. We can be so stubborn sometimes! We forget that we are all sinners saved by the grace of God. We all believe in the same God and we believe that His son, Jesus, was born of a virgin, lived a sinless life, died on a cross for the forgiveness and remission of our sins, and was resurrected from the dead and now sits at the right hand of God, our Heavenly Father. This is *essential* doctrine. It is the core of our belief system.

I will not go into this subject any further here, except to say, *please, please* seriously consider what it is that I am trying to say to you. If you find yourself offended by what I have said, stop and ask yourself, "Why?"

I am *not* attacking any denominations, but rather the idea that our denominations are only divisions within the church that *we* put there. God didn't put these divisions in place, but we seem to want to give Him credit for our "enlightenment." I believe, Satan, and Satan only, had a hand in creating this situation. In my opinion, he has been very successful in this endeavor. Our enemy is not our fellow Christian who flies the flag of a different denomination than ours. Our enemy is Satan. We need to recognize him and his deeds. He is very crafty, and we need to be on guard. In the meantime, we need to be more loving and accepting of our fellow brothers and sisters in Christ and come to terms with the fact that we are all on the same team and fighting in the same army. God's army.

> Put on the whole armor of God, that you may be able to stand against the wiles of the devil.
>
> Ephesians 6:11—NKJV

To *"deceive"* means to cause someone to believe something that is not true (typically to gain some personal advantage). In verse 11, the word *"wiles"* means crafty methods. Satan will use any tool or any method he can to get us derailed, and he is good at it, if we let him. He wants us to believe what is almost true in order to get us to take the bait and swallow the hook (believe the lie). Deception can seem like the real thing if we are not paying close attention. For example, consider Adam and Eve. Satan told Eve, while in the center of the Garden of Eden, if she were to eat the forbidden fruit that she would be "like God." He didn't say that she would become God, because he knew she would never believe that. Instead he told her that she would be "like God." He appealed to her pride and selfishness, and in doing so, through Eve and Adam, the sin nature, or fleshly nature, entered into the world. We have all been struggling with our depravity ever since.

We must remember that Satan is not threatened by someone without the knowledge of God's purpose. Satan's ideal situation would be to render us ineffective, therefore we are of no threat to him. He has no need or desire to mess with someone who is spiritually "neutral." When we are living out God's purpose for our lives, we are standing against everything that Satan stands for. Satan wants to render us powerless by attacking us where we are weak.

We all come under spiritual attack if we are trying to take a stand for God. We are all tempted to believe Satan's lies. Early in the process of writing this book, I felt the subtle, but effective power of Satan's deception in my thought life. As a first time author, I kept hearing a voice saying, *"Unlikely? Who are you kidding? You are not worthy of writing such a book."* I kept hearing this recurring thought. It got so bad that I scarcely wrote for over a month. Every time I sat to write, I just stared at the page and had nothing to say. Talk about writer's block! For a time, I completely lost my focus, but eventually, I got it back. When I did, I knew, without a doubt in my mind, that I was supposed to be writing this book. It is my God-given purpose! I now have that back in focus again. I rebuke the enemy for being so cunning once again. He will not stand in my way and short-circuit this work that God has given me to do.

As I sit here, I am pondering the thought that comes from Isaiah 54.

No weapon formed against you shall prosper.

Isaiah 54:17—NKJV

No weapon ... formed against you ... shall prosper. To me, that means that no force or power of evil will ultimately prevail in my life. I have God's Word on this subject matter. Let's think about what these so-called "weapons" look like. Believe me, we are hit with these weapons every day and probably don't recognize them for what they really are. Let us remember, the devil is a clever, crafty, and cunning adversary. We may be attacked with a weapon, but not realize that is even a weapon. This is one of the best tricks in the book. When Satan uses a benign method of distraction so that we don't even realize that he is the source of the problem; we fall down and don't seem to know why. Meanwhile, he pats himself on the back because he was able to trick us again by taking advantage of our short-comings and failures. He may have won that round, but we have God in our corner and if we will listen to His instruction and follow His lead, we will stand to fight another round. Ding. Ding. "Are you ready to rumble?" Come out of the corner swinging.

In regard to my writing, I was sucker-punched with doubt. It hit me right between the eyes because I had let my guard down. I didn't see it coming until I had been hit. Everything went blurry and I temporarily lost my focus (and my confidence). When I came to my senses, I was on the mat and the count was on. As I lay there, I had an epiphany. My writing-life flashed before my eyes. My mind settled on this clear, concise thought: *These thoughts are lies from the devil.* I know that this book is a work that God has entrusted me with and I am going to stand up and tighten the gloves and start swinging again. The rest is history.

I can do all things through Christ who strengthens me.

Philippians 4:13—NKJV

Maybe you have been attacked with criticism for standing up for your faith. We all face opposition in regard to our beliefs. Recently, my friend Bethany shared this awesome thought with me.

Key Thought:

People can argue your beliefs, but they cannot argue your experience.

Wow! No matter what other people believe, our personal experience, our living testimony, our silent example speaks volumes to people. Actions really do speak louder than words. This brings up our next thought.

Key Thought:

People will forget what you have said ... they will forget what you have done ... but they will never forget how you made them feel.

The truth is, our actions send an impression that is lasting and powerful.

Key Thought:

We all need to stop, pray, think, and then act.

Sadly, I think most of us get this completely backwards. We reverse the order. We *act*, *think*, and then *pray* about the consequences of our poor actions. Stop! Let this sink in. That is a profound statement! Read the previous "Key Thought" again and internalize it. Own it.

> But put on the LORD Jesus Christ, and make no provision for the flesh, to fulfill its lusts.
>
> Romans 13:14—NKJV

"Provision for the flesh?" What does that mean? It means that you have non-submitted areas of your life. To be more specific, it means that you haven't given every single area of your life to the Lordship of Jesus Christ. As I told you before, God wants all of you, not part of you. God does not like lukewarm (Revelation 3:16). When you make provision for your flesh, you are catering to the needs and wants of your fleshly nature. This is an area that Satan can work through, and believe me, he will use this "provision" to create a stronghold. What is a stronghold? It is a military term for "a fortress or castle of resistance."

> Submit yourselves, then, to God. Resist the devil, and he will flee from you.
>
> James 4:7—NIV

244 • Dr. George Goodman

Imagine that Satan is hiding inside the walls of a fortress in your life that you gave him permission to occupy. It's time to kick him out of your fortress and, by confessing your sin, allow God to demolish the walls of this stronghold. Every time you give in to Satan by making "provision" for your flesh, you are giving Satan brick and mortar to rebuild his fortress (stronghold) in your life. We need God's wrecking ball to clean house and make room for new construction. We need to pray that God would fortify our hearts and minds and protect us from the crafty methods of our enemy.

It is time that you understood the power of spiritual warfare. Yes, there is a battle to fight. It's time that you let out your battle cry and started fighting your enemy.

Question:

Why do we need warfare?

There are many answers to this question. First of all, we have an enemy. He has a name and his purpose has been made known to us. He is out to steal, kill, and destroy (John 10:10). Secondly, we have been given spiritual armor.

We would not be asked to go out on the battlefield without protection and without a weapon. It is interesting to note that all but one part of our spiritual armor is defensive. The only offensive part is the sword of the Spirit, which is the Word of God! Read Ephesians 6:10–18 again, this time, dissect it. See everything that it has to say to us as Disciple warriors:

> Finally, be strong in the LORD and in his mighty power [His strength, not ours]. Put on the full [complete] armor of God so that you can take your stand [defend] against the

devil's schemes. For our struggle [fight] is not against flesh and blood, but against the rulers, against the authorities, against the powers of this dark world and against the spiritual forces of evil [our enemy] in the heavenly realms. Therefore put on the full [complete] armor of God, so that when the day of evil comes [our enemy attacks us], you may be able to stand your ground [defend], and after you have done everything, to stand. Stand firm then [no retreat], with the belt of truth [defensive, protective armor] buckled around your waist, with the breastplate of righteousness [defensive, protective armor] in place, and with your feet fitted with the readiness that comes from the gospel of peace [defensive, protective armor]. In addition to all this, take up the shield of faith [defensive, protective armor], with which you can extinguish [neutralize] all the flaming arrows of the evil one. Take the helmet of salvation [defensive, protective armor] and the sword of the Spirit [offensive attack weapon], which is the word of God. And pray in the Spirit on all occasions with all kinds of prayers and requests. With this in mind, be alert [vigilant] and always keep on praying for all the saints.

Ephesians 6:10–18—NIV

This passage tells us to put on our armor daily and stand ready, prepared to fight. If you look at the battle armor of that day, a warrior's best protection came when facing his opponent head on. A warrior who turned away from the battle to retreat would lose the protection that his armor (shield, breastplate, etc.) were designed to provide. A retreating warrior would then be defenseless against an attack from his enemy (swords, spears, arrows, etc.).

If we do not have our spiritual armor on, we will quickly fall on the battlefield of life. We, in our own strength, cannot possibly win in a battle against our spiritual adversary. We must dress for success. By starting our day with focusing on God by meeting with Him on our knees, putting on His uniform, and running out into the world (our battlefield), we learn to lean on God to fight our battles for us. We have to show up and be prepared for the fight. When we learn to go to the battlefield with proper preparation and lean on Him to obtain our victory, we are strong because His strength is made known through us.

I heard Wayne Gretsky (one of the greatest hockey players who ever played the game) quoted once as saying that he never scored a goal he didn't shoot. Seems simple, but is it? How can you score if you don't take aim and "let it rip"? Conversely, how can we ever have a spiritual victory if we are not dressed for the battle, taking aim, and firing back at our enemy?

> For God has not given us a spirit of fear, but of power and of love and of a sound mind.
>
> 2 Timothy 1:7—NKJV

> No temptation has seized you except what is common to man. And God is faithful; he will not let you be tempted beyond what you can bear. But when you are tempted, he will also provide a way out so that you can stand up under it.
>
> 1 Corinthians 10:13—NIV

No matter what you are going through and no matter what trials or temptations you are facing, you must remember this solemn promise: God has made a way of escape for you. You *can* weather this storm. Nothing is bigger than God. No sin. No circumstance. No temptation. Nothing!

I have always found incredible encouragement from the following verse:

> For I am convinced that neither death nor life, neither angels nor demons, neither the present nor the future, nor any powers, neither height nor depth, nor anything else in all creation, will be able to separate us from the love of God that is in Christ Jesus our LORD.

> Romans 8:38–39—NIV

How amazing to know that we are secure in our LORD. Nothing can separate us from Him. Did you hear me? *Nothing* can separate us from Him. *Wow!* We are secure. We are safe. We are protected from any ungodly thing that would try to trip us, ensnare us, or imprison us. How liberating! God is love. Therefore ...

Key Thought:

Nothing can separate us from God's love.

> You believe that there is one God. Good! Even the demons believe that—and shudder.

> James 2:19—NIV

When you stop and consider that our enemy believes in God ... and shudders, we should get a sense of the true power of our LORD. He is supreme. He is the LORD almighty. He is the Alpha and Omega, the First and the Last, the Beginning and the End (Revelation 22:13).

Have I not commanded you? Be strong and courageous. Do not be terrified; do not be discouraged, for the LORD your God will be with you wherever you go."

Joshua 1:9—NIV

God has all the power and the authority. He has already won the battle. We are on the winning team! We are assured victory! Onward, Christian soldiers.

Go! Fight! Win!

Chapter 9

seeking His face

You do not have, because you do not ask God.

James 4:2—NIV

If you want something in this life, you usually have to work for it. You can set short-term goals, long-term goals; achieve those goals; acquire wealth, possessions, prestige; and so on. All these things are attainable to us in this life if we have the right attitude and if we are fortunate enough to be in the right place at the right time. These are all things that are within our grasp if we are willing to put some work into it and manage our way.

There are some things in life, however, that are not attainable with out special help. Think about eternal life. On your own, you can never attain eternal life. You could work tirelessly by caring for others, giving of yourself and your resources, and at the end of your life, you might be recognized for your contributions, but this will not earn your place in eternity. They might name a street after you or erect a bronze statue in your likeness, but this will not earn you immortality, it will only earn you notoriety. Eventually, people will forget about you and everything will turn to dust.

So many Christians today live out a faith that is focused entirely upon "good works." This is commonly known as a "works-based faith." What I mean is that these people live every day with the thought that they must somehow perform to be counted among God's "chosen" people. I want you to read the following verse slowly and very carefully and let it sink in:

> For it is by grace you have been saved, through faith—and this not from yourselves, it is the gift of God—not by works, so that no one can boast. For we are God's workmanship, created in Christ Jesus to do good works, which God prepared in advance for us to do.
>
> Ephesians 2:8–10—NIV

The Bible teaches us that we are saved by God's grace, and it is through our faith in God (not by any other means) that we receive this gift of salvation. Salvation is a gift! It is freely given to us, but we must ask for it by faith. We don't have to earn salvation by our good works, as so many Christians seem to believe, but rather, we receive salvation when we ask for it by putting our faith in God and in His son Jesus Christ.

Here is where so many believers get derailed:
• We were created by God to *do* good works.
• As believers, we are called *to* good works.
• We are not saved *by* good works.

Do you see the distinctions? Good works are *not* what gets us to heaven. Our faith in God is what saves us. Now don't get me wrong on this point: Works are very important because we are called by God to do good works, but we can't lose sight of the fact that we should be doing good works out of our obedience to

God and not in an attempt to earn salvation from God. If you never forget that your salvation is a free gift, then you probably won't get tripped up on this point yourself.

Key Thought:

If you want to find God's will, you have to ask Him for it.

We have not because we ask not (James 4:2). Translation: *We don't have because we don't ask.*

Just like I wrote earlier in this book about the perversion of the spirit of giving, I also believe that many Christians take this verse out of context and twist it to mean something like: *"You can ask God for million dollars and He will give it to you if you ask for it by faith."* How ridiculous! This isn't faith in action; this is panhandling God. Yes, if God wants you to have a million dollars, then He will deliver it to you, but why are you asking for it? Why are you asking our spiritual Father for worldly things? Wouldn't you be much better off if you asked God to reveal His *will* to you? That would really change your life for the better. The eternal consequences of a changed life grossly outweigh, and frankly don't even compare to, worldly riches.

I can't speak for you, but I can definitely speak for me and I say that I want whatever God thinks I need. Money is a tool, not a driving force, in my life. Yes, I want to be blessed, but I want to be blessed in such a way that I am drawn closer to God, not just bankrolled by Him. If he gives us something that makes us less dependent upon Him, we will likely drift away from Him due to our lack of necessity. God is my Father in heaven, not my *sugar daddy*. We need to evaluate our motives behind our requests and get our hearts right. What are we seeking: God or stuff?

Just like we have to ask God for our salvation, we also have to ask Him to reveal His will to us. (Remember the verse from Chapter 1 about *ask, seek, knock*?) You have to seek His face for the answer. You have to pursue it. He wants you to find it because that means that He has the relationship with you that He has been waiting for. He will love you no matter what, but He wants to be close to you, not just love you unconditionally from a distance, a distance that you created yourself by turning away from Him.

As I sit here and meditate on the thought of seeking God's face, I thought of something interesting. Take the word "seeking" and put a space in the right place and you now have "see king." Do we stop and take the time to see our King? I am not trying to be corny here; I am being very serious. Our God should be the LORD, and "King" of our hearts and lives. If we aren't seeking Him, then we must not really think (see) that we need Him (King) that much.

> But seek first the kingdom of God and His righteousness, and all these things shall be added to you.
>
> Matthew 6:33—NKJV

Throughout this book, I have been boldly pointing you back to God's presence. I know that I have hit you in the mouth and upside-the-head with a few spiritual two-by-fours along the way. I mean no offense by anything that I have said, and I just can't say clearly enough to you that having a *relationship* with God is so much easier than you think. We all want a secret formula and a twelve-step plan for getting to know God, when, in fact, after our salvation, all we have to do is talk to Him and read about Him in His Word and live out what we say we believe. It is really that easy. You don't need my book to tell you that, but hey, I don't mind being a friendly reminder.

We must seek His face if we really want His presence in our lives and if we really want the relationship with Him that we claim to desire. Don't make the mistakes that I have made. Don't look back with a heavy heart and wish you could have done things differently. Learn your lessons now the easy way and don't get led into the trap where Satan deconstructs your life and you find yourself utterly broken, on your knees, destitute, crying out to God. Not that being at that point is a bad thing, but I highly recommend that you listen and experience God and draw close to Him out of want and need, not out of desperation or tragedy.

Key Thought:

Sorrow looks back. Worry looks around. Faith looks up.

Sorrow:

As the old saying goes, *"There is no future in the past."* However, the past has a lot to teach us if we are open to accepting our mistakes and learning from them. Many of us are living in the past. If you saw the movie *Napoleon Dynamite*, you know what I am taking about (Uncle Rico). We need to grow from our experiences and learn the lessons that we need to learn and then move on. While we are on the subject of movies, in the movie *Shawshank Redemption*, Red (Morgan Freeman) said something

254 • Dr. George Goodman

that I can't seem to forget. He said, *"You better get busy livin'... or get busy dyin'."* To me, this means, we need to move forward. If we stay where we are, we will deteriorate. We need to quit feeling sorry for ourselves and get busy living—living the life that God intended.

Worry:

For all of you who spend (waste) time worrying about stuff, read Matthew 6:25–34 (awesome biblical perspective on the subject of worry). Worry is a sign of how little we trust God and seek His face for our answers. "Cast your cares upon Him." Don't waste another day worrying about something you can't change! If you believe or want to believe that God is in control, then step back and let Him take the reins. I promise, He will do a much better job of leading us through life's ups and downs, and who knows, He might just teach us something valuable along the way. It beats having an ulcer.

Faith:

> Now faith is the substance of things hoped for, the evidence of things not seen.
>
> Hebrews 11:1—NKJV

We must have real faith to have a meaningful relationship with God. Real faith will cause us to live differently. Real faith will cause us to trust our LORD and allow us to face anything in life with a calm reassurance that God will never leave us or forsake us, no matter what situation we find ourselves in. Just because our eyes cannot see God's hand at work, doesn't mean that He is not working in our lives behind the scenes. If we could see everything through spiritual eyes, what would we need faith for

Faith connects us to God, conviction

anyway? We need faith because it is what connects us to God. It is the substance of our hope in Him. It is by our faith that we come into a relationship with Him and continue to build on that relationship. Our life is not dictated by random chance, luck, or any other force. Our life is in God's hands. He knows our path and our destiny. We must remember that our time on this earth, in this physical shell, is temporary; it is but a vapor in the expanse of all eternity.

> Do not let any unwholesome talk come out of your mouths, but only what is helpful for building others up according to their needs, that it may benefit those who listen.
>
> Ephesians 4:29—NIV

I want to talk about something that I personally feel a strong conviction about. I believe that where God exists, there can be no room for words like *"luck"* or *"chance."* To me, these words are unwholesome in that they undermine God's sovereignty. As disciples of Christ, we absolutely cannot think that there is really such a thing as *luck*. I personally don't think we should use the word *"luck"* or *"lucky"* because it implies that God is not in control. How can we be seeking God's face if we are using words like *"luck"* or *"chance"*? These words steal His glory by not giving Him credit because we are insisting that the good things that occur in our lives did not come from Him. What a slap in the face to God!

Do we really believe that God is in control? If we do, we better *think* that way, *talk* that way, and *act* that way. The Bible says that as a man thinks in his heart, so is he (Proverbs 23:7). Let me put it this way: we subscribe to the thoughts, "Garbage in ... garbage out," and "You are what you eat." Well, what about the thought that "You are what you *think*"?

Key Thought:

Do your words and actions communicate to others that you really believe in God and trust Him to meet your every need?

If you truly want to find God's will, then you need to get your thinking in line with His character. God is sovereign. He is our supreme ruler. He has ultimate power. In this context, I believe that the concepts of *luck* or *chance* are offensive to God. What we need more of is real faith—the kind that moves mountains in our lives. What we need less of is luck, chance, fortune cookies, fortune tellers, astrology signs, astrological predictions, palm readers, tarot cards, "psychics," or anything else that distracts us from truly knowing and trusting God to provide for our needs. Think about what this paragraph has to say, pray about it and ask God to show you the truth and then make the change to your words and thoughts to conform to the knowledge of who God really is. This is part of the renewing of your mind that comes from being conformed into the image of Christ.

My good friend Ken was previously diagnosed with cancer. As anyone who is diagnosed with cancer will tell you, it changed his life, what he thought about life, and what he thought about the future. When Ken found out that I was writing a book about finding God's will, he asked me to include his thoughts on what he personally experienced while battling his cancer because, during his fight, he wrestled with many potentially faith-shattering emotions and wanted to share his thoughts with anyone who finds themselves in a condition of doubting God's purpose, plan, or His love for us.

As many cancer patients will tell you, Ken went through a period of being angry with God, as if by allowing him to have cancer, God let him down in some way. He even doubted God's very existence. Ken communicated to me that he felt trapped in a sick body and that he had an overwhelming sense of loneliness and abandonment. Some of the questions he asked God during that time included, *"Why does my prayer not bring healing?"* and *"What is the lesson if I live?"* It was a very trying time for Ken, and it made him bitter for a time, but ultimately he realized that God is in control and he eventually made peace with God.

Most people who face adversity often feel forsaken and ask questions like, *"Why me? Why did God allow this to happen to me?"* I will not pretend to understand God's methods, nor will I explain them away, but I will tell you that God's ways are higher than our ways (Isaiah 55:9) and He has a purpose for everything He does and we will not completely understand His reasoning this side of heaven. Regardless of how things may seem, He is actually doing a work in us by allowing these things to happen.

> Whereas you do not know what will happen tomorrow. For what is your life? It is even a vapor that appears for a little time and then vanishes away.
>
> James 4:14—NKJV

We all lose sight that this life is just a vapor. This life is boot camp for eternity. If we will keep this perspective and not lose sight that God is in the business of ...
• Building our character
• Perfecting our holiness
• Conforming us into the image of His son

... then we will be better able to face life's adversities with an eternal perspective.

Key Thought:

Where God guides, God provides.

A few months ago, I called my attorney, David, to ask him a legal question. David is a Christian man whom I consider to be a friend. During our conversation, David announced to me that he was leaving his practice to go to seminary. I was intrigued by the news and, I must say, I was very happy for him. He told me that for years he has believed that God was leading him into ministry (I related to his story because, for years, I have had the same thoughts that God has been leading me into ministry as well). Since college he had this notion, but at that time he decided to go to law school instead. After many years of practicing law and dealing with the nagging thought that he was supposed to be doing something different (seminary), he decided that it was time to act upon God's calling on his life.

Yesterday, I called him to see how he was doing. He told me that he was about two hours away from attending his first semi-nary class that night. We had not spoken since our conversation a few months ago. I thought to myself, "*How cool is that?*" The timing of my phone call was amazing to me, but then again, I remember that God's timing is always right on target. David said that his first class was about *hermeneutics*. If you remember, earlier in Chapter 2, we discussed this subject. Hermeneutics is the study of biblical interpretation (I really like this subject, in case you didn't know). I was so excited for him and, I dare say, a little jealous that he was embarking on this exciting new journey in his life. Just like God guided me to write a book, God guided David to attend seminary. It is so true ... where God guides, God provides.

> Rejoice always, pray without ceasing, in everything give thanks; for this is the will of God in Christ Jesus for you.
>
> 1 Thessalonians 5:16–18—NKJV

We have mentioned the *"good, pleasing, and perfect will"* of God throughout this book, but here is another facet to discovering it. Rejoice always! Pray continuously! Be thankful for everything! Seems simple doesn't it? If we would just get in the Word and read it for ourselves, we will learn so much more about God. The beauty of it all is that we will never stop learning about God's nature and character. As finite beings trying to learn about an infinite being, we are at a disadvantage, but not really. It just means that we will always be able to grow closer and grow deeper in our relationship with Him. That is amazing to me. It is too good for words!

> Then he said to them all: "If anyone would come after me, he must deny himself and take up his cross daily and follow me. For whoever wants to save his life will lose it, but whoever loses his life for me will save it. What good is it for a man to gain the whole world, and yet lose or forfeit his very self?"
>
> Luke 9:23–25—NIV

260 • Dr. George Goodman

Other translations say forfeit your "soul." Although they mean the same thing, the thought of forfeiting your soul just sounds so much more dangerous to me. Being a disciple means that we spend our time following our LORD, not leading. To follow someone, we are forced to sacrifice our personal agenda. If we deny ourselves and follow Him, we will gain our life eternally. If we look at this passage from an eternal and spiritual perspective and not just a temporal perspective, it makes much more sense to us. Denying ourselves means that we surrender our will and crucify our flesh (not literally, but figuratively it means that we live by the leading of the Holy Spirit—not live a life driven by our fleshly desires). This takes complete trust in Him and His plan for us. This is where our faith helps us.

When we begin to trust Him completely, we acknowledge His Lordship. At this point, the outcry of our heart is to pray that His will be done in our lives.

Most of us have heard this next passage numerous times and have it memorized in a particular translation. Don't get hung up on the translation of the following scriptures. I listed them here in the NIV translation, because most of this book references NIV. The specific translation chosen here is not what is important, but rather the content. I am asking you to just read it and hear its content, and not be swayed to just repeat it in your head, as you would normally, if you already have it memorized. (Remember—content, not translation!)

> This, then, is how you should pray: 'Our Father in heaven, hallowed be your name, your kingdom come, your will be done on earth as it is in heaven. Give us today our daily bread. Forgive us our debts, as we also have forgiven our debtors. And lead us not into temptation, but deliver us from the evil one.
>
> Matthew 6:9–13—NIV

I love that verse 9 says this is "how you should pray." The funny thing is that we hear the LORD's *Prayer*, but we seldom hear the preface to it (the beginning of verse 9). To me, I think this is one of, if not *the* best example of "how" to pray. Notice that I said, *how* to pray, not *what* to pray. There is a *big* difference. When I pray the LORD's Prayer, I try to personalize it. I try to pray everything that it communicates in its content, but in my own words. I want my prayers to be personal and relational. I don't want to get lazy and just brainlessly regurgitate a memorized prayer. I want my heart to connect with God when I pray and I want to focus on what He means to me.

It is interesting to note that in one of the verses that precede the LORD's Prayer (verse 7); it talks about *"vain"* and *"repetitious"* prayers. Some people think of the word "vain" as conceited, but in this instance *"vain"* means *"useless; producing no result."* Wow! Let that soak in. When I think that my prayers could be repetitious and "useless" (producing no result), it really makes me think about how my prayers are sent, received, answered, etc.

Questions:

What is required on our part to have assurance that our prayers are effective?

How do we make sure that our prayers are not just vain and repetitious?

The prayer of a righteous man is powerful and effective.

James 5:16—NIV

Key Thought:

The key to us having a prayer life that is effective and powerful (producing life-changing results) is our righteousness!

Question:

Can you be righteous if your heart is not in the right place?

Yes, we have Christ's righteousness imputed to us when we come into a relationship with our LORD, but what I am asking is this: *Can we really expect our prayers to be effective and powerful when our actions contradict our Christian beliefs and our hearts are not inclined to God?* I have a hard time believing that when our hearts are not inclined to God, our prayers are anything more than just vain, repetitious "noise." Frankly, the thought of this scares me. It should scare you too. I want to know that my prayers are heard ... and answered!

I especially don't want the LORD's Prayer to lose its potency to me. That is why I reword it and expound on it when I am praying it to God. I never want it to be simply repetitious. No matter how you look at it, I just believe that God wants to hear what is in my heart at all times, not what is memorized in my head. I think He is more delighted and impressed when He sees my heart connected to Him, rather than my mind regurgitating a "pre-recorded message" as if "the lights are on, but nobody's home."

> Choose for yourselves this day whom you will serve ... as for me and my household, we will serve the LORD.
>
> Joshua 24:15—NIV

This verse is familiar to many of us, but I wonder as I read it, how many of us make this proclamation in our hearts? How many of us will choose God today, because we have an immediate need, and then tomorrow, choose our own selfish plans, because we perceive no need to seek God with the mundane, everyday things in life that we think we can handle for ourselves? Read this verse again, hopefully for the "first" time. Look at the key words and let them sink into your heart: "choose for yourselves this day whom you will serve ... *as for me and my household, we will serve the* LORD."

> "No one can serve two masters. Either he will hate the one and love the other, or he will be devoted to the one and despise the other. You cannot serve both God and Money."
>
> Matthew 6:24—NIV

It is interesting to me as I write this, that just a few verses after the LORD's Prayer in Matthew 6:9–13 (which we just discussed), comes verse 24 about serving two masters. Although this verse references the differences of serving God or serving money (which we will talk about shortly), the concept is true of whether we serve God or serve ourselves. Think of the verse this way:

Key Thought:

No one can serve two masters. You cannot serve both God and yourself.

I pray that you receive the truth of this message: We make a choice every day of our lives to seek God and serve Him or live for ourselves. Either He is our master (LORD and Savior), or we are our own master—which makes us the owner of a stubborn, hardened, prideful heart. Like the old NFL film commentator would say, *"You make the call."* It is your choice. I encourage you to seek God with your whole heart. Let me put it this way: *As for me and my house, we will serve* ... (you get the picture).

In Matthew 6:24, it states that you cannot serve God and money. I also wanted to reference another couple of verses that speak about money:

> For the love of money is a root of all kinds of evil. Some people, eager for money, have wandered from the faith and pierced themselves with many griefs.
>
> 1 Timothy 6:10—NIV

> Keep your lives free from the love of money and be content with what you have ...
>
> Hebrews 13:5—NIV

Money, in and of itself, is not evil, but the *"love of money"* is evil. It is interesting to note that there are literally hundreds of references in the Bible about money, finances, investing, material possessions, etc. Why do you think this is? Maybe God thinks that we should really listen to what He is saying to us about money and how we are to handle our finances. If it is mentioned that many times, then obviously, it is important that we learn God's perspective on how we handle money.

Remember the following verse:

> For where your treasure is, there your heart will be also.

> Matthew 6:21—NIV

(This verse is also found in Luke 12:34.)

What is it that you treasure? Do you treasure your relationship with God more than you treasure your stuff (money, possessions, etc.)? If your heart is in your material possessions (in your wallet, jewelry cabinet, bank account, closet, or driveway), you are in for trouble. If your heart is inclined to God, then you have in your possession the most valuable treasure in all the world. When your heart is inclined to God, it makes it easier to open up and give back to Him what truly belongs to Him anyway.

> "Bring the whole tithe into the storehouse, that there may be food in my house. Test me in this," says the LORD Almighty, "and see if I will not throw open the floodgates of heaven and pour out so much blessing that you will not have room enough for it."

> Malachi 3:10—NIV

For many believers, tithing is a foreign concept—not in the sense that we have never heard about it before, but foreign in the sense that we don't all do it like we are supposed to. We may give some of our income to God, but are we doing what we are asked to do?

The word "tithe" means one-tenth. Tithing is giving a tenth of our income (also known as *"first fruits"*) back to God.

Imagine if the body of Christ really gave 10 percent of our incomes to God ...

- Our churches would be full of the most blessed people on the planet.
- God's supernatural blessings would be evident in all our lives.
- The ability of the church to reach out to our world would be unparalleled.
- This world would change.
- We would change.
- People's opinions of Christianity would change.
- Best of all, lives would change ... eternally.

When we finally come to the conclusion that everything we have is a gift from God, we will begin to evaluate our money and our possessions differently. Giving 10 percent of our income back to God as our *"tithe"* is biblical. As Christians, we do this out of obedience because we want God's best for our lives.

Many Christians get confused about the difference between tithes and offerings. An offering is when we give above and beyond our tithe. We give generously as God instructs us to do so. As we mature in our faith, we learn that being able to give above and beyond our tithe is one of the greatest blessings. As we seek God, He will impress upon us how we are to give. The best part is, you can never out-give God.

The Whole Tithe ...

Think about what Malachi 3:10 means when it says the whole tithe. It doesn't say "part" of the tithe; it says "the whole tithe"—all of it. It is exceedingly important to note that nowhere else in the Bible does God say, *"Test me in this."* Again, I will say that when God blesses us because of our obedience, He will do so in a manner that He sees fit. He may choose to bless us with safety, security, peace, or some other blessing like health, favor, joy, wisdom, or discernment. He may choose to bless us financially. Who knows? The important thing is that He is going to bless us in a miraculous way when we give *"the whole tithe."* Somehow, we will be much better off for having been obedient to His instruction. As disciples, we need to covet only what He thinks is best for us.

We don't tithe to receive financial gain as if we were investing. We tithe as an act of worship, out of obedience and we give cheerfully with a happy heart; ready to serve and be used by God to do His will. Somewhere along the way, God will open the *"floodgates"* and supernaturally shower us with whatever it is that He thinks we truly need for us to become even more deeply committed to Him. The Bible says that He will give us the desires of our hearts. The desire of my heart is to be in a close relationship with Him. I question anyone whose desire is for financial gain. If that is the desire of your heart, I think you are missing the point altogether. Our faith is about relationship, not tithing to plant money seeds that will grow into money trees.

Where our financial blessings come in is when we live our lives and manage our money according to God's financial principles. He wants us to be good stewards of His resources. He will bless us when we operate according to His sound financial principles. No, we probably won't get rich quick, but we will learn valuable lessons about Him, as well as ourselves, along the way. In the end, it all belongs to Him anyway.

> For every animal of the forest is mine, and the cattle on a thousand hills.
>
> Psalms 50.10—NIV

I included this verse because when I think about everything belonging to God, I always think of this verse. The symbolism of God owning the cattle on a thousand hills, to me, means that everything is actually His and that He just allows us to manage His resources. He entrusts us by giving us a lot of responsibility. He wants to see how we will manage the resources that He has placed in our hands.

Tithing is just one aspect of our faith where we are called to manage resources that we have been given. How we manage our time is also important. With the time we have, are we reading and studying His Word? Are we serving in some capacity in our churches? Are we ministering or witnessing to others? There are so many other ways that we serve our LORD as we follow Him. The important thing is that we have our hearts in the right place. We need to maintain our humility.

> Better is one day in your courts than a thousand elsewhere; I would rather be a doorkeeper in the house of my God than dwell in the tents of the wicked. For the LORD God is a sun and shield; the LORD bestows favor and honor; no good thing does he withhold from those whose walk is blameless. O LORD Almighty, blessed is the man who trusts in you.
>
> Psalms 84:10–12—NIV

What a great verse! I interpret verse 10 to say, *"I would rather have a lowly position in God's house than live like royalty with ungodly people."* Only a truly humble person could have this perspective. When we make it our mission to serve God and live a life that is obedient to Him, He will honor us and bless us in ways that we can't imagine. Once again, it is an attitude of the heart.

In Chapter 3, we mentioned that in the Jewish view, study

is the highest form of worship. Think about the next verse with this thought in mind.

 I have hidden your word in my heart that I might not sin against you.

Psalms 119:11—NIV

As we read and study God's Word, we hide it in our hearts. Through reading and studying God's Word, we learn more about God. The more we know about God, the more His wisdom permeates our lives. If we never seek wisdom, then we keep making the same mistakes over and over again. I had a boss that used to say that the definition of insanity was doing the same thing over and over while expecting a different result. If we insist on watching TV or surfing the web or finding some other means of successfully wasting our time and never find time to read God's Word and read books about our faith, relationships, finances, etc., then we shouldn't be so surprised when we fail in our faith, marriages, finances, etc. What an amazing thing that our enemy has done to distract us from feeding at God's table and getting His very best for us. Instead, we seem content to be lured into a trance and led away from the road that leads us home.

For the word of God is living and active. Sharper than any double-edged sword, it penetrates even to dividing soul and spirit, joints and marrow; it judges the thought and attitudes of the heart. Nothing in all creation is hidden from God's sight. Everything is uncovered and laid bare before the eyes of him to whom we must give account.

Hebrews 4:12–13—NIV

What a powerful verse. The Word of God is *"living and active."*

It is sharper than any sword. It penetrates and divides—soul from spirit—joints from marrow. It judges the heart's thoughts and attitudes. The more we read it, study it, learn it, and apply it, the more it sheds light on our personal areas of darkness.

> It is not good to have zeal without knowledge, nor be hasty and miss the way.
>
> Proverbs 19:2—NIV

This verse makes me think of two things:
- Enthusiasm (zeal) without wisdom (knowledge) is like a loaded gun with no aim.
- When we get in a hurry, we make mistakes.

Christ prepared for thirty years for a three-year ministry. It took ten times longer for Jesus to prepare for His ministry than it did for Him to live out His ministry. Jesus had zeal for the task at hand, but He also had the knowledge to back it up. He was patient—God showed Him the way.

> Being confident of this, that he who began a good work in you will carry it on to completion until the day of Christ Jesus.
>
> Philippians 1:6—NIV

> Be still and know that I am God.
>
> Psalms 46:10—NIV

Be *still* ... Hmm ...
Be still and *know* ... Hmm ...

Be still and know that ... *He is God* ... Hmm ... (Meditate on this for a moment.)

Question:

Why do we need to be still?

Is there a lesson to be learned here? Ask yourself the following questions:

- Why is it so hard for us to be still?
- Why is silence so hard for us to deal with?
- Does our being still (physically, emotionally, and spiritually) somehow teach us more about God?
- Could it be that God wants the distractions around us to fade away so we can get some quiet time together with Him? (I believe this to be true because we serve a relational God. He wants to spend time with us, but He wants us to make time for Him.)

I have heard of people praying in their closets to get alone with God. My brother Bryan used to get in his closet when we were kids so that he could pray (we came from a family of six kids, so alone time and quiet time were in short supply). I still remember people making fun of him for doing this, but I have to be honest, to this day, I still remember seeing him sitting on the floor in his closet when we would open the door to check on him. I have thought back on this many times and smiled because I bet God was smiling upon Bryan because of his desire and commitment to find a place to get alone and spend time with Him. I am really proud of Bryan for doing this. His heart was in the right place, and his actions to this day still speak to me.

Question:

When was the last time that you were really alone with God?

The act of finding a quiet, solitary place to seek God's face is so simple, yet profoundly important to our relationship with Him.

Key Thought:

When we do hear from God, it will generally come in the form of a revelation.

God will reveal His truth to you. What I mean is this: anything that you believe is from God, will *always*, without exception, line up with God's Word. The Bible says that God is the same yesterday, today, and forever; therefore, what was truth in the past is truth now, and that same truth will always be true. God's Word (truth) is eternally true. I say all this to refute the claims of some well-meaning Christians that I have heard say things that they claim came from God, yet did not line up with the Word of God—the final arbitrator of truth. If someone says God told them to do something that is directly opposite the truth of the Word, then I must say that that person is wrong! They may be sincere, but they are still totally wrong.

Key Thought:

God will never lead you to do something that violates His Word.

This is so important! It is another reason to get into His Word so that you will "know the truth," because "the truth will set you free." Learning truth will lead to the development of discernment. Don't forget, we have an enemy that would love to steal our testimony because he got us to do things in "God's name" that were nothing but lies from the pits of hell.

Let's get back to quiet time. Think about it: Why is it so hard to get away from everything, be still, and listen for the voice of God? Are we too busy for God? If actions really do speak louder than words, our actions often suggest that we are too busy for God.

Look at the life of Jesus. We see so many verses that show that Jesus regularly spent time alone talking with God. A great example that is familiar to us is when Jesus prayed in the Garden of Gethsemane. Another example can be found in the Gospel of Luke:

> Jesus often withdrew to lonely places and prayed.
>
> Luke 5:16—NIV

If we would follow Christ's example and get away to pray, we would grow in our relationship with Him. We have all heard about the "still, small voice" that most people call our "con-

274 • Dr. George Goodman

science," but is that still, small voice something more? In 1 Kings 19, we read about this very subject.

God told the prophet Elijah to go stand on the mountain and wait for Him:

> The LORD said, "Go out and stand on the mountain in the presence of the LORD, for the LORD is about to pass by." Then a great and powerful wind tore the mountains apart and shattered the rocks before the LORD, but the LORD was not in the wind. After the wind there was an earthquake, but the LORD was not in the earthquake. After the earthquake came a fire, but the LORD was not in the fire. And after the fire came a gentle whisper.
>
> 1 Kings 19:11–12—NIV

The LORD was not in the wind ...
The LORD was not in the earthquake ...
The LORD was not in the fire ...
The LORD was in the calmness that followed; He showed up in the form of a gentle whisper.

What amazes me about this passage is that, despite the fact that we imagine God showing up in a powerful, thunderous, earth-shaking way, He chose to show up in a way that confounds us. He doesn't make a grand entrance with "pomp and circumstance," but rather, He generally shows up in the moments of stillness, when everything around us is quiet. What a beautiful picture! God is not associated with chaos; instead, He is associated with peace. How appropriate. (It is interesting to note that in Revelation 9:11, Satan is referred to as the *Destroyer*, whereas in Isaiah 9:6, Jesus is referred to as the *Prince of Peace*.)

One night, a few months ago, my friend John and I sat down at his house to watch a video named *Noise*. I want to share some of the material from this video with you because I feel that it beautifully illustrates some truths that I think every Christian should hear.

Think about the following statements:

- Why is talking so much easier than listening?
- Is there a connection between the amount of noise in our lives and our inability to hear God?
- Does my schedule, my time, my life look like that of a person who wants to hear God's voice?
- Is it possible that you have been searching for God in the winds, the earthquakes, and fires, and He is waiting to speak with you in the silence?

These are great questions! Consider how they apply to your life and your relationship with God.

Another great thought that I got from this video is this: *How much time do we spend in complete silence* (no TV, radio, computer, or other distraction)? The truth is, probably very little. I believe that some of us are actually uncomfortable being in total silence. Sometimes we turn things on around us just to create background noise. Why? Is this our insecurity? Is this a tool that Satan uses to distract us and keep us from meeting with God and hearing from Him? Maybe we should allow ourselves more quiet time to meet with God and further develop our relationship with Him. Don't you agree?

Do you feel like God is nowhere in sight? Think again. If anyone has moved, it is us. God is right where He has always been. If we want to hear His voice, we need to get rid of the things that keep us from meeting with Him and hearing from Him. If we are not in a quiet, solitary place, being still and seeking His face, we may miss hearing from Him because we have too much "noise" going on around us. Our "noise" can come in the form of many things, most of which we can control. There is auditory noise, visual noise, emotional noise, and so on. Regardless of whatever it is, we need to turn it off, put it away or step away from it so that we can hear from God in the stillness. If we find a way to turn down everything else and focus on God, we would be more likely to hear from Him.

I don't know about you, but I sincerely wish that God's voice was more audible in my life. I admit that there are times that I don't spend as much time with Him as I should, but I recognize that and I know that what I am saying here, I am saying to myself as much as to anyone else. Working two jobs, raising four children, trying to be a good husband, writing a book, and everything else that I find myself doing, I am as guilty as anyone when it comes to quiet time alone with God. My prayer is that I would make more time to build my relationship with my LORD and Savior. My hearts desire is to seek His face.

I hope that you will make more time to meet with Him and "Seek His Face" for yourself.

Chapter 10

the importance of accountability

As iron sharpens iron, so one man sharpens another.

Proverbs 27:17—NIV

Accountability. What does this mean to the Christ follower? To understand the importance of this concept as it applies to our Christian walk, we must look to its root meaning. Think of it this way: *the ability to account*, or *the ability to give an account.* To give an account, there must be someone who is accountable. The definition of accountable is as follows:[13]

Accountable—(of a person, organization, or institution) required or expected to justify actions or decisions; responsible.

We, as members of the human race, are all accountable to God. As the definition says, we are required *and* expected to justify our actions *and* decisions; we are to be responsible. We, as believers, are called to live a life that is holy and pleasing to Him. We are to confess our sins to Him so that we may receive His forgiveness and be cleansed, so that we may approach a Holy God with freedom and confidence (Ephesians 3:12). Most Christians can grasp the concepts of confession and forgiveness. What many Christians don't grasp, or do not completely understand the value of, is the importance of having another Christian person in our lives that we can talk to about our experiences and struggles; someone who can hold us accountable on a personal, relational level. This accountability relationship is in no way to supersede our relationship with God, but rather, it is to be used as an adjunct means of growing spiritually through the process of "iron sharpening iron."

> The way of a fool seems right to him, but a wise man listens to advice.
>
> Proverbs 12:15—NIV

There is a seemingly innate tendency in many of us to feel like we can make it on our own. We may think that we don't need anyone else's help, especially when it comes to listening to their advice. Whether it is the proverbial statements like, *"I don't need any instructions—I know how to do it,"* or *"I don't need directions— I know how to get there,"* our list of excuses to justify our self-sufficiency goes on and on for miles. As if it were a good thing, we tend to pride ourselves in the fact that we have the resilience to weather most of life's storms on our own.

First of all, the Bible is clear on what God thinks about pride: He doesn't like it. In Proverbs 16:18, the Bible specifically tells us that *"pride goes before destruction."* What is pride? The definition of pride, as it relates to the Christian experience, is as follows:[14]

Pride—(1) A feeling or deep pleasure or satisfaction derived from one's own achievements; (2) the quality of having an excessively high opinion of oneself or one's importance.

The latter definition could easily be called the "sin of pride." Based on these definitions alone, we should be able to clearly see why God frowns upon our having a prideful attitude or outlook. The Bible says that God is a jealous God. He created us to be dependent upon Him and His sufficiency alone. When we think we have all the answers, we stop asking for help, and then we are headed for "destruction." At the very least, we will fail to live up to our potential in our spiritual lives because our focus is not on God, but on ourselves.

> I have fought the good fight, I have finished the race, I have kept the faith.
>
> 2 Timothy 4:7—NIV

The importance of finding an accountability partner cannot be overemphasized. To put it as an overtly simple thought, we need an accountability partner in our lives for the purpose of holding us accountable for our thoughts and actions. We also need an accountability partner to help us in our times of weakness or failure, with a consistent encouragement to *"keep fighting the good fight"* and *"keep the faith."*

We need to know that someone who knows us and cares for us is lovingly looking over our shoulders for our own good. We need to be able to answer to this person when our actions don't line up to our professed faith, and we need to be able to take constructive criticism from this person when it is offered. This is how spiritual growth occurs and how we develop godly wisdom.

Ideally, our accountability partner should be someone who is the same gender and who is willing to share their experience and knowledge of the truths of God's Word as it applies to everyday life, with all its struggles and challenges. Your accountability partner should be someone who is able to point you back to God at every turn, so they can help you stay on the straight and narrow path.

Key Thought:

If love is blind, then friendship is clairvoyant.

For the record, my accountability partner is my friend John. I owe an enormous debt of gratitude to John for his consistency with me during one of the most trying times of my life. I literally do not know how I would have made it through that long, dark valley in my life without the encouragement and support that John delivered on a consistent basis. He constantly redirected me to see God's hand at work in my life. Talk about a *"friend who sticks closer than a brother"* (Proverbs 18:24); John was that friend to me when I needed it most. There were many days that he patiently listened to me ramble on about the hardships in my life, and there were days that he figuratively punched me in the mouth to get my attention and directed me back to focusing on God's grace and sufficiency. He never allowed me to lose sight of what God was trying to do in my life. During that time, I struggled with the classic *"Why me?"* thought process, rather than seeing that God was preparing me for much more than I was able to understand at that time. Praise be to God for delivering me through that time and bringing me to such a time as this. My trial experience was instrumental in inspiring me to start writing this book. I thank God for allowing me to experience so much pain, in order for me to grow enough to be able to share my faith with others and encourage my brothers and sisters in Christ.

John and I are fortunate to have a wonderful church home. It is a blessing that we get to attend one of the fastest growing churches in the country. As I have mentioned previously, our church's mission statement is *Leading people to become fully devoted followers of Christ.* An accountability relationship should accomplish the same purpose. If we are fully devoted, then we should be following Christ and giving leadership (godly counsel) to others.

Another saying at our church is *God is good, all the time; and all the time, God is good.* I am here to tell you, there are times when you will question the goodness of God. It is during these times that having an accountability partner in your life helps you remember the goodness of God because sometimes we all lose focus of God's nature, especially His goodness. It is our own nearsightedness that keeps us from seeing the big picture, until God so graciously allows us to experience one of those mountaintop moments when we get a glimpse of what He has been up to all along. It is during these times that our faith is bolstered and we are reminded that we need to repent for not being more trusting in His infinite wisdom. It is also during these times that we learn to thank Him for allowing us to walk through those long, dark valleys where it seemed that He was nowhere in sight. He promised that He would never leave us, nor forsake us (Joshua 1:5). We need to learn to take Him at His Word and exhibit child-like faith and just accept what He says at face value. Oh, if we could just learn to consistently do that, we would be all the wiser for it!

282 • Dr. George Goodman

> For this reason, since the day we heard about you, we have
> not stopped praying for you and asking God to fill you with
> the knowledge of his will through all spiritual wisdom and
> understanding.
>
> Colossians 1:9—NIV

This verse says that we can pray for others and ask God to reveal
(fill you with the knowledge) to you His will (His *good, pleasing, and perfect will*) through all spiritual wisdom and understanding. To me, in an accountability relationship, I can not only
pray that God would reveal His will to me, but I also have the
freedom to pray that God would reveal His will to my accountability partner, or anyone else for that matter who is seeking "His
will through all spiritual wisdom and understanding." Seeking
Him this way could be through reading His Word, praying, or
through *"sharpening iron!"* How awesome is that!

> Therefore confess your sins to each other and pray for each
> other so that you may be healed. The prayer of a righteous
> man is powerful and effective.
>
> James 5:16—NIV

The first part of this verse says that we are to confess our sins to
each another and pray for each another so that we can be healed.
This can be healing of all types (emotional, physical, relational,
etc.). In an accountability relationship, this is so important. We
need to maintain this kind of openness, transparency, and willingness so that we can truly help each other grow toward maturity. Remember though, just like we discussed the second part of
this verse in Chapter 9, this verse doesn't say that the prayer of
a *lukewarm* Christian is powerful and effective; it says that the
prayer of the *righteous* man (or woman) is powerful and effec-

tive. We need to have an effective and powerful prayer life if we are going to be the Christians that we are called to be and the accountability partners that we were called to be.

Question:

Do you deeply desire to have a powerful and effective prayer life?

I know I do. If you want to know that God hears *and* answers your prayers, then I suggest that you concentrate on being righteous. I didn't say *pious*; I said *righteous*. There is a big difference, a night and day difference. You could say, the difference between *relationship* and *religion*. (Hmmm ... maybe he's on to something here ... this sounds familiar.)

There are many other obvious benefits of being an accountability partner, but the knowing that you can pray for each other (and seek God together for answers to life's toughest questions) is potent. When I know that someone is praying for me and interceding with God on my behalf, it speaks volumes to me. Just to know that someone out there cares enough about you to go to God on their knees and stand against the powers of hell and plead with God for your deepest needs to be met should communicate unfathomable, agape-like love to you.

> If we confess our sins, he is faithful and just and will forgive
> us our sins and purify us from all unrighteousness.
>
> 1 John 1:9—NIV

An accountability partnership is like a fraternal bond within the Christian brotherhood (without the secret handshake). Ideally, there is a mutual understanding between the parties that what is discussed in private, stays in private.

Key Thought:

To have a friend, you must be a friend.

Openness works best when trust is in place. It is so much more than just bearing your soul. It is the ability to fully express your deepest questions, fears, doubts, and needs, in an atmosphere that is not condemning or judgmental. When we are so deep in our own weeds, we generally can't see the forest for the trees. Having a relationship where your respected friend can tell you using "straight talk" what is going on and what God has to say about it, can be quite useful and extremely enlightening. We must be open enough and mature enough to really listen and accept constructive criticism and not resent our friend (accountability partner) for loving us enough to "say it like it is."

I really enjoy lecturing. Fortunately, I have had the opportunity to lecture within my profession on the state, national, and international levels, and outside my profession I have had the opportunity to speak at various civic events and college graduations. Once, before a lecture to a large group of physicians at a national meeting, I was experiencing some anxiety about standing in front of my peers on a national stage. My anxiety stemmed from the fact that this lecture was to be given to a large group of physicians from all over the country who specialized in the same field as I do. Though deep down I knew better, I had the feel-

ing that I was going to get up in front of a group of people who already knew the material I was going to present. I felt as if I could teach them nothing. I told my good friend Paul about this feeling and he gave me some very helpful advice. Paul is a very well known speaker and author in my profession and is a devoted Christian man (he also happens to be the person who wrote the foreword to this book). Paul is someone I deeply respect. When I expressed to Paul that I had some anxiety about the upcoming lecture, he said something to me that I will never forget.
He said ...

> George, you know more about the subject that you are presenting than probably 95 percent of your audience, but you must remember that 100 percent of them want to see you do well up there.

Prior to Paul's comments, I had been focused on how intimidating a thought it was to be lecturing to this kind of group and at this level, but with Paul's wise words of counsel, I began to look at my situation very differently. Needless to say, the lecture went off without a hitch, and I felt liberated after I walked away from the podium that day. I have never since been hindered by that anxiety before a lecture, thanks to another man's wisdom and perspective. Sometimes when we face our fears, we realize that we need not be so swayed by discouraging thoughts. God is always with us. We all need a reminder of this simple truth from time to time.

Recently, I was asked to lecture to another group of physicians; this time, I was scheduled to speak right before an internationally known and revered surgeon. In his respective field, he is easily one of the top surgeons in the world. Because of where we each were placed on the schedule, I knew that he was going to be in the audience listening to me, prior to stepping to the podium himself. At first glance, when I originally saw the schedule, I felt that twinge of anxiety because I was scheduled to lecture on a topic in which I knew that this surgeon was the expert. Literally, he had written the book on it.

To make a long story short, in my very next thought, I remember what my friend Paul said to me. It is relationships like the one that I have with Paul that continue to bless my life and my walk with the LORD. Not only did the lecture go well, but later, that same surgeon walked up to me and told me how well he thought I had done. He said he was surprised and impressed that I knew so much about that subject. Considering the source, those words of encouragement meant a lot to me. Again, I thank friends like Paul for giving people in their life, like me, words that encourage.

Sometimes I think we underestimate the value of encouragement. We all need to impart God's grace to others more often, especially through our spoken words. We never know that when we say kind, encouraging words to someone, it may leave a lasting mark that continues to bless that person for years to come. Our words have the ability to speak life into someone who may be riddled with doubt, fear, or insecurity. God can use our words to heal. We must not forget the potency of our encouragement.

> Wisdom is supreme; therefore get wisdom.
> Though it cost all you have, get understanding.
>
> Proverbs 4:7—NIV

> If any of you lacks wisdom, he should ask God, who gives generously to all without finding fault, and it will be given to him.
>
> James 1:5—NIV

If we ask God for wisdom, He promises us He will give it to us. It may come as an instantaneous revelation through the power of the Holy Spirit bearing witness with our spirit, or more likely, it may come through experiences that God will allow us to learn by. If we make it a point to concentrate on looking for the lesson in all things, we will grow in wisdom and God will reveal His truths to us through our circumstances. It takes a conscious decision to scrutinize the lessons we learn, looking for truth above all else. If we will retain an openness to seek wisdom and learn from our mistakes, we will find it easier to view the world with optimism, and not pessimism. We will be better (and wiser) for it.

> The fear of the LORD is the beginning of knowledge, but fools despise wisdom and discipline.
>
> Proverbs 1:7—NIV

> How can men be wise? The only way to begin is by reverence for God. For growth in wisdom comes from obeying his laws. Praise his name forever.
>
> Psalms 111:10—TLB

Fear of the LORD (reverential, respectful fear) is the beginning of wisdom. If we really gave serious thought to the idea of how great and glorious our God is, we would have a healthier, more reverential fear of Him. It is not as much about fearing God as much as it is about revering and respecting Him. As a Christian, I try to have a healthy reverence and respect (fear) of God.

> The LORD God said, "It is not good for the man to be alone. I will make a helper suitable for him."
>
> Genesis 2:18—NIV

Obviously, Genesis 2:18 is discussing when God created Eve as a partner for Adam. I reference it here for the sole purpose of establishing that we are not always meant to *"go it alone."* We really need someone in our lives to hold us to a standard and be a companion to us. We need accountability in our lives because we cannot always see in ourselves what others can see in us, and we need to have a mirror held up to our face once in a while so that we can really evaluate who it is that we see in the mirror. If the reflection is revealing, then we need to thank God for allowing us the opportunity to grow and learn from it. We also need to thank God for putting someone in our life to show us where this growth needs to occur.

> My brothers, if one of you should wander from the truth and someone should bring him back, remember this: Whoever turns a sinner from the error of his way will save him from death and cover over a multitude of sins.
>
> James 5:19–20—NIV

As an accountability partner, we have the chance to help our brother or sister by standing with them through their struggles. We have the chance to encourage them as they face their trials and tribulations. We have the chance to pick them up when they fall, "walk the extra mile" with them (Matthew 5:41), and help them defend their faith during the most difficult times of their lives. We also get to help turn them away from going down the wrong path and help them to find the right path, the straight and narrow path that leads to life—abundant life. Far too many Christians wander down the wrong path and don't even realize it until they have fallen down and then find themselves utterly broken and in desperate need of help.

Two are better than one, because they have a good return for their work: If one falls down, his friend can help him up. But pity the man who falls and has no one to help him up! Though one may be overpowered, two can defend themselves. A cord of three strands is not quickly broken.

Ecclesiastes 4:9–10, 12—NIV

When we have a good accountability relationship, we have the peace and comfort of knowing that the "third strand" that binds us together with supernatural strength is the Spirit of God. He is our comforter and our counselor. He will never leave us, nor forsake us (Joshua 1:5).

If you don't already have someone in your life who fills this role for you, I strongly recommend that you seek out an accountability partner by seeking God and asking Him to provide this unique, special person for you. It is a commitment for both of you, and it is a very serious proposition. Pray, seek God, read His Word, fast ... do whatever it takes to make this connection, but be patient and wait upon the LORD to place the right person on your path.

But those who wait on the LORD
Shall renew their strength;
They shall mount up with wings like eagles,
They shall run and not be weary,
They shall walk and not faint.

Isaiah 40:31—NKJV

How could one man chase a thousand, or two put ten thousand to flight ...

Deuteronomy 32:30—NIV

As in all things, there is power in numbers. It is easier to get something accomplished when you have help. In all human relationships, including accountability partnerships, I like the analogy of pulling in the same direction (yoked) compared to pulling in the opposite direction (tug-of-war). When two people share the same vision for anything and strive to work together, there is a synergistic effect that comes from their duplication of effort. Always strive to actually listen, truly hear each other, and give godly counsel, so that you can both be pulling in the same direction.

Contrast this to the thought of pulling against each other. If two people are involved in a tug-of-war, there is a maximal exertion of effort on both sides with little or no forward progress in either direction. Imagine two cats with their tails tied together. In this situation there is union, but there is no unity! Relationships fail when two people can't nurture one another's visions. They get tired, frustrated, and want to just give up. It is during these times that we really need to get on our knees and ask God for forgiveness and guidance.

Although I am writing about accountability partnerships, I cannot help but think of marriages when I am having this type of discussion. Imagine if our marriages were a true union and we were pulling in the same direction and not having our own selfish tug-of-war. I am not saying that we have to sell out our individual dreams in order to have unity, but I am saying that if both people were pulling in the same direction—along the straight and narrow path that leads to life—we can realize our dreams together as God reveals His *"good, pleasing, and perfect will"* for each of us along the way as we travel together down the path. God is not the author of confusion (1 Corinthians 14:33); therefore, if we are struggling in our marriages, we need to focus more on God. Together we will find the grace, strength, forgiveness, patience, love, and hope that we need to continue.

I once heard a sermon on unity. I will never forget one of the key points in the sermon. If you take the word "*united*" and switch the letters "I" and "T", you get the word "*untied.*" Think about that for a minute. Let that sink in. The difference between being *united* and *untied* is the position of the letter "I." Now imagine (in the selfish sense) that *we* are that letter "I." Where you put the "I" makes a big difference to the outcome. We are the difference between being *united*, and being *untied*. As always, it's all about the "I" (self-centered). "I" this, or "I" that. We ("I") are either the "tie that binds," or we ("I") are "un-binding the tie." It is our job; our obligation, to promote unity in all our relationships. This is true in accountability relationships, and this is especially true in our marriages. We need to tie knots that can't be untied.

Unlike being in a marriage, which is a "covenant" relationship (binding and permanent), if two people who are in an accountability relationship cannot seem to "feed" each other, then I suggest that each of you seek God and work it out, or, worst-case-scenario, find someone else who will be uplifting to you, but hold you accountable and not be afraid of speaking truth to you, no matter how painful. Remember, we are in accountability relationships for our growth, not our comfort.

Key Thought:

In an accountability relationship, if you find that you are the one who can't take constructive comments to heart without finding them to be too critical, then you need to consider that maybe you are not receptive to change. That should concern you!

We should always maintain the state of mind that we might possibly be wrong. If we happen to be wrong, we need to be willing to freely admit it, without reservation. Maybe you are not ready to grow; otherwise you would receive truth, meditate on it, internalize it, and make the necessary changes that this truth reveals to you about yourself.

An accountability relationship is not one that is always going to be happy and warm and fuzzy. You are going to get your toes stepped on and you need to stand there and take it, for your own growth and development. As iron sharpens iron, there will be collisions and confrontations that will help shape us into the proper form. Remember: No pain, no gain!

Key Thoughts:

Pulling against each other gets you nowhere.

Pulling in the same direction gets you moving forward.

In life, in dealing with other Christian people, we need to find more unity in order to grow and learn more about how to live the life of a disciple. In our walk with God, we need to develop a deeper relationship with Him in order to grow and learn more about His nature and character.

When running in a race, moving forward is the right direction. This life is a journey. As long as we are racing toward God, we are moving forward. When we learn to race toward God and take those around us with us on the journey, we all benefit. If you are in an accountability relationship (or in a marriage), grab your partner and get moving. We all have a race to run. We all have a path marked out for us. Sometimes, we may need the support and encouragement of our accountability partner to help bolster us to reach the finish line.

Chapter 11

running the race

Therefore, since we are surrounded by such a great cloud of witnesses, let us throw off everything that hinders and the sin that so easily entangles, and let us run with perseverance the race marked out for us.

Hebrews 12:1—NIV

We are all running in some form of race. Whether we are running to the cadence of our own drumbeat while we are pursuing our own selfish paths, or whether we are running *"the race marked out for us,"* we are all, in essence, running somewhere. We are either running toward God or away from God. Either we are coaching ourselves and telling ourselves how to get the job done our way, or we are being coached by God and instead we are listening to His wisdom and following His instruction.

Some of us are in an all-out sprint, as if our hair was on fire. What's the hurry? Are we possibly missing the point and missing God along the way? If this is you, I have words of caution for you: *Watch Out!* Burn out is around the corner for you. It is impossible to run full speed without giving out early; we cramp, dehydrate, collapse, etc. Maybe an analogy will spell it out to you. Imagine you were to put your car in first gear, put the pedal to the floor, and then rev up your engine to the point of red-lining it. A wonderfully made engine that could take you well over 100,000 miles down the road when driven responsibly could be completely burned out in a matter of a mile or two when driven this way. It is no different for our bodies, our minds, or our spirits. There is a balance that needs to be maintained. The journey is a long one, and we need to pace ourselves if we intend to finish the race God's way.

Some of us are sitting on the sidelines resting and catching our breath and are content to just sit and watch others pass us by. We are losing our position, our role, our passion. We haven't gotten back in the race since we decided to sit down and take a break. Why did we sit down in the first place? Why haven't we dusted ourselves off, stretched, loosened up, and headed out toward our ultimate destination? What happened to our conviction and that fire that was burning in our bellies? Have we forgotten our inspiration that keeps us running? Where are we going? Do we even care to go there? Why are we so apathetic? What happened to our endurance and motivation?

Think about what the previous verse (Hebrews 12:1) is saying to us. First of all, we do have an audience (*"cloud of witnesses"*) that surrounds us every day of our lives. Just imagine the thought that everyone is watching us to see how we are "performing" as we travel through this life. Rather intimidating, isn't it? If more of us would live as if everyone was watching, perhaps we would have better behavior, or at least, more consistent behavior and not be so lazy, apathetic, or hypocritical.

Speaking of audiences, I like to imagine my close friends seeing my spiritual progress. I also like to picture my loved ones who have already completed their journey through this life being able to watch my progress from heaven. I even picture God, Jesus, and the angels in heaven witnessing my progress. Thinking about the far-reaching aspects of our "cloud of witnesses" helps me personally not lose sight of the finish line. Whether the world is watching me or not, I know that God is watching my every step. His opinion of how I am running my race is of much greater value to me. God is the only one that needs to be impressed with my performance in my race.

Key Thought:

How we run our race matters.

What we seldom think about is the impact that we have on other people's lives as a result of the way in which we chose to live our own lives. While running our race, we come in contact with thousands of people and we touch these people in the most subtle of ways, but we are able to leave a lasting impression on them without even knowing we have done it. It is so important as a disciple of Christ that we leave people that pass through our lives with a touch of God's loving grace. It is like a saying that I have always loved: *"Leave a place better than you found it."*

Key Thought:

We should leave people better than when we found them.

It should be said of us that we left a lasting "good" impression—

an impression of God's loving grace and mercy—on all those with whom we have come in contact. The truth is, if people don't see God's love in us and in the way we live our lives, treat others, and communicate God's truth, we have somehow missed the mark.

We need to decide which race we want to run in. Maybe you are running hard, but you are running with the wrong motivations. Perhaps you are running in the wrong race altogether and haven't stopped to notice the road signs (warning signs) along the way that tell you to turn around. Caution: Danger Ahead—Turn Back!

The Bible says that a tree is known by its fruit. As professing Christians, we should always be ready to give an answer to the following question.

Question:

What fruit is your life producing?

As hard as it is to ask ourselves tough questions, the hardest part is being honest with ourselves and having a willingness to admit that we might be running in the wrong direction. Does your daily walk (daily race) show any sign to others that God is in control of your life? Do people see that your life bears witness to the life-changing power of God? If it doesn't, you have a choice. The beauty of God's plan is that you can call to Him and ask Him for directions and He will lead you back to the path that leads you home.

I know the world is watching my progress because I know it is harder to live the life of a disciple of Christ than to live without a moral compass and stand for nothing sacred. The world (and sadly, often our Christian brothers and sisters) loves to pounce on a Christian when they fall because it gives them "proof" that all disciples of Christ are nothing but hypocrites. You and I know that this is not true, but the world sees our falls and our failures as opportunities to discredit the Christian faith that much more—all the more reason to run the race with integrity and steadfastness.

Anyone can lead a life of self-indulgence and be morally bankrupt, but I dare anyone to attempt to live out the Christian lifestyle without the life-changing power of Christ. It is impossible. We need God. Yes, we fail again and again and again. Who cares? What matters is that we consistently look to God for wisdom, guidance, direction, etc. Christians are easy targets when they falter. I am no better than anyone else. I think I have probably made more mistakes than most people. I have failed at so many things, but the difference with me is that I recognize my own weakness and my need for a Savior. Without God in my life, I would be lost in every sense of the word. With God in my life, I have been able to learn from my failures, recognize my need and dependence upon Him and go on to accomplish so many wonderful things.

Let's look at Hebrews 12:1 again:

> Therefore, since we are surrounded by such a great cloud of witnesses, let us throw off everything that hinders and the sin that so easily entangles, and let us run with perseverance the race marked out for us.
>
> Hebrews 12:1—NIV

Something that stands out to me in this verse is the thought of *"let us throw off everything that hinders and the sin that so easily entangles."* I have heard it said probably about a million times that we all have *"baggage."* Imagine running a race while literally carrying baggage. Talk about a hindrance! It would be hard to get into a rhythm if, while we were running, we were lugging around a backpack, a suitcase, a briefcase, etc. We need to put it all down ("throw off everything") and take off running ("with perseverance"). The only thing that we should be carrying is our cross that we pick up daily. We have no chance of winning the race if we are so bogged down with everything else.

We all have sinned (Romans 3:23), and our sin hinders our ability to run the race. As we learned in Chapter 8 in regard to strongholds, we need to confess our sin, give it to God and walk, or even better, run away from it. Sin only entangles us when we give it power over us by making provision for our flesh (Romans 13:14).

In Genesis, our adversary (Satan) is referred to as a serpent. At some point, we have all knowingly flirted with the danger of being bitten by this serpent when we choose to ignore what we know is right. Some of us choose to run through snake-infested territory (hoping not to get bitten), while others stop, stare, sense the temptation, and then reach out and grasp what they know they shouldn't.

Key Thought:

If you don't want the snake to bite you, then don't pick it up and try to play with it.

Another thing that stands out of Hebrews 12:1 is the statement, *"let us run with perseverance the race marked out for us."* The race we run is a marathon. It is a long distance, cross-country (spiritual country) race. No marathon runner ever wins by sprinting the course. The race is won through perseverance. Without perseverance, we could never finish the race.

> Do you not know that in a race all the runners run, but only one gets the prize? Run in such a way as to get the prize.

1 Corinthians 9:24—NIV

Why run the race if you don't know what the prize is? What is at stake? What do you stand to win? Better yet, if you don't run the race, what do you stand to lose? (Think about the implications.)

As a follower of Christ, I know that the prize that I run for is the promise of eternal life. As I run the race on the course that is "marked out" for me, I see so many opportunities to share my faith with others. The Bible says in 1 Peter 3:15 to *"always be prepared to give an answer to everyone who asks you to give the reason for the hope that you have."* The hope that I have as a believer is more than the fact that I will spend eternity with God. It is much more. I have hope that He will never leave me or forsake me (Joshua 1:5, Hebrews 13:5). I also have hope that nothing can separate me from the love of God (Romans 8:38).

> However, I consider my life worth nothing to me, if only I may finish the race and complete the task the LORD Jesus has given me—the task of testifying to the gospel of God's grace.

Acts 20:24—NIV

About a year ago, I received an email with a link to a website[15] about Dick and Rick Hoyt, a father and son team who compete in marathons and triathlons. If that was all you knew about them, you might want to know more, but I am afraid most people would just shrug their shoulders and move on to the next thought of the day. What makes Dick Hoyt (father) and Rick Hoyt (son) so truly amazing is the fact that Rick has been paralyzed since birth. When Dick is running marathons, he pushes his adult son in a wheelchair. When Dick is competing in a triathlon, he swims while pulling his son in an inflatable raft, and rides a customized bicycle that his son is able to ride on the front of. Think about this: he runs, bikes, and swims the full distances required in a triathlon, which, in case you don't know, is 26.2 miles of running, 112 miles of bicycling, and 2.4 miles of swimming. Most of us couldn't do any one of those three things by themselves, much less do all of them in one day, but Dick Hoyt does all of this while transporting his son. He carries the weight of two people in his races while he is competing with people who are only carrying themselves. This story is worth reading about. It is all very touching. The bond that exists between this father and son team is truly special and very inspiring.

When I think about the powerful image of a father carrying his son, I begin to think about our Heavenly Father carrying us. We are all spiritually paralyzed to some degree, and we need our Heavenly Father to push us and pull us and carry us where we need to go. As disciples, we each try to run our races, but we often forget that the only way we can cross the finish line is to be carried over by our Father.

When we lean on God for our strength, He will give us the strength to continue. What an awesome opportunity to testify to the goodness of God. When other people see that we trust God in all things, it is a powerful message to others that God's grace is truly sufficient. We must remember that God provides opportunities for us to testify of Him to others in our lives. While

302 • Dr. George Goodman

running in our race, we get to run across the path of other runners and sometimes alongside others and, if we are fortunate, we sometimes get the amazing opportunity to pour ourselves into others and minister to them. When God uses you as His instrument to touch the life of someone in need of God's grace, it is such a blessing. We should long for these moments and be on the lookout for them because sometimes as we run, we need to help others by running alongside them and support them and point them towards the narrow path that leads to life.

> You were running a good race. Who cut in on you and kept you from obeying the truth? That kind of persuasion does not come from the one who calls you.
>
> Galatians 5:7–8—NIV

There are so many distractions along the course of our journey. As we are running our race, we come in contact with our enemy. He is there at every turn whether we see him or not. He has set up stumbling blocks for us along the way. He wants to bait us to slow down and savor things that look appealing, but that only end up distracting us from our primary objective: keep running! Even though he has set traps for us and designs detours to lead us off the narrow path and through some deep weeds. We have the choice. We can run on the path "marked out for us," or we can run through the weeds and briars.

> Do you not know that your body is a temple of the Holy Spirit, who is in you, whom you have received from God? You are not your own; you were bought at a price. Therefore honor God with your body.
>
> 1 Corinthians 6:19–20—NIV

Another very good way to live a life that is pleasing to God is to take care of ourselves. We are all made up of body, soul, and spirit. Each of these areas needs our attention. The Bible teaches us that the body is the temple of the Holy Spirit. If God's spirit resides in us, then we shouldn't abuse our bodies. We need to take care of our "temple." Obviously, as in anything in life, we can take this to extremes. For some, the extreme may be not watching what we put into our bodies by eating and drinking the wrong stuff. For others, we may be so obsessed with our bodies that we make our physical fitness routine look something like idolatry. I believe that the Bible teaches us to find balance. We need to eat right and protect the "temple" through our management of our diet and exercise, but we also need to focus on the health of our soul and spirit in order to have the balance we seek. I truly believe that the way in which we manage all these areas is another way that we can show God that we respect Him and it is another form of worship in action.

When I think of finding the balance that I am speaking of, I think of getting on the road to "wholeness." We are made to strive to maturity and completeness. As we grow in our faith, as we learn how to live a life that is truly pleasing to God, we learn so much more about the nature and character of God. I cannot say enough that to get to know God, we must keep running the race. This means we must continue to talk with God (pray). We must continue to read about God (get in His word and "hide it in our hearts"). We must give back to God what He has provided for us (tithes and offerings). We must incline our hearts to seek Him and be patient in the process as He mysteriously molds us and shapes us into something spiritually beautiful.

Blessed is the man who perseveres under trial, because

when he has stood the test, he will receive the crown of life that God has promised to those who love Him.

James 1:12—NIV

You need to persevere so that when you have done the will of God, you will receive what he has promised.

Hebrews 10:36—NIV

In writing this book, I am reminded of many things that I am thankful for, especially the many challenges and difficulties that I have faced throughout my Christian experience. These experiences were extremely difficult and, at times, definitely painful, but nonetheless, they were absolutely necessary for my spiritual development. We should never desire to stop the growth process just because we become uncomfortable. Things that grow stay fresh and alive. Things that stop growing can decay and become rancid.

In Chapter 8, I told you that I would tell you more about perseverance, and what is produced by perseverance. Well, here it is, plain and simple.

Key Thought:

Perseverance produces patience and patience produces character.

As disciples of Christ, we need to have a willingness to accept whatever comes our way, knowing that by God's grace we will survive the situation, trial, or difficulty and come out stronger in the end with a deeper faith in God. When we look at our present situations, we can't always see God's hand at work, but we know by faith that "all things work together for good for those who love God and for those who are called according to His purpose" (Romans 8:28). When we look back on our Christian experience, we have so much more actual experience to draw from.

In my life, it is much easier to look back and see how God was orchestrating my life in order to teach me what He thought I needed to learn. I will be the first to say that these lessons leveled me at times and left me wondering about the goodness of God, but I cannot say clearly enough or convey the level of conviction that I have when I say that God loves me, God provides for me, and God wants what is ultimately best for me. My life is a testimony to that fact that God is good ... all the time! The sad part is that many people don't see this truth because they won't trust Him to guide their path. Instead, like me, they run off the road and crash before they realize how much they need God to be their LORD. I thank God for guiding me down the roads I have traveled. I appreciate the person that I have become as a result of the life experiences that have guided me to His loving embrace.

If we would develop a determination to stand firm in what we know and believe in while those around us are falling or running away from God's guidance, we would develop the insight to see the character-developing hand of God in it all. If we will persevere, we will develop patience, and with this patience, God will develop our character. This perseverance, patience and character are what allow us to finish the race and grow in faith and maturity.

> I have fought the good fight, I have finished the race, I
> have kept the faith. Now there is in store for me the crown

of righteousness, which the LORD, the righteous Judge, will award me on that day—and not only to me, but also to all who have longed for his appearing.

2 Timothy 4:7–8—NIV

Chapter 12

a more excellent way

All scripture is God-breathed and is useful for teaching, rebuking, correcting and training in righteousness, so that the man of God may be thoroughly equipped for every good work.

2 Timothy 3:16–17—NIV

What an awesome thought it is to be *"thoroughly equipped for every good work!"* Think about the following questions and how they *presently* relate to your spiritual journey versus how you *wish* they related:

Questions:
- Are we so grounded in the Word of God that someone else could say of us that we are *"thoroughly equipped"*?
- Could we say that about ourselves?
- Are we so familiar with the Word of God that we can recognize when other people are twisting the Word (taking the Bible out of context) to prove their own point or further their own agenda?
- Do we have enough scripture hidden in our hearts that

when we hear even a portion of a verse, we can finish it from memory?

- Do we long to have a better grasp on the Word of God so that we can communicate it to other people with confidence and authority?
- Do we have the message of the Gospel in our minds so clearly that we could, at a moment's notice, present the message of salvation to someone and explain it to them in a way that is easy for them to understand (can we present the Gospel message with the necessary passion, conviction, and clarity)?

These are extremely tough questions that we need to be able to give honest answers to. If our answers are not what we wish they were; be encouraged because, if you really want to be able to say *yes* to these questions, you can, with time and some effort. It will take the kind of effort that, as disciples, we are all called to give. Again, this is a portion, a facet, of our spiritual identity and calling. We all need to know God's Word to have spiritual maturity and live up to our calling!

"All scripture is God-breathed and is useful ..."

Based on 2 Timothy 3:16, if we really knew the Word of God like we should, we would be actively doing the following things:
- Teaching others all about God.
- Standing up to those who are defiantly disobeying the Word of God out of rebellion.
- Correcting those who don't adequately understand the Word of God due to ignorance, misunderstanding, or misinterpretation.
- Training other believers how to live a holy and righteous life.

This verse says that we are to do these things so that we may be *"thoroughly equipped"* for every good work. That is a lot to process, especially if we aren't currently doing these things. What a big responsibility!

We should know what we believe and why we believe it so that we can expound the Word of God to anyone that God puts in our lives. If we would commit to learning more about the God we serve, we would then better understand our roles as disciples and we would be more effective in our service to our LORD.

> In the presence of God and of Christ Jesus, who will judge the living and the dead, and in view of his appearing and his kingdom, I give you this charge: Preach the Word; be prepared in season and out of season; correct, rebuke and encourage—with great patience and careful instruction. For the time will come when men will not put up with sound doctrine. Instead, to suit their own desires, they will gather around them a great number of teachers to say what their itching ears want to hear. They will turn their ears away from the truth and turn aside to myths. But you, keep your head in all situations, endure hardship, do the work of an evangelist, discharge all the duties of your ministry.
>
> 2 Timothy 4:1–5—NIV

This is an awesome passage if you think about it. It has a lot to say to us as believers. Read it again and think about it as a charge (an order, a command) from God to His children.

- *Preach the Word*—Be prepared at all times.
- *Correct, rebuke, and encourage other believers—with great patience and careful instruction*—Don't use the Bible to whack people like a sledgehammer (patiently, carefully, and lovingly instruct other believers).
- *Keep your head in all situations*—Stay focused on God and His Word no matter what is going on.

- *Do the work of an evangelist*—Sow seeds for God to harvest in His time.

This passage says in verse 3 that there will come a time when some of us will not put up with sound doctrine anymore, but instead believe only as it suits our own selfish desires. I have spent a lot of time thinking about this passage and I have come to some conclusions. "Sound doctrine" is biblically based, true, and defensible.

> Anyone, then, who knows the good he ought to do and doesn't do it, sins.
>
> James 4:17—NIV

If a person knows the truth of the Word and willfully chooses not to obey it, they are sinning against God. There are no two ways about it. We have choices every day. We can live up to the values that God gives us in His Word, or we can sell-out to our own desires and tell God that His ways are old-fashioned and not worth living for, because, to us, our ways are so much better. Sadly, this reckless, uncaring attitude is evident in so many areas of the church.

Key Thought:

 If you are living for God, you will be called a hypocrite.

It is sad to me that when Christians lose the desire to live for God, they are considered to be the worst type of hypocrite. A hypocrite says one thing but does another. If you are living for

God, get ready, you will be called a hypocrite whether you deserve to be called that or not. I have been called a hypocrite before—and I *hated* it! At the time I heard it, it was true about me, and deep down, I knew it. It hurt for me to hear it because it stabbed me in the heart. I had a form of godliness but no real change of heart to go along with it. It was all for show. Someone had seen through my mask. My hidden identity was out in the open. I was exposed. This form of godliness was my Christian veneer, my mask of artificial righteousness. I think many Christians walk around with their masks on because they don't want the world to know that they are a phony, a fake, a poser.

Many Christians have tried to live for God but failed and then taken criticism for it. Standing up for your faith is not easy. It takes guts. There will always be a person around you who will criticize your walk with God. So what! We are to be God-pleasers, not people-pleasers. God knows us intimately; He knows our hearts.

Key Thought:

God's opinion of us is the only one that really matters.

Our values are under attack every day. When society pushes us to conform, we should find out what God has to say about it, and not give in to anything or anyone who opposes God's plan for our lives. When we succumb to the pressures and sell-out our faith so we don't "make waves" or upset anyone, we are being *"politically correct."* I don't know about you, but I am so tired of hearing this term. It seems to me that for a Christian to be politically correct, they are dangerously close to selling out and being "lukewarm" about their faith. We all know how God feels about being lukewarm (Revelation 3:16).

People argue and insist that we should be politically correct so that we don't offend anyone. The problem with being politically correct is that our faith gets watered down (or obliterated) to a point where it is unrecognizable and powerless. When we experience external pressures that infringe on our spiritual beliefs, why do we feel the need to "go with the flow" and deny what we know is right? What about being *"biblically correct"*? Do you honestly think that God would have us to be politically correct, or do you think that He would rather us be staunch about what the Bible says above all else?

We were not put on this earth to have our light hidden. We were put here to be a beacon to a dark world. We should be more concerned about pleasing God and living out His will, rather than conforming to the pressures placed upon us by the world around us. So goes the song we learned as children (abbreviated version) ...

> This little light of mine, I'm gonna let it shine ...
> Hide it under a bushel? No! I'm gonna let it shine ...
> Don't let Satan blow it out, I'm gonna let it shine ...
> Let it shine til Jesus comes, I'm gonna let it shine ...

Think about it: Do you think that Christ was a people-pleaser? No way! Jesus was loving, but He had a specific mission. He knew His God-given purpose. He stayed focused on God's Word and perfectly lived out God's will for His life. Unlike us, Jesus lived a selfless life. He constantly served others. When you get right down to it, most of us tend to be pretty selfish. We typically serve ourselves and we cater to our wants, our needs, and our desires, rather than seeking God to discover how we ought to live. We have a biblical obligation to die to self and allow God to renew our minds so that we can live out His will for us and not continuously fail and be accused of being a hypocrite.

Look at the following examples. Think about it and see if you don't agree with me that these areas in the church and in the general Christian community have been areas where we, as disciples, have been extremely negligent and subsequently hypocritical:

Adultery

> You shall not commit adultery.
>
> Deuteronomy 5:18—NIV

"You shall not commit adultery" (plain English), yet affairs, premarital sex, and pornography are becoming more commonplace in the lives of people in the church. We don't value purity anymore, and it shows in how we live. We live to satisfy our lusts instead of asking God to make us complete and protect us from temptation.

Divorce

> "I hate divorce," says the LORD God of Israel.
>
> Malachi 2:16—NIV

God hates divorce (plain English), yet the divorce rate in the church (believers) is *higher* than outside the church (non-believers). We are not practicing what we are preaching! We deserve any criticism that we get, because, as a whole, we truly are absolute hypocrites in this area. Are there biblical grounds for

314 • Dr. George Goodman

divorce? Yes, there are, but the majority of divorces that occur are not covered by the biblical grounds (as if we cared to know that). We just want out of our marriages, so we justify it, make excuses, and get divorced anyway. *"Who cares what God says about it? Our 'happiness' is more important." Is it really?* Show me that verse in the Bible! Trust me, you won't find it!

I am personally under the impression that God wants us to be holy. This concept is in the Bible, numerous times! If we would get over the lie that *"God wants us to be happy,"* then we would move on to the truth that God is much, much more concerned about you being holy. When you have holiness, you will have joy. Joy beats happiness any day.

Sinful Acts

> The acts of the sinful nature are obvious: sexual immorality, impurity and debauchery; idolatry and witchcraft; hatred, discord, jealousy, fits of rage, selfish ambition, dissensions, factions and envy; drunkenness, orgies, and the like. I warn you, as I did before, that those who live like this will not inherit the kingdom of God.
>
> Galatians 5:19–21—NIV

Most of you would look at this list and say, "Nope. Not guilty." Look again. Just because you don't worship idols, practice witchcraft, or participate in orgies, doesn't exclude you from anything else on this list. Remember, this is only a few verses. There are many other verses that deal with many other issues (lying, stealing, murder, homosexuality, jealousy, gambling, etc.)—need I say more? Whether we're drunk, stealing, telling "white lies," or any other inappropriate act or deed, we are *sinning.* Why? Because God said so! We can argue about it, but frankly, your opinion doesn't matter and neither does mine—only God's opinion really matters. If God said it, that should settle it. Enough said! End of debate.

Key Thought:

Let's quit making excuses to justify things that God says are wrong!

When will we learn to accept His Word as the ultimate truth and just live by it as the governing law of our heart, regardless of our opinions of right and wrong? God is infinite. We are finite. If He said it is wrong or bad for us, then obviously, He knows more than we do.

> "Do not judge, or you too will be judged. For in the same way you judge others, you will be judged, and with the measure you use, it will be measured to you.
>
> Matthew 7:1–2—NIV

No matter what the sin, we can't grade it. We can't say this sin is bigger than that sin. Sin is sin. We can't look at someone else and think poorly of them because of their sin and judge them in our hearts, when we are just as guilty of committing sins of our own. Get it? It is not our job to judge such things. We are called to live a life of purity. We should be concerned for our own walk with God. We need to put the gavel down, step out from behind the bench, and allow God to serve justice as He sees fit.

Sin is a monster. It controls us sometimes, but it doesn't own

316 • Dr. George Goodman

us. We may be tempted from time to time, but God has something to say about that.

> No temptation has seized you except what is common to
> man. And God is faithful; he will not let you be tempted
> beyond what you can bear. But when you are tempted, he
> will also provide a way out so that you can stand up under
> it.

> 1 Corinthians 10:13—NIV

He will provide a way out. Did you hear me? A way out of the situation, no matter what the temptation! Anyone who is tempted is not tempted beyond what they can bear. Also remember that your temptation is not unique to you. Regardless of your sin or your circumstances, God is always faithful. He *always* gives us an escape so that we can "stand up" for what we know is biblically right.

At the beginning of this chapter, when I was asking all the questions about how well we know the Bible, I was asking those tough questions for a reason. Mainly, because I feel strongly that all Christians should have a healthy understanding of the Bible.

> If we don't know God's Word, we can easily be deceived ...
> as many have been.

> If we don't know God's Word, we can easily be led astray ...
> as many have been.

> If we don't know God's Word, we can easily get caught up
> in false doctrines ... as many have been.

Do you see the pattern? Does this sound familiar?

Key Thought:

Lack of knowledge leads to deception, which leads to propagation of false doctrine.

We need to know the facts! We need to know the truth so that we can have discernment. How can we be a light to the world and tell them about the love of Christ if we don't know the truth contained in the Bible? We have an obligation to dig in and learn God's Word.

Okay. It's time for a departure. I felt the need to elaborate on the importance of knowing the Word. Now, I think it's time to talk about spiritual maturity. If we plan to grow in spiritual maturity, we must understand a few things. First of all, we need to know who God is. We need to understand more about His nature and character. As a Christian, we also need to know who we are *in Christ* (we have already covered this in detail). Next, we need to have a healthy prayer life. Our communication with God is how we build our *relationship* with Him. Trusting Him is how we build our *faith* in Him. There are times when we are experiencing hardships and trials, yet in all of it, God has a purpose.

> Consider it pure joy, my brothers, whenever you face trials of many kinds, because you know that the testing of your faith develops perseverance. Perseverance must finish its work so that you may be mature and complete, not lacking anything.

> James 1:2–4—NIV

For those of you who are still reading this book looking for the secret formula for a great Christian life, let's break it down. Get ready ... there is no secret, scientific, or mathematical formula for a great Christian life! The real formula lies in the relational aspect of our faith. The truth is, when our faith is challenged and we keep on believing, our faith grows (like the "tree by the river" that we talked about). As our faith grows, we develop perseverance. As perseverance develops, we grow in maturity. As we mature in our faith, we find ourselves in the wonderful position of completeness; totally dependent upon God, totally in love with Him, totally secure in Him, and lacking ... *nothing!*

Most Christians are familiar with King David. Most of us remember him as a boy from the story of "David and Goliath." There is another story of David as a grown man that I had never heard until I was in my early twenties. I was at a men's retreat and I heard a message about David's charge to his son (Solomon) as he was nearing the end of his life. At the time I heard this message, I remember being a young man who was still unsure of himself. This passage spoke to me as to someone who was just entering into the world of manhood.

> When the time drew near for David to die, he gave a charge to Solomon his son. "I am about to go the way of all the earth," he said. "So be strong, show yourself a man, and observe what the LORD your God requires: Walk in his ways, and keep his decrees and commands, his laws and requirements, as written in the Law of Moses, so that you may prosper in all you do and wherever you go."

> 1 Kings 2:1-3—NIV

In a discussion of maturity, I believe this is a perfect fit. David was known as "a man after God's own heart." David led an amazing life. His life events are recorded for us in the Old Testament. What is most interesting to me is that as much as the Bible shares with us David's successes in life, it also shares with us David's failures. David did some wonderful things that required enormous faith, yet he occasionally did some terrible things because he lost sight of God's plan. However, in all of this, David never lost His love for God. As Christians, we could learn a lot about God by studying the life of David. If you will take the time to study David's life, you will be blessed by what you learn. The love that he had for God is truly intriguing. It is a story with all the great elements ... best of all: forgiveness and restoration.

At the end of David's life, he told his son exactly how to be a man (in God's eyes). When you consider that this passage is about a dying father (and king) communicating to his son the most important things that he has learned in his lifetime, this passage really takes on new meaning, especially when you consider that it was David, the man who loved God like no other. In my opinion, there is no better example anywhere than this of what it means to be a man in God's eyes—a real man!

Read the passage again. Think about it from the standpoint of it being the ultimate pearl of wisdom:

> Be strong, show yourself a man, and observe what the LORD your God requires: Walk in his ways, and keep his decrees and commands, his laws and requirements, as written in the Law of Moses, so that you may prosper in all you do and wherever you go.

Now, think about who David's son is—it's Solomon. Solomon is a very interesting figure in the Bible. He is known as the wisest man who ever lived. Imagine being David's son and living in the shadow of such a great man of God. It must have been amazing. If you had a father that was blessed and befriended by God to

320 • Dr. George Goodman

the extent that David was, you would probably have a healthy respect for the person of God. For this reason, I believe that Solomon had a better grasp on God's greatness than we do.

At the very end of the book of Ecclesiastes, the last two verses sum up the entire book. Here is Solomon's conclusion regarding life:

> Now all has been heard; here is the conclusion of the matter: Fear God and keep his commandments, for this is the whole duty of man. For God will bring every deed into judgment, including every hidden thing, whether it is good or evil.

> Ecclesiastes 12:13–14—NIV

According to Solomon, fearing God and keeping His commands is the *"whole duty of man."* When I first heard the verses about David's charge to Solomon (1 Kings 2:1–3), I fell in love with that passage. Since then, I have always put the end of Ecclesiastes with the verses from David's charge to Solomon. When you look at it like this, you get the picture that if we follow what God says in His Word and live our lives accordingly, we will be performing our duty as a child of God and a disciple of Christ.

The beauty of the message of the New Testament (the message of the Gospel of Christ) is that now we can have a true, open relationship with our LORD and Savior. Christ's substitutionary sacrifice on the cross paid our sin debt. We can now approach a loving God with freedom and confidence. Why has God made Himself so available to us? It is because He loves us more than we can begin to fathom (read John 3:16 again in case you need to be reminded of just how much He loves us).

But eagerly desire the greater gifts. And now I will show you the most excellent way.

1 Corinthians 12:31—NIV

Question:

What does "the most excellent way" mean?

Many believers can quote the location of the *"love chapter"* in the Bible (1 Corinthians 13), but I have found that most do not know the verse that comes right before it. In 1 Corinthians 12:31 (the last verse in 1 Corinthians 12), it says that we should *"eagerly"* desire the *"greater"* gifts. These *"greater"* spiritual gifts are mentioned in 1 Corinthians 12 and 13. In 1 Corinthians 13:13 (the last verse in the chapter), the *"greatest"* gift (among faith, hope, and love) that we should desire is Love.

I want you to read 1 Corinthians 13 (below) as if you were reading it for the first time. Meditate on its message. *Please,* don't hurry through it.

> If I speak in the tongues of men and of angels, but have not love, I am only a resounding gong or a clanging cymbal. If I have the gift of prophecy and can fathom all mysteries and all knowledge, and if I have a faith that can move mountains, but have not love, I am nothing. If I give all I possess to the poor and surrender my body to the flames, but have not love, I gain nothing. Love is patient, love is kind. It does not envy, it does not boast, it is not proud. It is not rude, it is not self-seeking, it is not easily angered, it keeps no record of wrongs. Love does not delight in

evil but rejoices with the truth. It always protects, always trusts, always hopes, always perseveres. Love never fails. But where there are prophecies, they will cease; where there are tongues, they will be stilled; where there is knowledge, it will pass away. For we know in part and we prophesy in part, but when perfection comes, the imperfect disappears. When I was a child, I talked like a child, I thought like a child, I reasoned like a child. When I became a man, I put childish ways behind me. Now we see but a poor reflection as in a mirror; then we shall see face to face. Now I know in part; then I shall know fully, even as I am fully known. And now these three remain: faith, hope, and love. But the greatest of these is love.

1 Corinthians 13:1–13—NIV

"The most excellent way"—think about that for a minute. It doesn't say *"the good way"* or *"the better way,"* it says *"the most excellent way."* To me, this communicates that there is no better way. This is the very best way. You could say that it is the ultimate way.

We are to eagerly desire having spiritual gifts, but, more specifically, we should desire to have the gift of *love* above all else, above all other spiritual gifts. This is *"the most excellent way"* that 1 Corinthians 12:31 is talking about. It is not the world's perception of what love is, but instead, it is a heavenly perspective of real *love*—God-like "agape" love, which is love in its purest form (sacrificial love).

Think back on what Jesus said were the two "greatest" commandments in Matthew 22:37–39:
- Love the LORD your God with all your heart and with all your soul and with all your mind. This is the first and greatest commandment.
- Love your neighbor as yourself.

Love God ...

> But the man who loves God is known by God.

1 Corinthians 8:3—NIV

Love others ...

> Whoever does not love does not know God, because God is love.

1 John 4:8—NIV

When we love God with all our heart, soul, and mind, and love our neighbors (those around us) as ourselves, we are living out a very important part of God's will for us as believers (disciples of Christ). A life that is focused on living up to the full potential of these two commandments is the best example of "the most excellent way" in action.

> One day Peter and John were going up to the temple at the time of prayer—at three in the afternoon. Now a man crippled from birth was being carried to the temple gate called Beautiful, where he was put every day to beg from those going into the temple courts. When he saw Peter and John about to enter, he asked them for money. Peter looked straight at him, as did John. Then Peter said, "Look at us!" So the man gave them his attention, expecting to get something from them. Then Peter said, "Silver or gold I do not have, but what I have I give you. In the name of Jesus Christ of Nazareth, walk." Taking him by the right hand, he helped him up, and instantly the man's feet and ankles became strong. He jumped to his feet and began to walk. Then he went with them into the temple courts, walking

324 • Dr. George Goodman

and jumping, and praising God. When all the people saw
him walking and praising God, they recognized him as the
same man who used to sit begging at the temple gate called
Beautiful, and they were filled with wonder and amazement
at what had happened to him.

Acts 3:1–10—NIV

What I love about this story is that Peter and John could have
done the *"likely"* thing (ordinary) and given the man money, but
they didn't. Instead, they did the *"unlikely"* thing (extraordinary)
and they gave him Jesus, the greatest gift of all.

This story is a great example of two things:

- *Action*—Peter saw through the surface problem and to the
deeper need of this crippled man. Peter loved God enough
to respond in obedience to what God prompted him to do,
so that God would ultimately be glorified. Peter also loved
this man enough to show compassion on him and give him
what he needed most.
- *Inaction*—This story is an excellent example of the church
today. For years, this man had sat right beside the temple
gate as believers went in and out every day, yet no one
helped him. I am not saying that no one ever gave this
man money (silver or gold), but obviously, no one had ever
shared the life-changing message of Jesus with him.

I wish the church today would strive harder to do things through
God's power and less through human strength and ingenuity.
We need to exercise faith first and muscle second, if we are going
to reach a lost world. This is what *"the most excellent way"* is all
about—being led by God to love others.

"As the Father has loved me, so have I loved you. Now

remain in my love. If you obey my commands, you will remain in my love, just as I have obeyed my Father's commands and remain in his love. I have told you this so that my joy may be in you and that your joy may be complete. My command is this: Love each other as I have loved you. Greater love has no one than this, that he lay down his life for his friends."

John 15:9–13—NIV

We need God's wisdom and guidance to know how to best reach out and love those that need it most. Everyone has needs. Everyone needs something. What we have to give these people should originate from the love of God. A love that guides us to act and minister to people out of our obedience and gratefulness to God for what He has done for us. If we truly are God's hands and feet, then we need to be guided continuously to *reach out* and *step out* in faith through His love.

"A new command I give you: Love one another. As I have loved you, so you must love one another. By this all men will know that you are my disciples, if you love one another."

John 13:34–35—NIV

Once again, the key word here is *love*. To understand God's will for your life and to personally learn what *"the most excellent way"* really means, you need to learn to show God's love to a world that desperately needs it.

Key Thought:

In order to show God's love, you need to find God's love for yourself.

There are two common problems that plague many Christians today:
- They haven't found the joy in their own salvation.
- They are too critical of other Christians.

We need to concentrate on both issues. We need to become more like Christ ourselves and stop looking for differences among other believers and judging them for it. We need to look for commonality.

Find reasons to love others. Jesus showed love in many ways. He exemplified love in His very life by freely giving of it before, during, and after the cross. As believers, we need to do a better job of demonstrating God's love by reaching out to others. My personal goal in life is not to be just a *Christian*. I want to be a *disciple*!

I want to be a follower of Jesus Christ. What does being a follower of Jesus Christ look like? Well, in order to be His disciple, I must try to *live* as He lived and *love* as He loved. If I am not willing to *"pick up my cross daily"* and crucify my own personal will and selfish desires, I will never fully know the depth of God's amazing love and His perfect, wonderful, and satisfying will for my life; nor will I be able to demonstrate to others what God's amazing love is all about.

Do you want the relationship with God that you have always

dreamed of? Do you want to see God's hand at work in your life? It seems that everyone wants to know the "formula" or "recipe," yet the answers are right in front of us. It is so very simple. Seek Him! He is there waiting for you to call out to Him. All it takes is a desire to have all that God has for you and to be willing to pursue Him with all your heart. If you call out to Jesus and you know Him as your LORD, you are a child of the Creator of the universe. The rest is a matter of seeking God and being obedient to living like a disciple.

Key Thought:

You are not "unlikely" at all.

God loves the so-called *"unlikely"* and *"unlovable"* people of the world. He always tends to root for the underdog. No matter how you see yourself, God sees you as important, lovable, and necessary. I urge you to seek God and pray every single day that he would reveal to you His will and purpose for your life. The more you discover God's *"good, pleasing, and perfect will,"* the more you will see that in God's eyes, when you lean on Him and trust not in your own understanding, you are the right person for the task that He has prepared for you.

It's time that you got on the right path and ran the race marked out for you. It's time to get going. The journey begins on your knees. Go before God every single day and ask Him to reveal to you His will for your life. Be willing to allow Him to shape you; step into the pain if that is what it takes. Allow Him to sift you and refine you into something pure. Confess everything to Him and hold nothing back. Bear your soul to Him. Cry out to Him for answers to life's toughest questions—the answers will come at the right time. Be ready for it. Trust Him in all things and He will guide your steps.

Good News:
God uses *imperfect* people to carry out His *"good, pleasing, and perfect will."*

For such a time as this ...
We were placed here on this earth, at this specific time in history, and in this place to make a difference for the kingdom of God. God has equipped you with special gifts, talents, and experiences that are completely unique to you. No one else can do what God calls you to do as well as you can. Where God guides, God provides. Spend time searching the heart of God. Ask Him to reveal His plan for you to you. Ask Him to orchestrate the events that need to take place to bring you to the place where you are ready and able to step through the door that only He can put in front of you and that only He can open for you. Walk by faith, not by sight, and you will one day look back and see how incredibly faithful God has been. He will bless you and use you to bless others. He will use you to make a lasting impact on this world.

Now it's your turn to show others *"the most excellent way."* It's time to take your faith out into the world and share the greatest gift of all—the gift of life through Jesus Christ. Thank God that He calls the seemingly *"unlikely"* people of the world, like us, to live extraordinary lives by living out His *"good, pleasing, and perfect will."*

Appendix A

tate publishing's statement of belief

The Author understands the Statement of Belief of Tate Publishing, LLC, which follows:

We believe in the reality of one true God, eternal and infinite, existing as three persons—Father, Son, and Holy Spirit. Man was made in the image of God. The fall of man from God's grace by sin put man in the position of needing forgiveness in order that his fellowship with God might be restored. He sent His son, Jesus Christ, into the world to take man's sin upon Himself. Jesus was begotten by the Holy Spirit, born of the Virgin Mary, and is true God and true man, the only sinless man who ever lived. As the Lamb of God, He took man's sin upon Himself as He died on the cross, thus satisfying God's holy demands for all mankind. He was buried, and was resurrected on the third day following His crucifixion. After appearing to various people during a period of forty days, He ascended into heaven and is the only mediator between God and man. All who personally receive Him, through faith, are declared righteous on the basis of His shed blood. When a person confesses the fact that he is

330 • Dr. George Goodman

a sinner and acknowledges Jesus Christ as his LORD and Savior, his spirit is reborn. He becomes a new creation, a member of the true church, indwelt by the Holy Spirit. This salvation is not the result of any human effort, but is the free gift of God's grace in Jesus Christ. Jesus destroyed all the works of Satan, who as god of this world, is allowed to continue, for now, to blind the eyes of those who do not believe. Satan leads a host of fallen beings who are his aides in warring against believers. Believers must be aware of the reality of spiritual warfare and know that victory is theirs through the application of spiritual truth and the presence and power of the indwelling Spirit of Christ. God sent His Holy Spirit with gifts to the church to empower believers for witnessing of Jesus, as well as to be comforter and teacher, until Jesus comes again. The Holy Spirit convicts the world of sin, righteousness, and judgment. The Holy Spirit witnesses not unto Himself, but to the risen Christ. He regenerates, seals, anoints and sets apart the believer to a holy life. Christ ordained the observance of water baptism and the LORD's Supper until He returns. The Bible was written by men who wrote under the direct control, inspiration, and anointing of God. The Bible does not contain the Word of God, it is the Word of God—the infallible, inerrant, only written revelation which God has given to man. It increases man's faith, as well as instructs and corrects him that he might become holy, separated from the world and unto God. The main theme of the Bible is God's plan of salvation in Jesus Christ. Everything in the life of every human being is directly or indirectly affected by his attitude about the Bible—whether or not he accepts it as the inspired Word of God. It is the supreme and final authority in all matters about which it speaks.

endnotes

1 See Appendix A.

2 The New Oxford American Dictionary (Second Edition)

3 An Orthodox Jew follows traditional Jewish doctrine and ritual very strictly. For example, they often eat only Kosher food. Kosher food is food that is prepared by following rules from the books of Leviticus and Deuteronomy. According to Leviticus and Deuteronomy, there are some animals that are considered clean and unclean. If an animal is considered clean, it can be consumed, but the meat has to be prepared according the requirements of the Jewish law in order to be deemed Kosher.

4 www.lifechurch.tv

5 "I Surrender All," written by David Moffit and Regie Hamm, *My Place Is With You*, sung by Clay Crosse, Reunion Records, 1993.

6 The New Oxford American Dictionary (Second Edition)

7 "The Anchor Holds," written by Lawrence Chewning, Ray Boltz, Steve Millikan, *Allegiance*, sung by Ray Boltz, Word Entertainment, 1994.

8 "You've Got To Stand For Something," written by Aaron Tippin and Buddy Brock, *You've Got To Stand For Something*, sung by Aaron Tippin, Acuff-Rose Music, Inc., 1990.

9 "Onward Christian Soldiers," hymn written by Sabine Bar-
ing-Gould in 1865, music by Arther Sullivan in 1871.
10 The New Oxford American Dictionary (Second Edition)
11 The New Oxford American Dictionary (Second Edition)
12 www.teamhoyt.com/history.shtml

9 781606 048436